TIME

of

TRIAL

ROBERT M. ZELAZO

TABLE OF CONTENTS

For Sandra

Acknowledgements

Thanks to Barbara Lagowski and Helen Newton

PROLOGUE

It was 2:45 in the morning. In the nursing home, the darkness was almost palpable, thick and nebulous. The lack of sound was extreme, with most of the ambient noise absorbed by the thick carpeting and heavy curtains. From out of one of the radiating corridors came what at what first appearance looked like an indistinct and ghostly white blur. The blur moved quickly out into the light of the main nursing station and resolved itself into the figure of a pale young woman dressed all in white with white stockings and white shoes. Like an acolyte approaching the altar at a high mass, she slowed her approach as she neared the central desk. There is a middle-aged nurse, also dressed in white, with grey hair and a prognathous jaw looked up from what she was doing. She was wearing a pair of half glasses and had to look up over them to return the gaze of the younger woman, but it quickly became apparent that she was the superior. There was a piercing intelligence and a resolute personality behind her bright blue eyes. 'Yes, Hence, what is it?" she queried. Without preamble, the young nurse responded, I think that the man in 115 is in trouble, Mrs. Callahan. He doesn't look good at all. Something is seriously wrong." 'Damn!' retorted the older woman. "And I thought that I was going to make some headway with this ungodly paperwork." Impatiently, she thrust aside some of the pile of documents in front of her and put her pen down. "Well," she sighed in exasperation, let's go and have a look at him then." She rose with an alacrity that belied her middle-aged physique and moved out swiftly from behind the desk. The two uniformly dressed women quickly hastened down the corridor to room 115. No further words were spoken between them until they arrived there. As soon as she entered the room, the more experienced nurse could immediately see that the patient was indeed in real trouble. He was breathing very rapidly and was drenched in sweat. She efficiently took his vital signs. As sshe later noted in the chart, his pupils were fixed and dilated and everything that could be done had already been done. At 6:30 A.M., three hours after he had been brought by ambulance to the emergency room, Martin Wennar was pronounced dead in the chart, the temperature was 104 degrees Fahrenheit, the pulse was 126 and thready and the blood pressure was 80/50. Grasping with both hands the thin sheet that covered him, with one sweeping movement she threw it aside exposing his entire lower body to the light. The sight that was revealed was not a pleasant one. The patient's left leg had been previously amputated just below the knee and, though the muscles were thin and atrophied, the stump was well healed and without any visible acute abnormality otherwise. The right leg, however, was another matter. In the heel area there was a large fungating ulcer that was only partially covered by a sterile dressing that had slipped a bit to the side. Surrounding this ulcer for about four inches was an angry red halo with ragged edges. From this halo-like pair of scarlet contrails two red streaks ran up the medial aspect of the leg to just below the right groin.

Taking a small penlight from her breast pocket, the nurse leaned over, opened the right eye of the patient with her left hand and shone the light into his eye with her right hand. The pupil of the right eye contracted briskly to a pinpoint.

"He's still in there, alright." She muttered.

The bright flash of sunlight through the trees caught him by surprise and he blinked involuntarily. He was running along a broad path bordered on both sides by tall pine trees whose needles had carpeted the path to the point that the impacts of running shoes made almost no noise as he ran. It had been a long time since he remembered running and it felt good. The effort of each stride, the alternate contraction and relaxation of leg muscles and even the slight discomfort of labored breathing filled him with a sense of joy. He wasn't sure just where he was. The unfinished path and the surrounding trees would indicate that he was running cross country but there were no other runners in sight. The path was quite regular and even and the trees were strangely uniform in size and separation. They were more like pillars than natural trees though the needles that covered the path felt real enough beneath his feet. The path stretched straight out in front of him as far as he could see, without deviation. Looking far far up ahead, he thought that the trees were thinning out some. He got a strong feeling then that he was running toward something, though he could not have said what that was. As he ran, this feeling became stronger and stronger. There was no wind. The light was generally diffuse and subdued other than that quick flash that had brought him to awareness in this place. There were no further flashes of brilliance. He had a feeling that this all had a distinct purpose to it and that this was where he was meant to be. With joyful resolution he put his head down, shortened his stride, and bent to his task.

"He's septic from his heel ulcer," said the nurse. "We had better get him right up to the ER right now." She re-covered the patient and marched rapidly back to the desk where she immediately placed a phone call to the home of the doctor who was providing the coverage that night.

"Sorry to bother you at this hour, but we have a man here who appears to be going into septic shock. He has a high fever, tachypnea and tachycardia and it looks like an infection from a decubitus on his right heel to me. He's a full code." This quick synopsis that the senior nurse had provided was all that the doctor needed to know, and he concurred with her plan without hesitation. The nurse disconnected the first call and immediately placed another to the emergency response system to obtain an ambulance. She next dialed the ER itself and gave a precise and professional report to the nurse who answered the phone there. In less than 15 minutes, the paramedics had arrived, and the patient was efficiently loaded aboard the ambulance which departed at high speed, lights strobing and siren wailing into the dark tunnel of the night.

It took only a few more minutes to get to the small local hospital where the patient was quickly unloaded from the ambulance and wheeled into the largest examining room which contained the cardiac monitors, a respirator, and the crash cart. The ER team, which consisted of a doctor, two nurses and two aides as well as a respiratory therapist, went into efficient action in a series of operations that were so well coordinated that they seemed scripted, which indeed to a certain extent they were by dint of extensive experience and long habit. The patient's vital signs were again taken, as per protocol. They were unchanged from those taken at the nursing home.

He was hooked up to the cardiac monitor by means of four separate electrical leads which provided a visual confirmation of the fast heartbeat on an LED screen. An intravenous line was placed in the right antecubital vein to gain access to the circulatory system. As this line was put in, two blood cultures, a complete blood count, electrolytes and kidney function blood tests were drawn. The respiratory therapist took a sample of blood from the radial artery in the left wrist with the patient breathing the two liters of oxygen per minute that had been started by means of a nasal cannula as soon as he was brought in the door. Even before these tests returned from the lab, the ER doctor, acting on his initial clinical impression, ordered two grams of Rocephin and one hundred milligrams of Gentamicin, two potent systemic antibiotics, to be given through the intravenous line. (Two days later, both of the blood cultures grew out a bacteria called Pseudomonas aeruginosa, a deadly gram-negative organism that often is the cause of a cellulitis in a compromised patient. The antibiotic sensitivities demonstrated that this bacteria was sensitive to both Rocephin and Gentamicin.) A catheter was placed into the patient's urinary bladder to accurately record urine output and to obtain an initial sample of urine. Large amounts of intravenous fluids were given over a short period of time in an attempt to bring the blood pressure back up. These measures were largely unsuccessful. The blood pressure remained low and the shortness of breath and fast heartbeat continued.

Within twenty minutes, the results of the various blood tests began to come in from the lab where several technicians had put any routine work on hold and had run the samples through the sophisticated lab instruments as quickly as possible. First was the arterial blood gas result that was done on its own machine in the pulmonary lab where the respiratory therapist had personally carried it and run the test herself. This showed a partial pressure of oxygen of fifty five percent, a partial pressure of carbon dioxide of twenty four percent and a pH of 7.22. All of these numbers were bad news to the medical team. They indicated that the patient's blood was acidotic due to the massive infection and low blood pressure. His lungs were working mightily to compensate for this situation by blowing off the carbon dioxide but were not succeeding. Also, in spite of the fact that he was breathing very rapidly and that he was getting supplemental oxygen, the oxygen level in the arterial blood was still abnormally low indicating a significant degree of respiratory compromise.

The complete blood count showed a good volume of red blood cells so there was no anemia, but the white blood cell count was low at two thousand five hundred. This was an extremely poor indicator since, in any person with an active infection, the white blood cell count should normally go up dramatically as the body attempts to marshal its defenses to fight off the infection. The low white count would indicate that either the immune system is inadequate in the first place or that it is being overwhelmed. Either scenario, of course, is problematic. The blood urea nitrogen or "BUN" and the creatinine levels were moderately elevated, indicating that the patient was probably somewhat dehydrated to begin with even before the massive infection had lowered the blood pressure acutely. All of the other tests, liver functions, blood sugar, and calcium levels were within normal limits.

The old man, the focus of all of these diagnostic studies and laboratory tests, lay pale and inert on the ER gurney in the center of the room. He did not appear to be suffering so much as working very hard. The thin chest rose and fell rapidly like that of a distance runner, but the facial expression was blank and placid. His hin arms and leg were motionless. There was no response when the needles used to obtain the various blood samples pierced the paper-thin skin. Without much effort, one could imagine that the medical team was working feverishly on a training dummy rather than a real live patient. The eyes were held closed so there was no visible eye movement, but still, in an exception to this general tenor of inertness, the eyelids would flutter almost imperceptibly every once in a while. One had to look very carefully and with some concentration to see it.

Even before she had drawn the blood gas sample, the respiratory therapist had placed a pulse oximeter on the patient's left index finger. This device measured on a continuous basis the level of oxygen saturation in the blood. The readings on the oximeter had begun to decline gradually since the patient had arrived, and they were reaching life threatening levels even though the supplemental oxygen had been turned up as high as it would go.

At this point, the ER physician said something to the effect that it would be best at this juncture to simply step back and let nature take its course.

"Sorry, Doctor," spoke up the nurse who had been looking through the prior hospital records, "but this patient is listed as a full code."

"What?!" responded the physician incredulously. "Let me see that." He snatched the chart not particularly gently from the nurse and quickly scanned the page where the resuscitation status had been noted.

"Unfuckingbelievable!" he expostulated. "This poor bastard is seventy years old and has been completely out of it with dementia for
the last fifteen of those years. This says that he can't speak coherently, express a formed thought of any kind, or even feed himself, dress himself, or go to the bathroom. And they make him a full code? I'm supposed to stick a tube down his throat and put him on a machine to maintain his oxygen levels? Jesus Christ! The inmates are running the asylum."

With ill concealed disgust he literally threw the hospital chart onto the little metal desk that stood in one corner of the large examining room, but, after some more grumbling about getting the ethics committee of the hospital involved with the case the next morning (Provided, of course, that the patient survived until the next morning.), he proceeded in his usual professional way to insert a breathing tube down into the patient's main airway. A balloon or "cuff" was inflated around the tube to keep secretions from sliding down around it into the lungs and to stabilize the position of the tube. The tube was then connected to a machine that pumped oxygen into the patients' lungs at a controlled volume and rate.

And so, intensive treatment was continued. The patient was moved to the ICU. Very powerful drugs called vasopressors designed to increase the blood pressure at all costs by increasing the vascular tone were given. This was a double-edged sword because the increase in vascular tone would further compromise kidney and other organ function as the amount of blood getting to these organs would be limited. Fluid resuscitation was continued along with constant monitoring of the blood pressure, oxygen and cardiogram. All of these measures were ultimately unsuccessful. At 6:19 A.M., the ICU nurse noted that the patient's heart rate began to slow markedly. Despite the vasopressors, the blood pressure had been uncontainable for some time at that point. She gave me a milligram of atropine intravenously, but the heart rate did not go up and, in fact, continued to slow.

Up ahead now he could see that the trees were definitely thinning out and that there was a large open area coming into sight. In the middle of this clearing was a figure, a female figure of some familiarity to him though her back was turned. Though he was sure that he had run some great distance, he was not feeling tired at all. In fact, he felt quite good. As he approached the woman, he slowed his pace and walked up to her. She turned and smiled at him. It was her.

She looked as he remembered her, not cachectic and wracked with pain as in those final days, but young and vibrant and alive as he always thought of her. As she turned, the setting shifted around them, and they suddenly were sitting on a white stone bench on the shore of a large body of water. The sun shone brilliantly above them, illuminating an azure sky and an equally blue lake that stretched out to the horizon. In the distance, he could hear the cries of a flock of geese as they lifted off from the lake. She smiled at him and reached out to touch his hand. And then, just at that very instant, he knew that everything would be all right, that he had come home, that there would be no further trials or suffering. A great peace suffused his being.

At 6:26 A.M., the patient's heart stopped altogether. Obedient to her training, the ICU nurse called a "Code 99" over the hospital intercom. This was the euphemism that this hospital used to designate a cardiac arrest. The "code team" which basically consisted of the same emergency room personnel who had attended the patient in the ER, responded promptly, but the ER physician, who was also the leader of the team, quickly determined that the patient's pupils were fixed and dilated and that everything that could be done had already been done. At 6:30 A.M., three hours after he had been brought by ambulance to the emergency room, Martin Wennar was pronounced dead.

THE BEGINNING

"Cry 'Havoc' and let slip the dogs of war."

Shakespeare

The world around me had receded into silence and there was a buzzing in my ears as if I had dropped down a long tunnel in the earth where sound could not penetrate. In my hand was a thick sheaf of papers the first of which started off, "Peterson, Faulkner and Beiderbecke, Attorneys at Law, Specialists in Medical Malpractice." This alone was enough to shock my system, but the words that followed ensured that my life would never be the same from this time forward. "Now comes the plaintiff, Katherine Weimar on behalf of Martin Wennar with an action of malpractice against the defendants, La Place D'Espere Nursing Home and Jon Ziebaska, M.D." My eyes raced desperately to the end of the page trying to elicit the precise nature of the charges that were being made against me but without success. There was a long list of allegations, none of which were very specific, but the gist of it was that this patient, Martin Wennar had died as a direct result of poor nursing care that had been provided to him at a local nursing home and that I, as the treating physician, had contributed to, and, in the final analysis, was responsible for, his death. Again, there were no specifics that I could address directly. Phrases such as "poor oversight of care," "egregious lack of supervision," "failure to coordinate specialty care," and "lack of response to ongoing changes in medical condition" were used; but this was so much legal gobbledygook to me, and there was nothing that I could get ahold of. Basically, the charges were most ominous but most undefined. At the end of the list of allegations was an even longer list of questions and demands for information. Again, none of these was specific. For example, one demand read as follows, "Provide any and all records and information as to how many times, on what dates and in what regard you did render medical care to the aforementioned Martin Wennar in your office, at the La Place D'Espere Nursing Home, in the Northwest Medical Center and in any other venue." It was also requested that I provide the names of any and all personnel who might have contributed to such care or interacted with the patient in any of these places. In this regard, the demands were quite universal and, when taken as a whole, appeared to demand that I give these people the specifics of every medical encounter with the patient that had occurred while he was under my care and with the name of every person who had ever been involved with such care. This would be a herculean task, to say the least, and the thought of it was daunting and depressing. Was I obligated to do the legwork for these lawyers in fleshing out their own case against me? Obviously, I was loathe to do so. Wasn't it their responsibility to find their own witnesses and to develop their own line of argument? I vowed that I would be as nonspecific in my responses as they had been in their questions, but even so, it appeared that I would have to devote considerable time and effort to answering these interrogatories. A bit later, I would learn from the malpractice lawyer that my insurance company provided for me that I would only be providing the preliminary details and that he himself would screen all of the information and decide exactly what parts of it would be passed on to the plaintiff's attorneys and in what form. He also would inform me that, while I was required to provide all of the information that I myself had in my possession (office notes, etc.), I was in no way obligated to provide information from other sources such as the hospital and nursing home. Plaintiff's attorneys would have to get that themselves.

The date was June fifteenth in the year two thousand. My day had been proceeding as usual. In the morning I had made hospital rounds which took approximately two hours. I had five patients in the hospital that day, one man in the CCU who had a recent heart attack, an elderly woman with an exacerbation of chronic obstructive pulmonary disease who was slowly improving on steroids and antibiotics, a middle- aged man with pancreatitis, an elderly man with a gastrointestinal bleeding of unknown source, and a young woman who was recovering from an episode of deep venous thrombosis of the left leg. She was on her fourth hospital day of intravenous heparin and her clotting studies were now therapeutic on oral medication, so she was ready for discharge, and I filled out the appropriate forms and prescriptions and dictated the discharge summary. There were no admissions for me from the night before, so I had no new patients to catch up on that morning and was able to get to the office at a reasonable time. There I began to see the patients for that day in the order in which they were listed, completing what paperwork I could and returning phone calls between patients up until the time that my office manager, Rachel Cobb, had entered my office and handed me what at first appeared to be a thick letter. I doubt that Rachel had any idea what was contained in that letter as she gave me her usual brilliant smile as she handed it off to me and remarked that we seemed to be getting some higher-class mail than usual these days. The paper was rich, and cream colored and the return address was that of a legal firm operating out of Burlington, Vermont. Naive as Rachel in these matters, I actually had thanked her before she left my office. Now that the upscale looking packet had divulged its message, I was sorry that I had opened it.

Mind racing, I feverishly tried to recall what I knew about the patient, Martin Wennar, and to determine why his wife should be suing me. Martin was one of my more celebrated patients, and I easily remembered just who he was. The more specific details of his life and just how he ended up on a collision course with me remained a mystery. Martin Wennar was a self-made millionaire, a local boy who had made it to the big time by starting a premium ice cream manufacturing business and building it up into a franchise system that extended into all of the New England states. His first ice cream shop was located in a renovated garage in Burlington, Vermont. Initially, his success was limited, and his sales were small and local. Then he hit upon the idea of wedding rich, flavorful ice cream to various solid ingredients that enhanced the flavor of the basic ice cream and provided a luscious mouth feel that was positively sinful. He popularized such flavors as "Very Cherry," which consisted of a cherry flavored ice cream that was replete with halves of real cherries which were interspersed generously throughout and "Heath Bar Crunch," a premium vanilla ice cream that was almost forced out of its container by solid chunks of the original Heath Bar candy bar. His slogan became "Wennar's Ice Cream, It's a Real Winner!" The citizens, first of Burlington, then of the Northeast and ultimately the entire world to some degree (Franchises were started in Russia, France and a few other countries as well) quite literally ate it up. At some point, a multinational food company bought out his share of the business, which was considerable since he was the business; and he stayed on as a "consultant" at some enormous salary over and above the sale price of the business. This was all common knowledge, and, if you lived in St. Albans, you would have to be comatose or dead not to know about it.

I had even met Martin Wennar a couple of times in the early days of moving to town to start my medical practice. Our paths had crossed at some hospital fundraisers, but we hadn't exchanged much in the way of conversation and the only impressions that stayed with me were general ones. Basically, I recalled him as a friendly bear of a man with one of those hail-fellow-well-met personalities that people found easy to like. His wife was much younger than he and was drop dead gorgeous. I remembered that I immediately had pegged her as one of those trophy wives that are a societal cliche though, to be fair, I hadn't had so much as one word of conversation with her so I really had little to go on. Apparently, he became ill some short time after that and dropped out of sight, or at least out of the consciousness of St. Albans society because I heard nothing at all about him until he became one of my patients many years later. John Greenleaf had been Martin Wennar's personal physician for many years and, in fact, was the only doctor that Martin had ever had aside from various specialists that were consulted early on in his illness. Once the diagnosis of presenile dementia or Alzheimer's Disease was established and it was determined that little could be done for the patient, Doctor Greenleaf had continued to provide Martin's primary care. However, when his condition deteriorated to the point where he could no longer continue in the home setting, Martin was hospitalized briefly and then transferred to a custodial care home which had an Alzheimer's wing, the Madonna of the Mountains in Richford, Vermont, a small town on the Canadian border just north and east of St. Albans. There he first became my patient as I was at that time the medical director of the Richford Health Center and, working with a physician's assistant named Rosaire Archambault, was delivering most of the ongoing medical care to the residents of that facility.

As I vaguely recollected, the primary reasons for his being institutionalized at that time were frequent falls and multiple escape attempts. In his confused state he would try to "get away" from wherever he was whether it was his own home, a hospital, or a nursing home; and, because he was at that point frail and unsteady, he would often fall and would sometimes injure himself. Despite the best supervision that the custodial care home could provide, he continued to have problems there with inappropriate ambulation and frequent falls. In fact, he fell a total of nine times there and on two of those occasions suffered injuries, once breaking a finger, and once suffering a compression fracture of the lumbar spine. Rosaire had tried putting his mattress on the floor to eliminate nighttime falls, but this proved to be ineffective since most of the falls were not at night anyway and he was generally up and walking some distance away from his bed when he did fall. He also continued to wander and made several attempts to escape from the home. Once he actually got out of the building and was found walking rapidly west on route 105. Luckily, he did not fall on that occasion, and he stayed safely to the side of the road. Because of the dementia and wandering, Mr. Wennar was on the locked wing at The Madonna of the Mountains.

Ultimately, it was decided by the nursing administration at the custodial care home that they could no longer deal safely with him in that setting and that it would be necessary to transfer him to a level two facility, or true nursing home, so that he could be watched more closely. Arrangements were therefore made to move him to La Place D'Espere, a nursing home in the city of St. Albans where I follow patients on a regular basis, and I continued to remain his physician of record there. The transfer diagnoses at that time were: 1. Senile Dementia and 2. Frequent Falls. While living at La Place D'Espere, Martin continued to get up and try to walk away at all hours. He continued on multiple occasions to attempt to leave the facility; and, most importantly, he continued to fall. The nursing home tried multiple interventions to remedy these problems but with only partial success. The escape attempts were thwarted to a significant degree by a bracelet that was attached to his left ankle. This would set off an alarm whenever he went through a door that he wasn't supposed to. Most of the doors to the outside had alarms that were triggered when they were opened, but certain inside doors which visitors and nursing home personnel used to get from place to place within the facility did not have their own alarms, and the main door off the lobby did not have an alarm either. Thus, it was necessary for certain individuals to have their own personal alarm bracelets. Like many nursing homes, and in fact, all of the nursing homes in the state of Vermont, La Place D'Espere is a "restraint free" facility. Physical restraints of any kind are seldom, if ever, used on any of the patients there. This is so that patients will not injure themselves because of the restraints and because it not only makes the patients feel bad to be restrained, especially the patients that have the uncontrollable urge to wander, but it also makes the facility look bad in the eyes of visitors and family who may understandably look askance at seeing residents tied down in their chairs.

Other measures such as tab alerts, motion sensors that would sound an alarm when the patient gets up, frequent toileting to ensure that the urge to void would not cause the patient to get up in the night, mild sleeping medications to ensure bedtime somnolence, closer observation, etc., were all tried, some with partial success; but the bottom line was that Martin Wennar continued to fall. Finally, he took that one fall too many and fractured his left hip. This required a brief hospital stay and a surgical repair of the hip by an orthopedic surgeon. After the surgery, he was returned to the nursing home where, in spite of blood thinning medication, special mattresses, special booties and heel protectors, and careful nursing attention to keep the heels off the bed and prevent pressure sores, he developed a pressure ulcer on the left heel which, in spite of intensive local care to that wound, did not heal, became infected and subsequently led to a below the knee amputation of the left leg. It was noted at the time of that amputation that the circulation in the remaining leg was very poor, and it was the opinion of the operating surgeon that the right leg would also probably need to be amputated in the near future. Indeed, as predicted, Mr. Wennar did develop a pressure ulcer on the right heel, but before any amputation could be considered; he came down with a massive infection and died within a matter of hours. Obviously, death is not a good medical outcome, but I could see no reason in any of this for a lawsuit. By my recollection, he had been provided with the best medical care possible, and there had not been any treatment that had been overlooked or delayed.

I called Rachel back into my office and asked her to pull the office chart on Martin Wennar to see if there was something in it that I may not have remembered or that would provide a clue as to what was happening. When I told her that I was being sued by the patient's wife, she expressed shock and outrage. "Kathy Wennar is suing you. Why that money hungry, gold-digging bitch!" she exclaimed. "Everyone knows that she married him for his money anyway. I suppose that this scheme this is just more of the same. Why, it's criminal." she fumed. "I agree one hundred percent," I said, "but there must be some reason for the suit, at least theoretically. I've been trying my best to figure it out but coming up empty. Maybe there will be something in the record that will help."

"I doubt it." Rachel sniffed. "Kathy always was a low life. Always will be. Why, she's slept with half the eligible males in town and a lot of the ineligible ones as well? I know for a fact that some of that was going on when Martin was still at home. In fact, some of that was going on in his own home while he was home. And she's suing you? What chutzpah!" It was touching and gratifying to have Rachel on my side, but I would have expected nothing less from her. I had been very lucky in my office staff from the first day of my practice. Rachel Cobb had been my first employee, and from the beginning she was more like a partner than an underling. In fact, there were many times that I felt that she was the one who was running the business which was perfectly all right with me. I could concentrate more on the medical aspects of the practice while Rachel ensured that the lights stayed on, and the rent was paid. In the early years, it was just Rachel and I. I did all of the things that an office nurse would do (blood drawing, EKGs, blood pressure checking, etc.,) myself. She did all of the billing, record keeping, typing etc. In time, I taught her to do all of those medical things and she was able to do some of that as well. Then we found Peg Dumont who had just come out of nursing school at the time and was working at the local hospital. She had just had her second child and was looking for a job with regular daytime hours so that she could spend more time with her family. Rachel and I both agreed immediately that Peg was just the right person for us, and we hired her on the spot. The three of us have been working together ever since and it is most amazing to me (and to all of my jealous medical colleagues) that I have had literally no turnover of office personnel the entire time that I have been in practice.

Rachel and Peg can only be described as the best of employees. Though they are different from one another in many ways, they are the same in their professionalism, their common sense, their can-do attitudes, their compassion, and their loyalty. In spite of what many of my male patients have lecherously implied, neither one of them was hired for their looks, but both of them are strikingly good looking. Rachel is slightly on the thin side with chiseled and delicate features but nonetheless a womanly figure, and her complexion is dark, and gypsy like with jet black hair that has no grey in it though she is as old as I am. Peg is as fair as a summer day with a full and buxom physique. She is the youngest of us all and keeps us energized. Both women are great with patients, knowing whom to kid and whom to coddle. They are also great with me, knowing when to humor me and when to put me in my place. They have both saved me from myself on innumerable occasions when I was about to lose my temper or to inappropriately snap at a patient. They provide a buffer and protect me from many of the strains to which a private medical practice is prone. They suffer overtime which, much to my shame, is seldom compensated, but I try my best to make up for it with flexible scheduling and with bonuses and Christmas presents. Every physician in town envies me for my office staff.

"Also, Rache, please call the insurance company that carries my malpractice and notify them that a suit has been brought against me. They'll need to mobilize the lawyers so that we can prepare a defense as soon as possible." She said that she would.
A few minutes later, Rachel re-entered my office and handed me the office chart of Martin Wennar. It wasn't very thick at all, and it also wasn't very helpful. There was a problem list, a medication list, and some insurance information. Since he had never actually been seen in the office, there was nothing else of any consequence. Dead end.

TELLING CASSIE

"Yet the first bringer of unwelcome news hath but a losing office, and his tongue sounds ever after as a sullen bell, remember'd knolling a departing friend."

Shakespeare

T he rest of that working day blurred by. Luckily, there were no emergencies or hospital admissions, so I was able to get out of the office at a reasonable hour. I'm not sure that I would have been good for much anyway, given my distraction and general anxiety about being the target of a lawsuit. As a practicing physician, I was usually very good at compartmentalizing my emotions and thought processes, but this was threatening to overwhelm my abilities. Driving west down the lake road to our house on the shore of Lake Champlain, I couldn't stop running the few facts about the case through my head. What had I done wrong? Why was I being sued? Was there any merit to the case? No answers came readily to mind. This was a moderately elderly man with progressive senile dementia who had died a natural death as a typical consequence of typical complications of that disease. At first blush, there was no reason to think otherwise, and I couldn't imagine what the plaintiff had in mind. I finally concluded that I would just have to wait and see, and that perhaps an intensive review of the medical records, the nursing home records, and the hospital records would provide some answers in this regard. Certainly, the preliminary questions from the attorneys had not shed much light on the situation. They had been so broad that they might include just about anything and everything and gave no clues as to what the meat of the matter might be. It was frustrating and inconclusive. I must have been on autopilot for the entire drive because I have no recollection about anything in the external environment on my way home. I remember leaving the office, and the next thing that I recall is turning into the long dirt driveway that led to the house. Cassie's red Mazda convertible was parked in front of the house so I knew that she was home already. As soon as the car door closed, the frenzied barking of Orion, our great brute of a black lab, announced that my presence was duly noted. When I opened the side door, he was there to greet me, still barking exuberantly, his great tail lashing back and forth uncontrollably, his tongue hanging out with a drool of pleasure. I bent to give the big dog a vigorous head pat, and to scratch behind his ears. Orion was an immense black male lab, weighing over one hundred pounds and gave the lie to the idea that a rugged hunting dog should not be raised as a pet or coddled in any way. Since he was a pup, he had been spoiled almost constantly by the three female members of our household. Until the girls had gone off to school, he had mostly lived in the house where he reigned supreme pretty much doing what he liked and listening to no one but me. Cassie, Alexandra and Tatiana had never disciplined him, and basically had treated him like a lap dog, carrying him everywhere and allowing him to climb up on the furniture with them where he could cuddle in a nice warm human embrace. This wasn't so bad when he was a small pup, but as he inevitably and gigantically grew, it became more than a little difficult to support this type of behavior. Not to mention the embarrassment of having guests on the receiving end of a big furry black bundle of drooling affection when their only crime had been to sit down for a conversation in our living room. In spite of this affectionate upbringing, Orion was a terror in the field, and was one of the finest waterfowl retrievers that I have ever seen. Out of the house, away from his mistresses, he was a duck hunter's dream. He obeyed the usual commands to "sit," "come," and "hie on" to a fault, and would go anywhere I asked him to go in the heat of battle. In fact, he would go anywhere he needed to go to complete his genetically ingrained mission to retrieve any and all ducks that were brought to earth by his master's gun. At least once in every hunting season, I would have to pull up my floating blind from its resting place to motor into the middle of Missisquoi Bay to save the big lab from drowning in his quest to bring a wounded duck to hag. For rather than give up the chase and given his own proclivities he would prefer to drown than not succeed in his mission. Not that he was a macho dog. Where others might snarl, assume a vicious look or exude testosterone, Orion would happily thump his tail. Still, he was not one to be taken lightly or disrespected by his peers. On one occasion, another dog had the temerity to pick up a duck that I had wounded and had sent him to retrieve. Apparently, the dog had broken from his own boat without the command of his owner when the temptation of a wounded bird swimming by the boat had just been too much for him and, since he was closer to the prey than Orion, he had gotten there first. Big mistake. As soon as the other dog had picked up the fleeing duck, there came from Orion a sound that I have never heard come out of the mouth of a dog before or since. It was more like a roar than a bark or a snarl and sounded like something that might be produced by a lion rather than a dog. In two great bounds, Orion was on the back of the offender, slashing and biting viciously. The other dog dropped the duck, yelped piteously, and high tailed it back to his own boat dropped it as if pursued by demons, which, in a sense, he had been. Orion picked up the fallen duck as if nothing had happened and brought it back to me with his tail high and proud. After praising him for the retrieval and making him sit and stay, I waded over to the other blind to offer my apologies to the other hunter and to offer to pay half of the vet bills. In time honored duck hunting tradition however, the owner of the other dog allowed sheepishly that his dog was in the wrong and had bolted from the boat without permission to go after someone else's duck. He opined that the lacerations that his dog had received were "his own damned fault" and adamantly refused my offer. Nothing I could say would change his mind, so I waded back to my own boat where an unrepentant Orion awaited me. He lived a double life in this way. Adorable and huggable pet at home, terror of the swamp in a duck boat. This dual doggy existence had its downside since no one but myself could control the dog at home. There he was completely undisciplined, sort of like one of Cassie's unruly schoolchildren, doing what he wanted when he wanted when the master wasn't around. Since Cassie invariably got home before I did, and Orion spent his days in a fenced in run at the back of the house while we were at work, she was tasked with taking him for a walk each afternoon. This was good exercise for both her and the dog, and she enjoyed it for the most part. However, since he would not heel or come to her when called, she was forced to use a retractable leash to perform this activity. The leash did its job for the most part, but Orion was so big and powerful that every once in a while, he would jerk her off her feet, and it was only by some luck that she had avoided any major injuries up to this point. I tried on several occasions to get her to assert her dominance over the beast, and do some serious training in this regard, but it never happened. The other main problem was that Orion was never trained to avoid the road. Since our driveway was so long, and he was always walked on a leash while at home, there was no pressing need to do so. Out in the field, I would make him heel, if necessary, but usually we were out on the rivers or lakes, and there was no concern with traffic. Still, I knew that this could be a potential disaster, and there was always some niggling concern in the back of my mind that one day he might just get off the leash and wander merrily into the middle of a well-traveled roadway.

Though it was early summer, and the day was still bright and hot, the interior of the house was cool and dark. As I walked down the shadow entryway to the main living area, Orion at my heels, I could hear the muted murmur of television voices. The shades over the large living room windows that overlooked the lake had been drawn shut and there was a solitary light on. My wife, Cassie, was lying on the couch watching the television. She had a down comforter spread over her up to her chin and her fine-featured face looked pale and drawn as she turned towards me. I sensed that she was tired and remarked as much.

"Yeah," she said, "the little monsters were particularly obnoxious today. They totally exhausted me before lunch and after that I was running on fumes and caffeine. It was murder."

Orion was annoying us both at this point, making a pest of himself and trying to insinuate himself under the comforter, so I ordered him into his cage. Cassie started to protest, saying that he had been on his run all day, but she soon also saw that there was no way we would be allowed to talk to one another with him on the immediate scene, so she agreed to his exile to the pen. There the big lab whined until I covered his cage with a heavy blanket.

I made some commiserating noises concerning the ongoing battle to maintain discipline in the public schools, and Cassie, in turn, asked me how my day had gone. Rather than dissemble, I decided to bite the bullet, and gave her the bad news without any preamble.

"Well," I responded, "the day itself didn't go too badly, but I'm afraid that I do have some bad news. It seems that I am being sued for malpractice by the wife of a patient who died while he was under my care."

What happened next was disorienting and deeply disturbing to me. I knew that Cassie had been more on edge than usual in recent weeks for unclear reasons and she had just told me that she had a bad day and was physically wasted. Also, the news that I had just delivered so abruptly was obviously not good. Nonetheless, I was completely surprised by the intensity of her reaction.

Cassie's face took on a sudden and profound change. Her eyes widened and her pupils dilated. In that instant, she appeared on the average of screaming or crying. This transformation went from mild concern to hysteria in a millisecond. I was rocked back on my heels.

"My God, Jon," she exclaimed, "what have you done? Will we lose the house? Will we have to move? I don't think that I can stand it." And then she did burst into tears, sobbing uncontrollably into the comforter that she now pulled up to cover her face.

I was dumbfounded. Wasn't this something of a bizarre overreaction? For a few moments I was rendered speechless but on partially recovering, I responded, "Don't be ridiculous, Cass. As far as I know, I haven't done anything wrong in the first place. And even if I have, you know that at the very worst I have malpractice insurance that will take care of everything. There's no way that we would lose anything, except for my pride, and there is no way that we would have to move anywhere unless we wanted to. Why would you even think such a thing?"

Her face crumpled and she began to sob even harder. Her entire body shaking in a paroxysm of grief. "I don't know, Jon. I DON'T KNOW. But I have heard that these things can happen. How do you know that they can't? What if the insurance company refuses to pay? What if the settlement is more than they will cover?"

I thought that any of those scenarios would be highly unlikely, if not impossible. And said as much, but it was clear that my beautiful wife was determined to be worried no matter what I said. And it took almost another ten minutes before I could calm her down to the point where she agreed that we should attend to more mundane matters such as getting something to eat and try to put off intensively evaluating our position until we knew more about the facts of the case and knew just where we stood with the malpractice carrier. Personally, I wasn't worried in the least, or, in any event, I pretended not to be. After all, as I had said, even if bad things happened, I was covered. And, in my experience, bad things rarely occurred in totality. There were always some mitigating factors. Right?

It was obvious that no one was going to be up to cooking that evening, so we ordered out for pizza, our usual large cheese lovers with pepperoni and jalapeno peppers, a pizza that only those of us with cast iron digestive tracts could love. Still, while we waited for its arrival, neither one of us could resist worrying about the case again.

"You know," Cassie said, "I think that I actually remember meeting Kathy Wennar at one of those money raising functions that we attended a long time ago. I think it was at the Heart Ball, one of the benefits for the American Heart Association that the hospital auxiliary put on. I remember that she was quite young at the time, much younger than her husband, and that she was very good looking. She seemed a bit intimidated by her surroundings as I recall and was watching her husband like a hawk to imitate his table manners. Every man in the room was aware of her, and don't say that you weren't, but she was actually a bit scared and didn't say a word to anyone. I was feeling sorry for her, in spite of her good looks. When I went to the ladies' room, she was there, and she actually asked my advice on which fork to use and how to use the napkin. Me, a total stranger, she asked. I remember thinking that she was naive and vulnerable at the time. Apparently, I was wrong."
"I don't think that you were necessarily wrong," I retorted, "but she may have been a little out of her social depth at the time. I would guess that she learned to swim quite quickly. Martin Wennar is, was, a wealthy and powerful man. Money can buy a lot of social grace and power rubs off on those who are close to it. This woman may be beautiful but it doesn't follow that she's stupid. She certainly knows how to pick a lawyer."

We conjectured back and forth about the motives and the possible underpinnings of the lawsuit, but again came inevitably up against the fact that we simply did not have enough information to develop any solid theories so our discussion provided little enlightenment. Thankfully, the pizza arrived at last, and our obsessive turning over of the events was brought to an abrupt and welcome close. We both found that we were ravenous, and we attacked the pie like starving wolves. No pieces remained for breakfast the next day. Then, bellies warm with culinary fire, we went to bed.

To my surprise, sleep came quickly. In the night, however, I suddenly awoke. At first, I was confused and disoriented because I invariably slept soundly. Many years of taking night call had conditioned me to falling asleep almost at will and, when I wasn't on call and did sleep, almost nothing could wake me. Cassie often tells the story of how, when we were living in Boston, and I was doing my medical residency, there was a fire in the apartment across the courtyard from us. When she shook me awake to tell me this, I had asked her if the fire was touching our building. When she responded in the negative I rolled over and told her to wake me when it was. I soon realized that the events of that day had made their mark upon my psyche, and I was soon again reviewing the case in my head, what little I did know of it. Those same questions raced over and over wildly through my brain. My mind ran uncontrollably in circles for some undetermined period of time that seemed like forever. Beside me Cassie slept unconcernedly on as if nothing had happened. Eventually, some time before morning, I was able to get back to sleep. Unfortunately, this would be the harbinger of many similar nights to come when my thoughts would be overwhelmed with the firestorm of ongoing accusations and defenses, ripostes and parries, and I would be at times anxious, unsettled and even fearful in the hours of darkness. The worst part about this was that I had no conscious control over the process at all. These thoughts, alien and unwelcome, came in the night like merciless Visigoths and laid waste to my rest without remorse. There was no defense against the but to come to an end of the lawsuit

A LITTLE BACK-GROUND MUSIC

"...those inquires who desire an exact knowledge of the past as an aid to the interpretation of the future..."

Thucydides

Cassie and I had met in college when we were members of opposing debating teams. She had gone to a small women's college in Northampton, Massachusetts, Smith College, and I had gone to Harvard College in Cambridge, near Boston. At that time, to my everlasting shame in later years, I had actually entertained some thoughts of being a lawyer and had chosen the debating team as a means of honing my speaking skills as well as developing logical arguments. Truth be told, I was at something of a loss as to how to decide just what to do with the rest of my life, not being one of those folks who always felt destined to become one thing or another. There were just too many interesting occupations. Unfortunately, if you chose one or another of them, it would almost invariably rule out most of the others. To keep my options open, I took the law boards and the medical boards and majored in psychology rather than biology or the social sciences. This uncertainty ultimately brought me a fine reward as I met my Cassie because of it.

It was the time of the Vietnam War, and the topic of debate that day was the legitimacy of the war itself, a topic that was both highly charged and extremely relevant. As is usual in these debating contests, each team would get a certain amount of time to present one side of the case, and then the roles would be reversed, and the same team would then go on to take exactly the opposite position. The Smith team turned out to be one of the toughest that we competed against that season. In fact, they mopped the floor with us though I would never admit that to Cassie. Not that it mattered, because the judges knew who the winners were without doubt, and the score wasn't even close. I often told Cassie that I was so distracted by her presence on the other team that I couldn't do my usual superb debating job, but she believed that about as much as the judges believed that Harvard had beaten Smith that day. Physically Cassie was an average young woman about five feet four inches in height and one hundred and fifteen pounds in weight. Her most outstanding features were her eyes and her smile both of which were shown to best advantage in the situation of a debate where the contestant stands behind a podium and uses the force of reason to make points. A couple of times during the contest, Cassie's gaze locked upon my own, and I immediately felt a strong connection. Those eyes, large and dark brown almost to the point of blackness, were mesmerizing, and I was strongly drawn into them. Perhaps I have some masochistic tendencies, but the idea of a good-looking woman who can best me in an intellectual endeavor really turns me on, and I wasted no time in making the acquaintance of the beautiful young lady whose sharp mind had torn my best arguments to shreds. We felt a common bond immediately (or she felt sorry for me in my defeat) and, after talking together for almost two hours after the debate had concluded, we agreed that I would get out to Smith the following weekend to see her. After that, we were inseparable, and it was rare that one of us would not be found in the room of the other on any given weekend. This was our sophomore year. At the beginning of our senior year, we had agreed that we would marry in the fall after graduation. Neither one of us knew exactly what we would be doing at that time. I was about to apply to medical school, and Cassie had determined to get a job in publishing or library work, but none of these plans was yet a reality. Nonetheless, we both felt that we should follow this path. To me, it just felt right. In later years, I had often asked Cassie if she was worried or nervous about getting married at that time with so much uncertainty regarding our mutual futures. Invariably, she had said that she was not concerned in the least. I know that I felt the same.

As luck would have it, things worked out just as we had anticipated. I was accepted to Boston University School of Medicine, Cassie got a job working for the library Association of Massachusetts, and we rented a studio apartment on the backside of Beacon Hill for one hundred and forty dollars a month. Although the place was decidedly small (One of Cassie's friends remarked after seeing the apartment for the first time that her father's boat was bigger than it was.), we really didn't care. We were too involved with each other to worry about creature comforts or living space, and we each had other interests as well, Cassie with her job and I with my studies.

It turned out that Cassie came to actually hate that first job pretty quickly as the work was just not intellectually stimulating and the people involved in it were so caught up in bureaucratic infighting that there was little comradery there. She was determined to leave that place as quickly as possible and, to that end, enrolled in a master's program in Library Science at Boston University where she could take courses in the evenings. In two years, she had her master's degree, and was able to get a job as a school librarian at Christopher Columbus High School, a private Catholic boys' school run by Franciscan friars in the North End of Boston. This job turned out to be a godsend, and Cassie just loved it. The friars, all male of course, and with a dedication and intelligence that was unmatched in the public sector, ran a tight ship. Since it was a private school, disruptive behavior on the part of any student would not be tolerated for long, and the boys who enrolled there would either toe the line or be forced to leave. Discipline, enforced by one of the friars who was specifically fitted to that role, was not a problem.

Teaching was a joy; and, as sole mistress of the library, a lovely female face in a sea of masculine endeavor, Cassie was in her element.

When I graduated from medical school, we determined that I would stay in the area to do my internship and residency, so I applied to most of the Boston area hospitals. Luckily, there are a lot of them to choose from, and I eventually did get into a program in internal medicine at University Hospital, the teaching hospital affiliated with Boston University. So it came to pass that we ended up staying in Boston for another seven years after college graduation while my training in medicine progressed and Cassie continued to run the library at Christopher Columbus. Those years were full and busy ones. In spite of the strains of a medical internship with its long hours and multiple stresses, I generally look upon those times as happy ones. Perhaps this is the rosy view of nostalgia where only the good times are recalled, but even when I try really hard, I can't bring up too many painful memories of that time. Cassie and I filled the hours that we had together with long walks, movies, occasional dinners with friends and a rare show or two. We were never bored and never tired of one another's company. Treacly but true.

This is not to say that life didn't have its problems. On one occasion our apartment was robbed. We concluded that it had to be kids who, having spotted our ten speed bicycles out on the back porch three stories up, had entered the apartment building during the day while we were out, and had kicked in the door to our apartment. They had taken the two bicycles and nothing else. In fact, it appeared that they hadn't even taken the time to look for anything else. No drawers were askew, and nothing else was missing. The two detectives who had responded to our call had taken the appropriate information, and happily assured us that it was highly unlikely that anyone would ever be apprehended for the crime. We consoled ourselves by saying that the kids probably needed the bicycles more than we did and that they were pretty inexpensive bicycles in the first place. Not that this would have prevented us from prosecuting the little miscreants to the fullest extent of the law had they ever been apprehended.

During the time that we were in Boston, the usual litany of street crimes took place. There was one terrible occurrence when a physician that I actually knew personally was out with his wife when they were accosted by a young black male who held the wife at knife point and demanded money. The doctor handed over his wallet but happened to be armed with a revolver, and when the robber let the wife go and turned to flee, he shot him dead. There were all sorts of inflammatory comments in the news at the time. Some felt that this was murder as the perpetrator was no longer a direct threat after he had released the wife and was making his getaway. Others felt that the shooter was obviously under great emotional stress as his wife had just been threatened with deadly force and that any actions that he took after that could readily be justified. Still others said that the young criminal was outside the law and was getting away with the man's wallet so that shooting him was perfectly appropriate under the circumstances. I don't actually remember how the situation resolved, but I have the general sense that it eventually all blew over and that the offending doctor was not charged.

When my residency came to a close and it was time to decide upon a place to go to live the rest of our lives, the city did not seem particularly attractive to me. I had been asked by a couple of internists who had finished in the year or two before I did to join them in medical practice in the Boston suburbs. This was flattering but not appealing. Cassie and I agreed that we would look for a position in a rural or semi-rural area where I could join a small coverage group in internal medicine. It so happened that, among a few others, there was an ad in the New England Journal of Medicine for just such an opening in St. Albans, Vermont. A four-man group had just lost one of their members who had had a heart attack and was retiring prematurely for that reason. The local hospital was guaranteeing a reasonable salary for the first two years, and it looked like a good deal. After we had traveled up to St.

Albans, we have seen the hospital and met the members of the call group, we were sure that this was the place for us, and we took the position.

Everything fell into place. We found a nice house off the Georgia Shore Road on the shore of Lake Champlain and, with the recommendation of the senior member of the call group, were able to purchase it with a mortgage that we thought was astronomically high at the time but in later years turned out to be the best financial investment that we ever made. Soon after we arrived, Cassie was able to get a position as a school librarian at the local high school to start immediately in the following fall.

Life went on apace. As we both settled into our new jobs, we felt secure enough to start a family and stopped using birth control Early the next summer, our first child, Alexandra, was born and, about two years after that we had another daughter, Tatiana. With active careers, children to raise, a fantastic natural setting for sports, recreation of all kinds and multiple interests outside of work, our lives were full to overflowing.

RECORD VIEW

"Let's look at the record."

Al Smith

T he next week found me, on a Wednesday afternoon, my afternoon off, at La Place D'Espere, one of the local level two nursing homes, where Martin Wennar had lived out his final days. My objective was to thoroughly review his records there. Rachel had called ahead the day before so that I could have allotted to me a private space in which to look at them and the nursing home had already gathered them together to make the onerous task as simple as possible. Still, my heart sank into my shoes when I realized the enormity of the task before me. There were three huge binders, each about six inches thick, which supposedly contained the full record, and, from the weight of them, I could well believe it. Three nursing shifts, twenty-four hours a day, seven days a week for three hundred and sixty-five days a year, and each shift would write at least one note, that is, if all was uneventful and going well. If there was an emergency, a fall, a bruise, or some other atypical problem no matter how minor, this would generate yet another note and possibly a separate incident report as well. So, just taking into account the nursing notes alone at a minimum would be one thousand one hundred and fifty-five notes. On top of that would be the notes of the nutritionist, the physical therapists, the social service people, doctor's progress notes, notes from any other medical consultants, hospital discharge summaries, living wills and durable powers of attorney, results of lab-work, x-rays and any other diagnostic studies, medication lists and on and on...

I was just about to dive into this swamp of information when Gail Casperson poked her head into the small conference room which I was using as a base for my assault. Gail was the administrator of La Place D'Espere, an outstandingly good-looking woman with a first-class brain who had essentially pulled herself up by her own bootstraps from merely graduating from high school as the daughter of lower middle class parents to going on to get her master's degree in business administration. She and I had come into contact many times in regard to nursing home policies, nursing home patients and just the day to day work of running an extended care facility of this type. All of our contacts hadn't necessarily been peaceful ones or even productive ones, and some of them had been downright contentious. Still, I respected Gail enormously and fervently hoped that the feeling was mutual. Besides, I liked her - a lot. It didn't hurt that she was five feet eight inches tall, weighed one hundred and twenty pounds, had luxurious dark blond hair cut into a pageboy and had a dazzling smile that could knock me right out of my socks. Above the smile were high cheekbones and a straight nose complemented by two brown eyes that were so large and dark that they suggested two luminous black pools. There was quite definitely an attraction there, but we were both married to people that we loved and cared about so there was little danger of anything more than a bit of harmless flirting going on.

The equation had been knocked somewhat out of balance about a year prior to this when Gail's husband, Mike, a long-distance trucker, had been killed in a bizarre accident on the job. He was piloting a big rig hauling transformers in Colorado somewhere when he came over a small rise to find a small passenger car broken down directly in the middle of his lane. A state trooper had arrived on the scene and had parked his car on the right shoulder just off to the side. The trooper was in the very act of moving flares and cones out of his car to guard against such a disaster as Mike's speeding behemoth represented, but he was just a little too late. Mike apparently could see that the car was full of people and that there was no room at all to get off the road to the right side. Naturally, there was a large black SUV approaching the scene from the other direction eliminating the possibility of simply switching into the oncoming lane. Braking to a stop was out of the question as the immense mass of the eighteen-wheeler would take far too much distance to come to a full stop. There was no obvious way to keep his gargantuan vehicle from simply riding over and crushing all in his path. In a heroic and masterful piece of driving skill, Mike was somehow able to get his truck all the way over to the left side of the road and to jackknife the trailer to the left away from the on-coming SUV. Unfortunately, in doing so, the truck careened onto its side and skidded in that position for over one hundred yards, There was was a wooden cattle fence there along the left shoulder of the road. One of the individual fence posts became airborne and lanced into the cab of the truck like a giant spear, impaling Mike through the abdomen and transecting his abdominal aorta. He died within a second.

Gail was devastated. They had two teenage children, Erin, and Sean, who needed to be comforted by her. Somehow, like most in such horrid and tragic circumstances, they all got through it one day at a time, and the residual family was surviving. I know that Gail herself was coming through the worst of it although she certainly had some dark days. More than a few times I had spotted some unaccustomed tears in those large brown eyes of hers and some days when I had looked for her, discovered that she just hadn't come to work. Initially, I think that she was moved to go on just for the sake of her children, but, as time passed, she actually regained a large measure of her basic joie de vivre and was, if only on the surface, back to her indomitable self.

Subsequently, the governor of Colorado posthumously awarded Michael Casperson the State Medal of Honor for his heroic and selfless action in undoubtedly saving the lives of at least four people and probably a few more at the expense of his own. Some cynics would say that the governor only did this because it so happened that he was a passenger in that black SUV that had been approaching the scene from the opposite direction and was so traumatized by the sight of the big rig coming directly at him that he had an accident of elimination right then and there. He was so happy and amazed to come through the situation in one piece that he had to do something memorable about it and thus the award. This medal came with a modest amount of financial recompense as well.

Mike also had insurance through the trucking company for which he was working at the time and the company itself had added to this another sum of money, a considerable sum, for service "above and beyond." Now once again, some cynics might say that the company could well afford this and that it was the least that they could do in view of the fact that, had innocent civilians been killed or maimed by one of their trucks driven by one of their drivers, they would be vulnerable to potential lawsuits for damages into the seven figures, notwithstanding the unavoidable circumstances of the crippled car standing in the middle of the lane in the center of a deep dip that prevented any visual warning of any kind before the truck driver was on top of them at speed. I was beginning to realize the truth of that old bromide that, in the good old US of A, anyone could sue anyone for anything and probably would. Gail did not question the reasons for the company's largesse but was merely grateful for it. With two young children rapidly approaching the age of college tuition, any financial help was greatly appreciated. These insurances and awards were very helpful, but they did not ensure her financial independence, and she resumed working at her administrative job. Knowing Gail, I suspect that she would have done this regardless of the circumstances as she was not the type of person that could simply sit back and live a life of unproductive leisure.

"Hey, Jon," she said, "what brings you out to these parts? From what Julia had told me, I thought that Bill Zarabedian would be working in this room today."

William Zarabedian was another internist who was a member of my coverage group. Because both of our last names began with the letter "Z," people would constantly be confusing the two of us. Bill and I had a standing joke that this was because we looked so much alike. Bill was five feet six inches tall, a bit on the portly side and balding. Cassie always said that he reminded her of an elf. I am six feet even, weigh one hundred and ninety pounds and have a full head of hair and a full beard. Even so, shortly after Cassie and I moved up to St. Albans and she gave birth to Alexandra, many people were congratulating Bill on the birth of another child. Bill said nothing to dissuade them and took all of the congratulatory remarks in stride.

Since Bill was also the medical director of this nursing home, it was not surprising that there might be some confusion as to which "Doctor Z" would be using the room.

"Nah," I responded, "it's me alright. I'm being sued by Martin Wennar's wife and have to review the records to see if I can find out why."

"Jeez," Gail said, "I'm sorry about that. Why that bitch on wheels! You know that La Place is also named in the suit, and they are making me the point person on the case. You and I may be seeing a lot more of each other in the near future."

"Well, Darlin'," I replied, "not that I wouldn't mind seeing a lot more of you, but I could do without all the lawyers as chaperones." She laughed. "But what exactly do you mean by those words, "that bitch on wheels." I went on. "You're the second person that reacted that way when I mentioned Martin Wennar's wife. What's the deal there?"

"There are some interesting things I can tell you about the good widow Wennar." she responded. "Most of this is gossip and rumor, you understand, but it's good gossip and solid rumor. I have a couple of younger sisters who are closer to Kathy's age and this is a small community to begin with, so my sources are pretty accurate. Ve haff our says you know."

"Okay, you've piqued my interest. Spit it out before I bring out the thumb-screws and the iron maiden."

"Oho, so it's a bit of the old whips and chains is it? Well, we can't have any of that. Let me try to fill you in from the beginning. In all fairness to Kathy, she really had it tough growing up. She came from a big family and grew up literally on the wrong side of the tracks. We can say that with some confidence in St. Albans, big railroad town that it used to be and still is to some extent. Her father, Jerry Sheperd, was a slacker and ne'er do well who never held a job for any extended period of time. He was on disability for chronic back pain, sold some of his prescribed pain meds and a little marijuana on the side and spent most of his time hanging out in bars and fathering children by several different women. I believe he was actually married to Kathy's mother, but it was a union in name only. Jerry probably slept in his own house about half the time. Worse, I think he thought that a marriage license was a license to smack your wife around. Still worse, rumor has it that he abused all of the boy children physically and the girls, including Kathy, physically and sexually. This I don't know for sure, but I do know for a fact that all of the kids were in foster care at one time or another. And given the way Kathy turned out, it would certainly fit. Have you ever seen Kathy? Do you know what she looks like?"

I acknowledge that I had seen her on a couple of occasions many years ago but not recently. I did know that she was very good looking, a real beauty.

"That may be an understatement." Gail asserted. "Kathy Wennar is, without a doubt, one of the most beautiful women that you will ever see. Whenever I see her in person, I am amazed all over again. She is really absolutely gorgeous. And I don't mean in any sort of fake , made up, artificial lower class sort of way. Her face is lovely, transcendent, the very embodiment of beauty. Her figure is flawless and proportional with all the curves and lines in the right places. By the time she got to high school, all of the boys and a lot of the men were already falling all over themselves trying to get close to her. And she wasn't standoffish in the least. In point of fact, she was incredibly promiscuous, using her looks and her body to get her whatever she wanted at the time. I firmly believe that this was a result of her father's abuse. Interestingly enough, however, she seemed to retain a high opinion of herself. At least she was no shrinking violet. If there was a competition that she wanted to enter or someplace that she wanted to be, nothing could stand in her way. She was homecoming queen, prom queen, and, except for the fact that the office required some little effort and a speech at graduation, she undoubtedly would have been class president. She wasn't a cheerleader, but she dated, at one time or another, all of the big jocks on campus. There never were any steady commitments, however, probably because the seasons changed, and football became basketball became baseball. Maybe if St. Mary's had some three- or four-letter men, her affections would not have been so transient. Rumor has it that she never dated any male that she didn't have sex with, and I have no reason to think otherwise."

"So," I interjected, "now you really interest me. How did this kind of a woman hook up with an upstanding citizen like Martin Wennar? I mean, outside of the physical attraction, which, from your description of the lady, must certainly have been considerable. Was that all there was to it?

"Just listen, my son, and all will become clear." Gail intoned. "Right out of high school, Kathy got a job on the line at the Fonda Container Corporation where she worked the third shift, from eleven at night to seven in the morning, stacking paper plates in cardboard boxes for shipment. I can't say if she had the intellect, but she certainly did not have the desire to pursue further education and there isn't really much else you can do in this area with only a high school education.

Lord knows what would have become of her if she hadn't met Martin when she did. She was twenty-two years old, never married, with a long string of multiple "boyfriends" by that time and had been working on the line for four years without a promotion and only the regular salary increases that the union had been able to negotiate. I imagine any other material need or desires that she had were satisfied by these off and on male companions.

In any event, Fonda Container, like many similar business-es, had some infrequent morale building events where the employ-ees might be given a day off, some free food and chance to enjoy some recreational activities at the expense of the company. One such event was the annual company picnic. Wennar's Ice Cream often donated free ice cream to these affairs as a public relations gimmick, another way of getting its product into the public con-sciousness. As the president and owner of the company, Martin enjoyed going out to some of these affairs and handing out the free ice cream personally. For him, it was better than playing Santa Claus at Christmas.

So now we come to the other side of the equation." Gail went on. "The Martin Wennar part. You know, of course, that Martin had been married before he met Kathy. In fact, as far as I know, he had been very happily married to his childhood sweetheart, Mary, long before he had achieved his huge business success. They had two children, both boys, who, luckily were both grown and out of the house by the time Mary had developed the non-hodgkins lym-phoma that ended her life. Mary and Martin were very much in love, and outside of Martin's work, were inseparable, going every-where together and sharing the same hobbies, reading, fishing and running. He remained at her side through all of the multiple tests, staging procedures, radiation and chemotherapy in an attempt to cheat the malignant crab of its prey but this was all ultimately to no avail. Martin was willing to spend all kinds of money and, in fact, did spend a considerable sum over and above their comprehensive medical insurance to try to move the universe and keep Mary with him; but, in the end, death took her inexorably.

Mary had been dead for eleven months or so by the time Martin met Kathy, who was to become his second wife. Martin, then at the age of fifty, was at the height of his powers. He was in good physical shape, still running regularly, knew what he wanted out of life, was enormously wealthy and was well grounded in the realities of day-to-day existence. He also was pretty good looking himself, at six feet two inches, two hundred and twenty pounds with thick black hair and a strong male face that was roman in feature and swarthy in hue. Many of his friends joked that, because of the way he looked, he was a "made man" in the mafia, which accounted for his business success. This, of course, was total non-sense, but he never attempted to set anyone straight on that issue, enjoying the nefarious association, fantastical though it was. At this juncture, he had been without any close female companion-ship for almost two years. He had not dated anyone since his wife's death, probably had not even consciously thought about doing so. And, of course, there was always the fact that he missed Mary a hell of a lot.

So it came to pass that the two of them met, like star crossed lovers, the fifty-year-old ice cream magnate and the twen-ty-two-year- old assembly line worker, the former looking for the companionship and the comfort that his wife's death had so cru-elly and prematurely taken from him, and the latter, as always in her troubled life, looking for the main chance. It didn't hurt that the assembly line worker was probably one of the most beautiful women in the whole wide world. Within six months, Kathy Shep-erd became the second Mrs. Martin Wennar.

To the surprise of many, the marriage actually was working out quite well for the first five years. Kathy enjoyed a life of luxu-ry, a palatial home, an expensive automobile of her own, frequent trips, cruises and social events of all description. Martin enjoyed her high spirits, her general devil-may-care attitude and her un-surpassed physical beauty which he delighted to show off at every opportunity. There was more than a little of the "Professor Hig-gins- Eliza Doolittle" aspect to their relationship as Martin intro-duced Kathy to heights of society that she might never have con-sidered scaling under other circumstances. He proved a thoughtful and considerate mentor in this regard. Sexually, Kathy had little to complain about though she may have found a constant companion a bit of a boring change. In the early days of their marriage, Martin's bottled-up sexual energies, which had been accumulating all too long since Mary's illness and passing, were a pleasant surprise and, indeed, a revelation to Kathy. In spite of her multiple previous sexual partners, she never had really experienced a thoroughly satisfactory sexual encounter until this time. The "affairs" in which she had been involved had consisted of back seat groping for the most part, with the rare single night in a motel room thrown in. It was the pleasure of the male partner that was paramount, indeed mandatory, from Kathy's perspective in those couplings. The youths that had accompanied her in these activities, while handsome enough and more than willing, were callow and inexperienced. Martin, on the other hand. was well versed in love making, and was a thoughtful, caring and also incredibly energetic lover. Kathy was transported. Many mornings she awoke feeling dreamy and pleasantly enervated. As far as I know, Kathy never cheated on Martin at that time, and though there have been some rumors to the contrary, my sources can't substantiate them. Once he got sick, though, she reverted to her previous behaviors. I think he began to show signs of dementia about five years after the marriage. Her behavior after that was unconscionable. She took multiple lovers, many times in their own house with Martin in it at the time. I don't think he realized what was going on though. By the time he went into the custodial care home he was long past caring about what his wife was up to. She herself made a complete psychological break with him fairly early on. It was as if he no longer existed in her world. He was no longer any use to her so she threw him out with the trash."

At this point, Gail took a long breath and gave me one of her dazzling smiles. "That's widow Wennar in a nutshell." she said. "At any rate, that's about all I can tell you about her. I wouldn't want to get in her path if I had something that she wanted."

"Wow!" I replied. "That indeed is quite a tale. You told it very well. Scheherazade has nothing on you."

"Why, thank you, kind sir." she acknowledged, blushing with pleasure. "And now, I really must go. Good luck with your other research. Some of us have to do the work around here. See you."

> With that she was gone before I could come up with a witty rejoinder, and I was left to face the mountain of paperwork that lay before me. For the next few hours, I pored over the medical records diligently looking for any clue that might give me an idea as to why I was being sued and what the specific allegations might be. As far as I could determine, there was no problem. Marlin Weimar had had a number of severe medical problems that were a direct result of his underlying senile dementia, and these, despite appropriate evaluation and treatment, inevitably led to his death. The dementia itself was a terminal condition anyway. The records appeared to be complete. Mr. Wennar's every meal, every activity, every bowel movement and every interaction were duly recorded. As his primary physician, I had reviewed and signed off on every medication order, every consult or order made by the specialty physicians, the ancillary personnel such as dietary and physical therapy, and my own physician's progress notes.

Now, it is true that many of my progress notes were very brief and, in the eyes of some, might be considered not very informative or perhaps not complete but I would argue that this was not the case. I simply did not embellish where simplicity would suffice and refused to be redundant in my verbiage. The notes that I had written in Martin Wennar's chart were similar to any other progress notes that I might write on a patient with senile dementia who had no other active medical problems. Up until the time of his fall, and to a large degree in between his relatively few medical crises, this was the case with Mr. Wennar. My notes were written in the typical format of the day for physician's progress notes and were in what is called the S.O.A.P. format. The S is subjective, what the patient says or describes as the complaint, the o is objective, what the doctor or other personnel actually observe, the A is the assessment, what the diagnosis is, the P is the plan of treatment or plan of further evaluation. A typical note in Martin Wennar's chart might read as follows:

S: Nothing. Patient demented.
o: V.S. (Vital Signs) stable.
A: Stable.
P: Same.

So, as can be seen, there may be little of substance in such notes unless something new is happening with the patient. Again, some might consider this to be a bit cursory, but I have always maintained that such notes simply reflect the situation as it is and require no elaboration. Besides, truth be told, a physician's time is often short with always another patient to be seen and always another problem with which to deal. Personally, I would rather deal with the problems than spend more time writing notes in the chart. Not that documentation isn't of some value other than protecting us from lawsuits. It can provide a covering physician with vital information when we ourselves are not available and ensures continuity of care for our patients. Still, notes should be succinct and to the point. If there is anything unusual going on, then they should reflect that as well. After several hours of chart review, I was no further along in my quest. I had not uncovered any smoking gun, or, for that matter, even a leaky squirt gun. The care appeared appropriate, and the records appeared to be complete. I would have to await the arguments of the lawyers to understand the exact nature of the allegations against me and the nursing home, but the former were obviously of dearer interest to me than the latter. By this time, my eyes were blurring, and I had developed a raging headache. I figured that it was time to quit and so I did. Without further ado, I packed the three huge binders into one of those fold-up cardboard file boxes that was there especially for that purpose threw the box onto the table with some disgust and walked rapidly out of the nursing home. I couldn't quite bring myself to run, but believe me, I felt like it. There was no one to engage me in conversation on the way out but a little old man sitting on the end of a redwood bench just at the entryway, and he appeared lost in his own murky thoughts if his steady, low, and unintelligible mumbling were any indication. The remainder of the day, such as it was, beckoned.

THE PIPES, THE PIPES ARE CALLING

"Piping down the valleys wild, Piping songs of pleasant glee."

William Blake

My home was only a few miles away from the nursing home, and it took a mere ten minutes to drive there. I changed quickly into running shorts and shoes and was back out the door within another ten minutes to do my five miles. It's not that I run every day although I have every intention of doing so. Many days I end up getting home late because office hours run over or there is an emergency admission or two at the hospital that would require me to go there after office hours or there is some meeting or other, usually job related, that takes up another block of time or the weather is just not the sort in which any sane person would wish to go out running. In Northern New England this would not be rare, especially in the winter months when sleet, snow, hail, and vicious winds all might conspire on a regular basis to keep me from my appointed running rounds. Also, once daylight savings time went out, it would be dark so early that running on the roads would be like trying to draw to an inside straight in poker. Dangerous. Still, I did manage to run the majority of days; and it was the rare week that I couldn't at least get in three days of running, the Wednesday afternoon that I usually took off and the two weekend days when

I wasn't on call at a minimum. Though I do try to run regularly, I don't consider myself to be a runner. I never ran competitively in high school or college, and my body type, at six feet and one hundred and ninety pounds, is just not that of the archetypal runner.

And besides these, I have many other excuses. In spite of this, I do manage to compete on an irregular basis in some of the ten- kilometer races in the area. Where we live, these are the Sap Run in St. Albans, the Milk Run in Enosburg and the Swan Run in Swanton. On an even rarer occasion, when the entries in my age group are few enough and even slower than me, I have actually placed "on the money" in some of these events, and have collected some piece of dust catching hardware that Cassie just loves to see me bring home. This intermittent positive reinforcement only serves to keep me coming back. I also run as part of a five-man relay team in the Vermont City Marathon that is held in Burlington each year and participate in a local triathlon, the Bay Day Great Race in St. Albans Bay, as the runner in a four-man relay team that consists of a runner, a bicyclist and two canoeists. To date, we have the dubious distinction of having participated in every Great Race since the inception of the event. Notice that I don't say anything about how well we have fared in these races. We have taken, with great hubris, to calling ourselves the Bay Day Originals. Running is good for the body and good for the soul. It also helps to clear the mind and quite often leads to creative thinking. I have had some pretty good ideas while out pounding the roads and not trying to concentrate on the physical demands of the effort itself. Sometimes the brain on cruise control takes a creative turn of its own. There were no insights concerning the present lawsuit on this occasion, however.

By the time I had finished the run and taken a shower, Cassie was home from school, and we contentedly shared a light meal while we discussed the events of our mutual days. Cassie seemed a bit distracted to me, but she took my news of no news on the lawsuit front with equanimity, and I took that as a good sign. There were no hysterical reactions or inappropriate outbursts. If anything, she was strangely calm and indifferent. Her own day had been relatively benign. None of the little "angels" at school had maimed or killed anyone and, as far as she knew, the library was still intact when she had left it. Unquestionably a good day. After we finished eating, we both had to leave again. Cassie was a member of the local library board in Georgia, the small town in which we lived, and had a board meeting that evening. I had a standing date on Wednesday evenings for bag-pipe practice at the Saint James Episcopal Church in Essex.

The way this came about is an interesting tale in itself. A few years ago, the famous golfer, Payne Stewart, died in that freak airplane accident when his private jet plane lost oxygen pressure at high altitude and eventually crashed, killing everyone aboard. Since Stewart was one of the finest golfers of the time and a Scotsman as well, his funeral ceremony was conducted on national television on the eighteenth green of one of the country's most celebrated golf courses. The memory is strong in me. It was very early in the morning and there was a thick mist over the course. All was preternaturally silent. Then, from far off, came a low sound that gradually resolved itself into the wail of a solitary piper playing Dvorzak's "Going Home." The sound slowly came closer and closer until the lone figure came striding ghost-like out of the mist with the plaintive howl of the drones running on and the forlorn dirge of the basic tune soaring above this background like some angelic demon. The camera panned in on the footsteps that the piper's brogues left in the heavy dew. The sound of his skirling pipes slowly receded into the distance and the world gradually returned to its original silence. The footsteps, formed as they were from the pressure of the piper's shoes on the short grass, also gradually faded away before the unblinking eye of the camera as the grass gradually sprang back to its original position, reflecting the fading away of the haunting tune. The hair on the back of my neck stood on end. I was strangely moved. Surely the highland bagpipes are the human equivalent of the loon's cry, the whale's underwater lament or the wolf's howl. They all somehow touch the deepest part of the human psyche and reveal the world to be both terrible and beautiful. I resolved that somehow, I would learn to play this powerful instrument.

The Christmas of my fiftieth year, my dear Cassie called my bluff and gave to me as a gift one of those kits to "learn to play the bagpipes". It consisted of a recorder-like instrument formally called a practice chanter, which reproduced the part of the bagpipe that carries the tune and allows one to practice the fingering without the ear-splitting noise of the full instrument assaulting the ears of innocent passersby, some simple directions as to hand placement and fingering techniques, a couple of tapes of bagpipe tunes and some sheet music for a few simple tunes, including the ubiquitous "Amazing Grace". From this point, there was nothing for it but to start to learn to play. And so, I did.

Serendipitously, a few months later we happened to attend a party that was given by one of the members of a duplicate bridge club that I frequent. In the course of a conversation with one of the wives of another player, it came out that she played the bagpipes! When I told her of my feeble attempts to master the instrument on my own, she informed me that the Saint Andrew's Pipes and Drums held practice at the St. James Episcopal Church on Wednesday nights at 6:00. It just so happened that I took Wednesday afternoons off, in the time-honored tradition of many physicians and this was a perfect fit for me. The rest was history.

Now don't get the idea that I learned to play the bagpipes easily or quickly, because this is simply not the case. The good thing about the bagpipes is that there are only nine notes in total and there are no sharps or flats. The bad things about the bagpipes (Note the plural.) are that they run off the bag and only indirectly off the player's breathing so that there is a constant stream of air that has to be managed effectively, there are three drones which must be properly tuned and also kept in tune with the chanter and with one another, and the notes of each tune must be separated from one another in novel ways, especially if the same note is played twice in succession because the stream of air never stops.

To do this, the writers of bagpipe music separate out the main, or melody notes from one another with a series of grace notes, ranging anywhere from one to five in number. Each of these grace note movements has a name of its own. There are buries, toluates, grips, strikes and several other grace note combinations that take place in microseconds between the melody notes of the tune. The listener usually keys into the melody notes and that is all that is perceived, but any bagpipe aficionado will notice the small pops and burps of the grace notes that are appearing between the melody notes. Needless to say, each of these grace note combinations takes many months of practice to perfect. Of course, for the player that is new to the bagpipes, there is the art of mastering the flow of air from the bag to produce an even sound in the drones and to keep the tune going forward. For someone who has played other wind instruments this may be counterintuitive, since when one is running out of air it usually feels right to blow harder but, where the pipes are concerned, this simply will not work. The bag should be kept constantly filled as much as possible and any extra air that is needed must come from the pressure of the upper arm on the bag. When I first tried to do this, I came close to falling on the floor from hyperventilation on many occasions. However, seeing that some elderly men and young children could play the pipes, I realized that it was all a matter of technique that could be mastered in time, so I persisted. Eventually, I succeeded and now consider myself a piper, albeit far from a great one. I have managed to stir some souls with my piping on occasion and have stirred my own soul on a regular basis, so it has not all been for naught.

THE FIRST LAWYER

"The charge is prepar'd, the lawyers are met;."

John Gay

A little over one week later, a small, dapper little man bounced into my office on the heels of Rachel who introduced him to me as Jacques Parent of the law offices of Courtney, Davis and Parent. This was the man that my insurance company had retained to defend me. Jacques was a small man, about five feet four inches tall and weighing somewhere around one hundred and forty pounds. He was dressed impeccably in one of those semi-shiny gray suits that seemed to change colors with the light with a blue and white polka dotted bow tie surmounting a light blue shirt. I would guess his age to be in the low to mid-sixties. His hair, though completely grey, was coiffed in layers that feathered forward on his scalp and ended abruptly about halfway down his forehead, making him look like a modern-day Caesar. When he spoke, it was with clipped and precise tones as if English were a second language or he were trying to achieve a perfect exactness of speech.

"Nice to meet you, Dr. Ziebaska." he said as he shook my hand. I had braced myself for one of those soft, "Oh, do I really have to?" handshakes, but Jacques' was firm and dry and gave the immediate impression of no nonsense, two serious men meeting for a serious purpose.

"Same here." I responded. "Please have a seat."

Jacques sat facing me across my desk, crossed his legs to reveal gleaming black shoes that appeared to be made of some sort of soft glowing leather without a scuff mark to mar their perfect surface and, without further ado, got to the heart of the matter.

"Rachel informed me that you had a chance to review the nursing home Wennar Case. I know that you got a long list of interrogations from the plaintiff's attorney. What do you think?"

"Well? I replied, "I may be biased, of course, but I can't see where they have any sort of case at all. The records reveal that Martin Wennar got good care and that everything that should have been done and could have been done was done. No question that he had a bad outcome, but I don't think that his doctors or his caretakers could reasonably have remedied that."

Jacques settled back in his chair and rested his chin on his hand, flashing a snow white cuff that was blinding in its whiteness.

"Hmmmmmm. Do you think that the fact that Mr. Wennar fell multiple times at the nursing home before the fall that fractured his hip speaks to any degree of negligence or suboptimal care?"

Now, of course, this was the crux of the case as I saw it. After all, the patient had been transferred to the nursing home in the first place because he was a fall risk. Then, he had fallen several times while there and, to top it off, had had the fall that resulted in a serious injury and that had led ultimately to his death. I was pleased that my lawyer had quickly come to this conclusion, but I was not so pleased that the lawyer for the plaintiff would, no doubt, make the same argument.

"No, I don't think so. If you review the record, as I have done, you see that all sorts of appropriate measures were taken in a stepwise fashion to ensure that the patient didn't fall, or that, if he did fall, the fall will not hurt him. They used tab alerts, motion monitors, direct visualization and observation, and multiple other means of ensuring his safety. Short of having someone following him around twenty-four hours a day, I don't think that anything else could have been done that would have been successful."

"Have you ever used hip protectors for any of your nursing home patients?" asked Jacques.

Again, I was a bit surprised, but secretly pleased, that the lawyer would be perceptive and familiar with the aspects of nursing home care for this type of patient. Nice to feel that your defender has some ammunition with which to defend you.

"No, I haven't used them." I said. I am aware that they exist, and there is some evidence that they may be somewhat effective in preventing hip fractures in patients that have frequent falls. However, those that I have seen are either very bulky and difficult to put on or keep in place. For a patient with dementia, it can be a problem just to get them dressed in the first place. In fact, I have never seen any of these protectors used by any of the nursing home patients where I visit on a regular basis. It would seem to me that such devices could well be of some use in a patient who is aware of the propensity to lose some motivation in keeping the padding in place. Otherwise, however, they are seen by the patients as a bulky nuisance. MY wife's aunt, for example, is currently in a nursing home because she is always unsafe on her feet and requires a walker. She has fallen a few times at the nursing home even so. They have offered her those hip protectors there, but she has adamantly refused to wear them.

"I see" responded Jacques. "Your wife's aunt, I presume, is in charge of her mental faculties. Martin Wennar was not. This is a double-edged sword. One might say that he was so confused that he would not be able to tolerate the hip padding or have any idea why it might be good for him. Therefore, it would be the duty of his caretakers to ensure that he wear such a device to insure his safety."

"Perhaps so," I replied, "but the other edge of that sword is that Mr. Wennar was so demented that his caretakers had all that they could do to keep his clothes on his body. This is documented in the records on multiple occasions in both nursing homes and while he was in the hospital."

There was a momentary pause in the conversation while Jacques pondered what I had just said and then he said, "Okay, that sounds reasonable to me. Now all we have to do is to make sure that it sounds reasonable to a jury. Do not worry. That will be my job, and I do my job very well. Now, I see that you have attempted to answer all of the questions that were put to you by the plaintiff's lawyers. Do not worry about those either. I will take care of it. Any documents or responses that will go back to them will be first vetted by me, and I will decide just what we will or will not say in our responses. You may have noticed that most of these questions are extremely vague and nonspecific. Our answers will be just as vague and nonspecific. If they ask for documentation in the record, for example, we will simply refer them generally to "the nursing home records" or the "hospital records." We, of course, will understand precisely to which we refer, page by paragraph, but they can do their own work in regard to fleshing out their case, if they indeed have one."

This was a lawyer after my own heart, and I said as much. Jacques seemed pleased at my reaction and told me that there was little else for me to do at this point since I had responded to all of the questions that the opposition had raised. He reiterated that he and his firm would take things from here, and that if there were further developments, he would keep me apprised. He got up from his chair briskly. We again shook hands, and he was out the door. I never saw him face to face again.

RUMPOLE AND THE NOVEL FROM AN ALTERNATIVE UNIVERSE

"It's a poor sort of memory that only works backwards."
The Queen remarked.

Lewis Carroll

A few days later, after an especially rough day on the job (I had had two hospital admissions that required my going back to the hospital after office hours and doing the histories and physicals and writing admission orders on those two patients.), I dragged myself home to be met at the door by Cassie, who had a big smile on her face.

"Hey, Jon, look what I've got."

She held up a small hardcover book.

"I got it off Amazon.com. It's the latest novel by John Mortimer, hot off the press."

I took the book from her and looked at it more closely. Sure enough, it was a Rumpole novel. Horace Rumpole was the English barrister who, behind the avuncular and rumpled facade that he cultivated, had a rapier mind that invariably pierced through the hypocrisy, class prejudices and pretensions of his fellow jurists and struck upon the truth in each and every case in which he was involved. John Mortimer had made a good living describing the adventures of the clever barrister in a series of novels and short stories that had even been made into a short series that had aired on PBS in the United States. Cassie and I had both thoroughly enjoyed reading the books and had watched the television shows as well. The title of this most recent work was "Rumpole and the Penge Bungalow Murders." Something about it struck a chord in my mind.

'That's great, Cass," I said, "but I already have read it and I think you have too."

The smile on her face slowly faded and was replaced by a puzzled expression.

"Impossible, Jon. It just came out."

"Maybe so," I retorted, "but I know that I already read the thing"

"No, Jon, you don't understand. This is the latest one. This is the one where Rumpole describes the first big triumph of his career, the one that he alludes to in many of the stories already published. That must be why it sounds so familiar to you."

"I know, Cass, but I swear to you that I already read it."

"Well then," she challenged, "why don't you just tell me what it was about then."

I knew perfectly well that I was right, but I couldn't for the life of me remember just what the novel was about. I could recall the generality of the plot where Rumpole had used the evidence of blood spatter to demolish the case against his innocent client but, as Cassie was quick to point out, that had all been mentioned at one time or another in the previous works so I might be simply extrapolating from these. At this point, I was almost starting to doubt myself but the recollection of having read the book already was so strong that I was still convinced that I was in the right.

"I may not be able to recall the exact details, but you know that we both read a lot and that often the details are not recalled. Besides, it was quite a long time ago that I read it."

"Oh, really," said Cassie, "Just how long ago do you think that you did read it?"

"I'm not sure exactly. But it was some time ago. Possibly

as long as two years."

"Aha," she crowed triumphantly, "then what do you make of this?"

She shoved the part of the book in front of me where the date of publication printed and pointed it out. Sure enough, it was listed as only two months ago.

"I don't know what to tell you, but I am quite positive that I have already read this book."

"You son of a bitch!" cried Cassie, her voice beginning to rise. "You just always have to be right, don't you? Why don't you just admit that you are wrong this time?" At this point, she was actually yelling at me. Her face was contorted, and her eyes were bulging. I was surprised and confused by the intensity of her reaction.

"Take it easy, Cass, I just remember having read the thing. That's all. Don't get all bent out of shape."

"No, no, no, no!" she screamed. "You always do this to me. You just have to be right all the time. Why don't you just admit that you are wrong? Just this one time. Admit it. You couldn't possibly have read the book. Admit it. Just admit it."

"Jesus, Cass, just relax. I can't admit it because I know that I am right. I can't remember how or why I was able to read it but I know that I did. Maybe we got an advanced copy somehow. I seem to recall some friends going to England and staying in a bed and breakfast which was owned by John Mortimer's publicist or something. I think that they were able to get ahold of an advanced copy of the book that way and brought it back to the States with them and gave it to us.

"Well, where is it then?"

"I don't know. We probably gave it back to them when we were done with it"

Cassie laughed almost hysterically. "You have an answer for everything, Jon. But you are wrong, wrong, wrong, and I am going to prove it." And with that parting shot, she stalked fiercely from the room.

I slumped down on the couch, turned on the television

and tried to lose myself in whatever program was running at the time. I have no memory of it. What I do remember is trying unsuccessfully to recall the exact details of just how I had gotten to read this book ahead of the printed publishing date. It was maddening, to say the least. I knew that I had read it, but I just could not figure out how. I resolved that I would talk to anyone I knew with some sort of English connection to see if they would remember receiving an advanced copy of the book. I had a few good candidates in mind, specifically Jay and Martha Carpenter who were good friends of ours who had traveled to England within the last few years. Maybe they were the answer.

My reverie was interrupted by the explosive reentry of Cassie who, eyes gleaming with a feral light of triumph, thrust some printed material in front of my face. It was information that she had printed off the Internet on the upstairs computer. There, in black and white, was a list of all of John Mortimer's work in chronological order with the "Penge Bungalow Murders" listed last and with the date of publication in England only a few months before that in the United States.

"There," she cried, "now what do you have to say for yourself, Mr. Perfect?"

I steeled myself for the reaction that inevitably would come after my next words.

"I remember reading it, Cass. That's all that I can say. Sorry."

The look on her face was simply one of sheer incredulity. "Unbelievable! You still say that you are right even in the face of this. I can't stand it. I just can't stand it anymore. Your incontrovertible proof? I can't stand it. I just can't stand it anymore. You are driving me crazy. I hate you. I really hate you."

With that, she began to weep and for the second time that night rushed out of the room before I could respond. I was too dumbfounded to follow and resumed my blank stare into the unblinking eye of the television until I fell asleep in my chair.

For several days thereafter Cassie wouldn't even speak to

me, and when she finally did, it was with sarcasm and malevolence. Against this attitude I had no defense, most particularly because I was completely unable to prove my case. I reached Jay and Martha by email, but they had no knowledge of "The Penge Bungalow Murders" before. I read much of the book that Cassie had bought and it was all quite familiar to me. Of course, I had already read it. Then again, maybe I was losing my mind.

SHIFTING SANDS

"Oh, dry the starting tear, for they were heavily insured."

William Schwenck Gilbert

A sense of normalcy gradually reasserted itself over the next two and a half weeks. Relations between Cassie and myself, initially strained due to the clashes that we had over our respective recollections of literary events, returned almost to the easy comradery and companionship that we had always known in our lives. Still, there was something not quite right in our universe. It was difficult for me to verbalize, but Cassie seemed, even in her quietest moments, to remain ever the slightest bit on edge. At first, I thought that this was a natural consequence of the uncertainty that the pending lawsuit assured, but as the days went by, I became convinced that there was something else going on, something both more complex and more sinister. There was no pinning it down and defining it, however. It was like a summer mirage on the highway. The more it was focused on, the more it shimmered and slipped away.

Cassie had always been very involved in the lives of our two daughters and obsessed over their activities and their happiness to almost a pathological degree, but this was what mothers did, after all, and could not be regarded as out of the bounds of that close familial connection that often asserted itself between mothers and daughters.

In my case, as the orbiting paterfamilias, I found myself feeling no small amount of envy at the female nucleus of three about which I rotated, and often I wished that I might join that tight interacting circle where the women in my life shared their most intimate thoughts and dreams. These feelings, jealous as they were to a degree, blunted whatever niggling sense of wrongness that I felt under the circumstances. If your wife obsesses about your daughters, it only means that she cares. Is this not the way of the world? If Cassie asked me for the eighth time in the same evening whether I thought Alexandra would be safe driving back to school or Tatiana would be happy majoring in art studies at Smith, that was only her being a good and watchful mother. It really wasn't that odd.

One night, when I got home from work, I reflexively opened the refrigerator door looking to see what edibles might be lurking there. I was surprised to find the yellow dustpan and short broom lying on the top shelf between the milk and the soda. This was odd. Not quite the order of things. Naturally, I removed these objects and placed them in the cabinet below the sink which was their normal resting place. Having assured myself that no exotic snacks were offering themselves up for consummation, I grabbed the newspaper off of the kitchen table and proceeded through to the living room where Cassie was again watching television. This in itself was a bit unusual as there was generally nothing of interest at that time and Cassie usually was either doing some school related work, reading for pleasure, or doing some word puzzle or another at this hour of the day.

"Hey, Bug," I said laughingly, "what is with the dustpan in the refrigerator?" For a moment, there was a fleeting look of sheer panic in her eyes, and I thought that I might once again be witness to one of those emotional storms that had marred our existence recently. But the change was brief, and before anything else untoward occurred, the anxious expression disappeared as if it had never existed. To my great relief, I saw an actual twinkle come to her eye.

"Must have had a senior moment there," she said, laughing in return. "I was sweeping up some dog food that Orion had spilled when the phone rang. I guess I was just so distracted that I shoved the dustpan into the nearest storage space before I could even think about it and then must have forgotten what I did with it. Oh, well, no harm done."

We both had a good laugh then and expressed a mutual wonderment over how strange the human brain could be and what bizarre events might unfold for lack of paying a little attention to the most common of our daily activities. Then we spoke no more of it. The remembrance of this event, however, did not quickly leave me, and it boiled to the surface of my thoughts on many occasions over the next several months.

The work of a thriving medical practice kept me more than occupied and I had little time to think during working hours except for those thoughts that directly involved patient care. I was considering the differential diagnosis of a macrocytic anemia in a young woman with lupus erythematosus when Rachel butted me over the intercom phone system to advise me that someone from the malpractice insurance company was on the phone.

"She says that it's a matter of great importance," said Rachel, rolling her eyes, "and that I should interrupt you no matter what you're doing."

That sounded ominous enough, and I punched the button that would access that call on the other line. "Yes. Doctor Ziebaska speaking." I spoke.

"This is Marjorie Flaxen from Transcorp Insurance." came a pleasant female voice. "I'm sorry, but I have some bad news for you, Doctor. Transcorp has decided not to cover you for the malpractice suit which is being brought against you by Kathy Wennar." There was a long pause. I was stunned speechless for a few seconds. The universe shifted.

"What do you mean? How can they do that?" I queried angrily once what she had said actually made some sort of sense to me through the raw impact of it. Denial is the most primitive of defenses, and it was the first thing that my mind was inclined to do. Perhaps I had heard her wrong.

"Well, Doctor, it seems that you did not give us all the information that you were required to when you applied for insurance after MedInsure left the state and you transferred your coverage to us last year."

I understood what she was referring to as far as it went. MedInsure, the mal-practice insurer that had previously covered all physicians in the state of Vermont and much of New England had gotten out of the insurance business over a year ago. Transcorp had agreed to take over all coverage previously assumed by MedInsure though at a slightly higher rate. They also had insisted that all physicians again fill out all of the paperwork that had already been required by MedInsure when they initially took on this malpractice function. Still, I couldn't imagine what Ms. Flaxen was talking about. As always, I had filled out the appropriate forms thoroughly, accurately and compulsively. I was sure of that.

"I don't understand." I spluttered back. "What exactly is the problem?"

"You didn't mention anywhere that a law firm had asked for the records in regard to Martin Weimar before you switched your coverage. As a potential lawsuit in the making, this was a violation of your obligation to notify us of the risk involved."

"Now, wait just a minute." I expostulated. "Lawyers ask for doctors' records all the time. They have to have information regarding a client's medical treatment for reasons of disability, for reasons of insurance, for reasons of payment even if the client is deceased and for many other reasons. There was no question of a pending lawsuit at the time. Do you mean to tell me that I was obligated to list all of the incidents where law firms had asked for information up to that point?"

"That is exactly what I mean." responded the pleasant voice, still pleasant and unemotional.

"Why, that's absolutely ridiculous!" I retorted. "You people are using a technicality to get yourselves off the hook here. There was no intention on my part to mislead you and I don't believe that I mislead you in the first place. This is - why this is - this is robbery!"

How would you feel if this happened to you? Now I have to find myself a lawyer and am potentially liable for a lot of money if the case goes against me. You should be ashamed of yourselves."

"I'm so sorry that you feel that way, Doctor. But I'm just the messenger. The claims committee has decided that we are not going to take the case and that's the way it is."

"Well, you might think that's the way it is, but you people will be hearing from the Vermont State Insurance board, the state medical society, and my lawyer." Of course, now I would have to find a lawyer.

"I understand that you have to do what you think is appropriate." declared Madame Flaxen. "When you have decided upon alternative counsel, please let us know, and we will forward all of the records and the preliminary work that we have done to that party. Once again, I am so sorry to have been the bearer of bad news, I hope the rest of your day is more pleasant." And, with that bar hypocritical pleasantry, she hung up.

"More pleasant than what?" I seethed. "More pleasant than a fine day with The Inquisition?"

Disaster. Cassie, like her classical namesake, had foretold it but I, like those ancient Greeks, had ignored her prophecies. Now what? The lawsuit had mentioned six million dollars as the amount that was being sought. Even a small portion of that, should a decision be rendered against me, might be sufficient to take all of my assets, house, IRA, medical practice and everything. Not to mention legal fees, which would now be incurred whether I won or lost the case. Could Transcorp get away with this? Obviously, they could in the short run. In the long run, I thought I had a pretty good argument and might very well prevail, but in the short run I would have to shore up my legal defenses and find some way to pay for them.

Once again, the rest of the afternoon was taken up by the lawsuit and its attendant difficulties. I called Chuck Taylor, the lawyer that I used to set up my medical corporation and to do legal work involving title searches, etc., so that he could recommend a good malpractice lawyer. He gave me the name of a woman, Beatrice Germanowski, who, he said, was the best malpractice lawyer in the state, and whose office was in Burlington. I then called my banker and requested a personal loan of ten thousand dollars, not nearly as much as I knew this was going to cost me in the long run, but enough to get the ball rolling. He was good enough not to even ask me what the money was for and said that I should come in and fill out the paperwork at my convenience, but that he saw no problem with obtaining the loan. Next, I had Rachel ring the law offices of Beatrice Germanowski, and was pleasantly surprised to get to speak to her immediately, as I assumed that she would be busy with other clients or other cases.

As I outlined the events leading up to my phone call, Ms. Germanowski listened silently and, I hoped, attentively. It was somewhat hard to tell, as she didn't make any of those polite noises of assent that most people do when listening to a prolonged diatribe. There were no "ahuhs," "yeahs," "I understands," or other affirmations from her side of the phone line. When I was done, however, she quickly dispelled any doubts as to whether or not she had been paying attention.

"Yes," she assented. "We'll be pleased to take your case. We'll take both the malpractice suit and the action against the insurance company. By the way, I think you have a very good case against Transcorp, and I would be very surprised if we don't eventually carry the day there. I understand that things do seem dicey at the moment but hang in there.

Now, the unpleasantness of the financial nitty gritty. We'll need a retainer of seven thousand five hundred dollars as soon as you can get in here. Our hourly fees for fellow professionals who doesn't have insurance and believe me, it would be considerably more if any of these did not apply, is two hundred and fifty dollars an hour. That may sound expensive to you, but the rates in Vermont are dirt cheap compared to other states in the union."

I readily agreed to her terms and asked if she might give me a general idea of just what those hourly fees might come to.

"Very hard to say. Obviously, it depends on the amount of research that needs to be done, depositions that have to be taken, hours in court, etc. I can tell you that, in general, for a case like this we are looking at upwards of fifty to one hundred thousand dollars."

This was not good news, and, in spite of the fact that I knew at the core that legal fees are always astronomical, I was shocked. But I forbore to make any noises of disappointment or outrage. I knew that my professional existence was now going to be in this lady's hands.

"Okay," I responded, "thanks for taking the case. I'll arrange that you get all of the pertinent information, and we can go on from there."

We said our goodbyes and ended the conversation. When I had hung up the phone, I held my head in my hands and moaned in frustration. Now it was on me. The expense, the risk, the exposure, it was all on me personally. No longer was there the buffer of a big insurance company to protect and defend me and mine from the ravening wolves of the impersonal legal system. And, worst of all, I would now have to explain all of this to my darling wife.

TELLING CASSIE
PART II

"Though it be honest, it is never good to bring bad news."

Shakespeare

G iven my wife's high state of anxiety lately, and the overreactions that she had exhibited not only on hearing some bad news but also with less important incidents such as the "Rumpole" business, I was not in the least sanguine about delivering to her the latest unpleasant details. Over and over, I rehearsed in my head just how I might break it to her in the least threatening and shocking way but, as usual, it appeared that I would best just tell things right out and deal with whatever came of it. That was my plan. But, like most plans...

I was in the door and halfway to the living room when I realized that something wasn't quite right. My mind had been occupied with the insurance debacle and telling Cassie, so it took a while before it sunk in, but at last I did become aware that there was a strange silence in the house. No barking. No dog!

"Where's Orion?" I asked as soon as I saw Cassie. "He's not on his run and I can't hear him barking."

"Oh, he ran off." she responded calmly. "I was taking him out for his walk and got distracted when he tipped over his water dish. When I bent to pick it up, he got past me and ran off before I could get the leash on. He wouldn't come back when I called him." She seemed oddly unconcerned by this, especially in view of the high level of anxiety that she had expressed in recent days. In the past, she had always been very solicitous of the dog's every move and would obsess over him like one of our daughters, so this was not typical behavior.

"Which way did he go?" I asked.

"He ran north along the shore," she replied. "I chased him and called him, but he just kept going. It was like he was chasing something, but I didn't see anything. Maybe he caught a scent or something. Do you think he'll be alright?"

"I'm sure he'll be just fine. He's a big boy and can take care of himself." I wasn't so sure that this was the case, particularly in light of the fact that the big doofus wasn't afraid of anything and hadn't been road trained, but I didn't think that Cassie needed to add my worries to her own at that point.

"I was going out for my run anyway. I'll take the whistle and a leash and look for him along the way."

Grabbing the hunting whistle from the hook on which it was hanging, I went first to the back door where I blew three quick blasts in succession, the signal to "come." In the field, Orion would drop whatever he was doing and instantly come to me on a full gallop whenever he heard that command. This evening, he didn't appear. I went to the front of the house and repeated the performance. Still no dog. I then changed into my running gear, grabbed a short leash, put the whistle around my neck and set off up the driveway for my usual five-mile run. Periodically as I ran, I would call the dog's name and blow the whistle, but each time there was no response. I ran north up the Georgia Shore Road for two and one-half miles and then turned around and ran back. Still no dog. I kept looking far up the road ahead fearing that I would see a black lump lying there in the middle of the road. Nothing. Thoughts of doggy funerals couldn't help but insert themselves into my brain as I ran along. Traffic was light, as usual, so that was a saving grace. Also, it was still daylight so the black dog would be easily seen by anyone driving the highway. As I came back to our driveway, I spotted the miscreant at last, sauntering nonchalantly right down the middle of the road as if he didn't have a care in the world. A big, black Silverado pickup truck was rapidly approaching from the south, coining up on the dog from behind. The truck was probably going sixty miles an hour, and I could see the front of the vehicle depressed as the driver hit the brakes. The dog, still in the middle of the road, turned to see the truck coming up on him and promptly swerved directly into the path of the vehicle as if to greet it. I screamed out the dog's name and blew on the whistle, trying to get his attention and to get him to turn out of the way of the oncoming truck. It looked certain that he would be hit and killed or severely injured at that point. At the last instant, however, the driver pulled right, and the dog jumped right, and they just missed colliding by what appeared to be only inches from my perspective. I quickly narrowed the distance between us, called Orion to me and put the leash on as soon as I was able. Safe.

The driver of the truck yelled something at me about taking proper care of my dog, and I shamefacedly agreed, hauling the dog behind me as I turned down the driveway. I have to admit that I gave him a few particularly hard yanks along the way. Once we arrived home, I immediately put him back on his run and figured that I would leave him there for the rest of the evening. Ordinarily he would spend the evenings in the house with us, but I was determined that some punishment was in order for the scare that he had given us. Once Cassie saw that we were both back and that the dog was unharmed, she immediately lobbied for leniency, but I stood firm. She went into the run and hugged him unmercifully, but, in the end, she acceded to my wishes and left him there to repent his ways.

Needless to say. I did not presume to chastise my wife over the fact that she had carelessly allowed the dog to run off or the fact that she had failed to train him properly to her commands in the first place.

This would not be a good move just before presenting her with the unwelcome news of our insurance problems, problems that she herself had predicted and which I had pooh-poohed. I bided my time through a lite meal of orange chicken and brown rice with a glass of chardonnay. I bided some more through dessert, a selection of summer fruit with an orange sherbet. I bided yet another few minutes while we cleared the table and rinsed the dishes before loading the dishwasher. Finally, I felt that I could bide no more, and I gingerly but quickly laid out the facts of my malpractice debacle before her. Once again, her reaction came as a complete surprise to me.

When what I said about the refusal of Transcorp to take up my legal defense in the Wennar case had sunk in, Cassie first looked at me in shock. Then she began to cry. She said nothing. There were no recriminations, no screams, no accusations, no "I told you so's." just tears. But there were a lot of those. She cried as though she would never stop, and, indeed, I thought then that she never would. She just looked at me with those big brown eyes and cried and cried and cried. This was worse than the screaming. At least then I could scream back. Against these tears I had no defense. I told her that the new lawyer had said that there was a good chance that I would prevail eventually and that Transcorp would be forced to pay any expenses that we had laid out, including the lawyers' fees that would be necessary to bring forth an appeal. I told her that even if Transcorp did prevail and were able to get themselves off the hook, the previous malpractice insurance company would surely then be liable for the coverage. After all, I had to have been covered by one company or another at any given time. There was no instance in which I had been denied insurance coverage or had been given any notice that my insurance had lapsed. It was the duty of the insurance company that had left the business to ensure that all of its policyholders were covered after all. These arguments, factual and rational, could not stem the flow, and the tears fell like the monsoons, heavy and without pause. I took her in my arms and held her close but could not comfort her. She continued without speaking. After a while, my arms tired and I arose.   Cassie was still crying. I kissed the top of her head.

"I'm sorry, Bug." I said. "I really didn't imagine that this would or could happen. I know that you said that it could, but I still can't believe it. Trust me, though, that all will be okay in the end. I promise."

Still no verbal response, but at least she met my gaze and nodded her head ever so slightly. I took this as an affirmation and released my grip.

While Cassie went about loading the dishwasher and completing the cleanup chores from supper, I went into the den and grabbed my bagpipes. I walked out onto the shore of the lake as the sun was just setting on the horizon. In contrast to my mood of depression and sadness, there was a magnificent sunset with purple clouds set off by fiery fringes over the Adirondacks to the west. I fired up the instrument of destruction and, after a short interval of tuning drones and chanter, began a long set of tunes starting with "Scotland the Brave" and "Rowan Tree" and segueing into "Shoals of Herring," "I See Mull," "Castle Dangerous," "Arales Crossing the River Po," "Green Hills" and "Balmoral." I then finished up with "Amazing Grace" and "Going Home," the two sad tunes usually played at funerals or memorials. The howl of the pipes raged out over the lake like a self-contained typhoon, and the sound filled my head, emptying my mind of any other thoughts or concerns. For that brief time there was nothing but that primitive music ruling overall, subjugating any quotidian worries and anxieties, asserting its dominance over time and space. At the end, I brought the music to an instant halt, as is the goal in pipe playing. First there was the wail of the chanter and the matching howl of the three drones, then, in the next instant, there was complete silence. A shock of silence. In that vacuum, where there was no sound, I walked slowly back to the house.

That night I slept well. I have no idea why. I was being sued, my wife was distraught, my malpractice insurance was not coming through; and I didn't feel that I had a good grasp of the case or my part in it. Nonetheless, I slept like the proverbial log. There were no dreams that I can recall, and there were no awakenings hat night. Cassie, though she turned her back to me as soon as she got into bed, did not recoil from my touch; and I held her to me as I slept like two spoons in a drawer. When the alarm clock rang the next morning, I found myself still in that position and I felt strongly a sense of optimism, if not of happiness.

ESCAPE ARTIST

"I love to go a-wandering,
Along the mountain track,
And as I go, I love to Sing,
My knapsack on my back."

"The Happy Wanderer"

J ohn Greenleaf had been one of those old-time physi-
cians who did it all, the last of a dying breed of general practitioners
who did general surgery, delivered babies and provided cradle to
grave medical service to his long list of appreciative and grateful
patients. For over thirty years he had largely devoted his life to his
medical practice and the service of his flock. Then, in distinct contrast to most of the other doctors of his kind, and rather than dying
with his boots on as was the time honored tradition, he had un-
characteristically and abruptly retired at the age of sixty-two. And
when he had retired, it was as though he had dropped off of the
face of the earth. Aside from a small circle of close friends, he was
rarely seen by anyone. Certainly, he was never seen at the hospital,
and I doubt personally that he had ever even crossed the threshold
of the place once he had ceased working as a physician. When I had
first come to town, he was the oldest member of the coverage group
that I had joined and, as such, was the guru and mentor that many
of the younger generation looked to for guidance and stability in
regard to the ongoing changes in health care that were proceeding
to mold the manner in which medical services were rendered. He

always took even the most wrenching transformations of insurance coverage and bureaucratic demands in stride and was able to steer us in the right direction while other groups were wringing their hands or running off on one unproductive path or another. At the time he had ended his medical career, none of us in the group had naturally stepped up to take his place and we were subsequently just a loose, leaderless collection of M.D.s I know that I missed his steadfast hand on the tiller, and I am sure that all of my colleagues did as well. Still, as he himself would have been the first to acknowledge, no man is irreplaceable; and our group had sailed merrily on in spite of the disappearance of our captain. This was the man whom I was now going to see. He had been the physician to Martin Weimar when the terminal diagnosis of senile dementia had been made and had hoped I treated him through the early and the middle stages of that illness. I was hoping that he might be able to shed some light on the case, and I was also hoping that he would be willing to do so.

John lived up near the top of Fairfield Hill, on a farm off a long dirt driveway off of the main road. On a fine, early fall day with the leaves just starting to turn, I drove up to his front door in my bright yellow New Beetle. The driveway was lined by long, low stone walls that were precisely parallel to the road and were so exactly constructed that they looked as though they had been machined. I knew that John had painstakingly built each and every one of them with his own two hands without the aid of mortar or cement and with only such primitive tools as a weight and a string. This was the old art of dry-stone wall construction at its finest. John would often spout on about it at some length when I knew him as a physician, but I had never taken him up on the invitation to come and see some of his work. Another missed opportunity. He had also been a model railroad buff and had combined the two avocations into a huge project in his backyard where he had overseen the building of over two miles of narrow-gauge railroad track on which he ran a twelve-car train powered by steam engines that could be sat upon. Each car was, naturally, machined, engineered and decorated by hand.

The two steam engines had been purchased, but everything else in the layout was personally "made by Greenleaf". This included several arched bridges, some of them double and triple arched, that carried the tracks over small streams and gullies. These bridges were also constructed with the dry-stone wall technique and were without mortar. I had heard about all of this from other acquaintances on the medical staff who had spent time at the Greenleaf farm but, until this day, had never seen any of it for myself.

When I knocked on the door, John's wife, Candace, answered. A rather petite, good-natured woman with a head of short grey hair, Candace was always pleasant and outgoing. I had never seen her in anything else other than an upbeat mood, and she greeted me warmly and effusively. I had called ahead out of courtesy, so she was expecting me.

"Why, hello, Jon," she said, "It's been a long time. Too long. You should have come out to see us ages ago. And where's Cassie?"

"I know." I rejoined, hanging my head in embarrassment "Somehow I just never got around to it. And now that I am here, I'm sorry to say it's sort of on business. That's the main reason I didn't bring Cassie with me. But some of us still have to work, you know."

She laughed merrily.

"That's true. You young folks have to support us in our old age, and in the grand style to which we have become accustomed. That's why John is out there working like a crazed slave to finish that new triple arched bridge over the Mallard Brook. He has a troop of cub scouts coming over next Saturday and, of course, the new line extension absolutely must be finished before they arrive. The usual two miles of track won't satisfy them because the troop has been here before and, after all, we wouldn't want to bore them by showing them the same old layout two years in a row. I was just about to take him something cold to drink. You can help me by carrying it out there."

I readily agreed to this, and when Candace had loaded me up with four cold beers and a bag of sandwiches, she provided me with detailed directions as to just where I might find her husband in the vast tract of land that they called their backyard and I set off on my mission. The instructions were perfect, not to mention that I could follow the railroad tracks, so getting lost was highly unlikely even for the directionally challenged and I got to my destination without taking any wrong turns. There, at the bottom of a small gorge through which ran a gurgling stream of the clearest water, I found the retired general practitioner, John Greenleaf, setting up the middle and final arch of a three arch dry-stone bridge that would span this miniature canyon and allow his train to roam another several acres of the small woodland that composed the northern section of the property. John was caught up in his work and didn't notice me at first. I took the time to admire his handiwork and to marvel at the intricate fitting together of the individual stones in the construction. The bridge, as I said, was composed of three arches, two of which, one on either side of the stream, were already complete. Resting on the pillars that supported each end of the completed arches and spanning the middle of the stream was a large wooden frame in the shape of an inverted U, the secret of the work. Extending over this frame were interlocking stones, all somewhat wider at the top than at the bottom. In the very middle of the U was the keystone, or in this case, the keystones, a group of rocks that were much wider at the top than at the bottom and that fit between the extending stones on both sides to complete the arch in the middle. Gravity would then press down upon the arch firming the strength of the bridge. The greater the pressure put on the top of the bridge, the firmer the arch would hold, up to the point where the rocks would be crushed, of course, but there would be little likelihood of that. The wooden frame would then simply be removed from underneath and the arch would stand otherwise unsupported. Basic and elegant.

After a few minutes, John stepped back to get a longer look at his construction and noticed me standing on the side of the stream. He smiled and came over to me. A tall rangy man, he stood six feet and two inches tall and was thin but solidly muscled. His close-cropped grey hair molded his skull like a thin helmet and his well-tanned face made him look more like a native American Indian than the progeny of Norse and Scandinavian ancestors that he was. He gripped my right hand in a grasp of iron and greeted me like a long-lost brother.

"Well," he declared. "The prodigal returns. And bringing gifts, I see." He indicated the beer and sandwiches that I was carrying.

Once again, I was a bit embarrassed, not having had the grace to keep up the acquaintance after his retirement, and now I was doing so, with an ulterior motive in mind.

"This is somewhat awkward, John, but I'm here to get some information from you, not just to make a social call."

"I figured that much, my boy." rejoined the stonemason. "It wasn't too likely that you drove all the way up here just to learn the fine points of dry-stone construction although you might reconsider your position on that. Nothing like a few hours of playing with rocks to cleanse the mind and purge the soul. So, what's it all about, anyway?" He motioned me to sit on one of the many large rocks that stood sentinel on the side of the stream and lie himself perched upon another nearby. Pulling a pipe from his right front trouser pocket, he proceeded to fill and light it as I began my questioning.

"Well, John, it's like this." I started. "The wife of one of your former patients, Martin Wennar, is suing me for malpractice, claiming that it was due to my poor care that he fell in the nursing home which led to his amputations, his skin breakdown and ultimately his death." I proceeded to outline what I did know about the case which wasn't really all that much considering that I had exhaustively reviewed the available records.

"What I would like from you, if at all possible, would be to get some background as to what had happened before he was placed in the custodial care home in the first place. Obviously there was no shortage of funds there so why didn't he just remain at home with round the clock nursing care?"

John looked back at me with a twinkle in his eye.

"Isn't this some sort of patient privacy violation? They might add my name to the suit if they found that I was talking out of turn to the defendant in the case. I'm not sure that I can take that kind of risk."

I must have let the disappointment show on my face, as he laughed outright and immediately proceeded to disabuse me of the notion that he would have any qualms about answering my questions as best he could.

"Relax, Jon," he went on, "the patient is long dead, and I don't consider this a breach of his privacy in any way. And besides, I never did like that young wife of his very much. A good-looking lady without a doubt but something about her always gave me the willies. You know how Gertrude Stein said about Los Angeles that "there was not there"? I had this feeling about Kathy Wennar that there was no soul there. I'll be happy to tell you whatever I can remember, and, if necessary, I can dig back in the old office records to come up with any further de-tails." He took a few moments here to light up the recently filled pipe and to take a few quick puffs to get the thing started as he gathered his thoughts.

"Until he developed Alzheimer's, I didn't see much of Martin as a patient. He was always too healthy and too busy to see his doctor. The only times I did see him was when he re-quired a physical exam routinely so that he could buy insurance or reassemble his business empire in one iteration or another. Before he became ill, I had last seen him for such a physical when his company was bought up by that big conglomerate. At that time, he was in perfect health, though he had gained some weight over the years. Did you know that he ran cross country in college? Well, he did. I guess he was pretty good too, though he was a bit too big to be a great runner. In school he weighed one hundred and seventy pounds; and after many years of long hours and minimal exercise, he ballooned up to two hundred and twenty. Still not really overweight at his height but not ex-actly svelte, either. He did manage to keep running, though, or so he spoke. Actually, I truly believe that he did. In any event, I remember noting that his resting pulse was in the low sixties at the time of that last physical. I especially remarked upon it.

The next time that I saw him after that, he was having some alarming memory difficulties and his wife and children were already dreading the worst. Naturally, I referred him to the best specialists immediately, and he was diagnosed by Jim Mitchell as having presenile dementia pretty early on. Nothing to do about it, of course, but there you have it. From that time, I saw quite a lot of him and his wife, trying to ameliorate the symptoms and to control the behaviors. He really became quite the handful towards the end there.

Maybe it was because he had been a runner for much of his life or maybe it was simply because he felt like a stranger in his own house with Kathy there, but almost from the beginning he was trying to get away from that place in one way or another. One time he took his car and drove to the site of the old ice cream factory in Burlington. The police picked him up there wandering around the unlit building in the middle of the night. Kathy tried hiding the keys to all the vehicles, but Martin still managed to find them and drive off a few more times. Luckily no one was injured in any of those escape attempts, and he was always returned unharmed. Eventually, she had to resort to disabling the cars by having the caretaker remove the distributor caps and place them in a locked cabinet. Once the automobiles were no longer accessible, Martin resorted to making his getaways on foot. He proved to be the most amazing escape artist, a regular Houdini. First, he would choose an opportune moment and merely walk out the open gate of the driveway. Then, when they kept the gates locked, he would manage to slip out alongside or in back of some vehicle or person who was leaving or entering. You know how high the gates are around that compound of theirs at the top of Congress Street? Well, believe it or not, after they got wise to him and watched all of the gates assiduously when anyone entered or left, Martin started scaling those walls and getting away that way.

No one ever saw him actually go over a wall, but there is no question that he got out. Time after time he escaped the grounds and was found running down the interstate headed toward Burlington. Each time the police or Kathy's private security force would have to bring him home. Eventually, three shifts of employees were hired to watch over him at all times and to literally shadow his every step. As the disease progressed, this propensity to escape, to run away at first and then to walk away when running became too great an effort for him became even more problematic. As time went on, he became more and more frail, in keeping with the natural course of the disease, and he began to have falls. It then became the duty of the watchers to not only follow him more closely so that he would not escape in the first place but to be there to catch him when he fell.

Things might have gone on this way indefinitely as there was plenty of money ' to pay the followers and the catchers. However, things weren't static in Kathy's life, either. Though her husband was old and sick, she was still young and vital and still had all of the appetites that any healthy young woman has. Not surprisingly, she began to take lovers to satisfy these desires; and being that she was who she was, her choices were not always the wisest. She might, for example, pick up some good-looking young hooligan in a bar and bring him back to her own bedroom for a one-night stand, not knowing anything about the man's background or morals, not knowing whether he was a thief, had HIV or was a mass murderer. But, let's face it, St. Albans is a small town; and, while it might be naive to think that such things don't happen here, they were less likely to do so than in, say, New York City. So far, she had gotten away with these peccadilloes without any major repercussions. Martin's children weren't too pleased with that state of affairs, but what could they do? Initially, they had gathered around and commiserated with their stepmother and had helped to care for their confused father to some degree. While they hadn't exactly welcomed Kathy into the family with open arms, they initially hadn't been hostile to her either, figuring that at least their father was happy. When it first had become clear that he was slowly losing his mental faculties, the older son had made the macabre joke that Kathy was "sucking his brains out," but such irreverent comments had ceased when the terrible nature of the progressive disease revealed itself. As Kathy's sexual dalliances became more and more outrageous and less and less circumspect, the boys turned away from her in disgust.

Matters came to a head one night when Kathy intimately coupled with a handsome young stranger, well on the way to achieving a glorious climax, was ignominiously interrupted by Martin and his caretaker of the moment as they walked unannounced through an unlocked door which Martin had joyously and triumphantly jerked open but one second earlier. Goodbye, orgasm. Goodbye, Martin.

That very evening, Martin Wennar was taken by ambulance to the Northwest Medical Center where he was seen and evaluated in the ER for "change in mental status and frequent falls." He was subsequently admitted by me (What else could I do?), had a short hospital stay where I evaluated him for any possible metabolic derangements that might have contributed to his dementia (Fat Chance) and was then transferred to Madonna of the Mountains Custodial Care Home in Richford. There, he could no longer continue as my patient as there was no way that I would be making a house call thirty miles away, and so you took over in your capacity as the medical director of the Richford Health Center. Essentially, your physician's assistant up there, Rosaire Archambault, became his primary caregiver. Thus, endeth my role in the care and feeding of Martin Wennar." John paused in this long narrative to thirstily quaff one of the beers that I had brought out and make some inroads on one of the sandwiches.

"So, anything else I can answer for you?" he went on, speaking around a mouthful of ham and cheese.

"Not really," I replied. "I don't suppose you could give me some idea of why she's suing in the first place? She can't possibly need the money. I don't see that she cared so deeply for the man that she feels an obligation to avenge his death.

And besides, I really don't see where there was any serious element of neglect or error in judgment that might motivate someone to take revenge. I just don't get it."

"Nope, I can't help you there, Jon." he said. "Who knows what evil lurks in the minds of heartless women? I can tell you that Kathy just stopped thinking about Martin as a person as soon as he became confused enough to lose his position as the alpha male in the relationship. You might think that she had some residual feelings for him, they say she kept him at home and spared no expense in hiring anti-fall personnel to watch over him and to care for him. But I was there to observe their personal interaction on many occasions. There was no respect or affection in the way she treated him. He was more like an unwelcome pet that required monitoring and feeding at periodic intervals. I would say that she treated him like a dog, but most people actually show some liking for their dogs. Maybe it's a legal thing. Do you know anything at all about their financial affairs, the will etc.?"

I had to admit that I knew nothing whatsoever about the Wennars' monetary business. It was common knowledge that Martin had been phenomenally well off, and I assumed that, as his surviving spouse, Kathy would inherit all of the money and the property. But perhaps I was wrong in the assumption. In any event, it appeared that I had reached a dead end here.

John and I spent some time catching up on one another's lives, children and, in John's case, grandchildren, all of whom were doing well and proceeding onward with the living of life. He then put aside his work for the rest of the afternoon and gave me the grand tour of the Greenleaf Railway. We spent the rest of that shining early autumn day playing with trains, riding them over bridges and through underpasses, whooping like children as we cruised through the small woods at what felt like breakneck speeds. John had built a number of structures including a station house with water and fuel tanks and a small village with a bank, post office and saloon situated strategically along the tracks. All of these were supplied with electricity and had their own lighting. There were functional switches for moving the train into storage and repair sheds as well as a couple of places where alternate routes of track could be selected. We tried them all that afternoon. It was just what the doctor ordered. For those few hours, I was able to completely put the case out of my mind and to enjoy the moment.

AT THE ZOO

"It's a fine and fancy ramble to the zoo

Simon and Garfunkel

J esse Calderone arrived at his job at the Franklin Park Zoo promptly at 6:45 A.M. on a very warm August day. He unlocked the doors to the Primate Center, that huge modern building that looked like something between a gargantuan circus tent and a flying saucer and made preparations for his initial morning tour of the public walkways, a task that he performed every morning that the zoo was open to the public. His mission was to power wash the pathways clear of any detritus, dirt, or other debris and to pick up any litter that might have been deposited by the paying customers the day before. As is usually the case, the work was routine, and he found it to be boring in the extreme. The exotic setting notwithstanding clearing off dirt was not that exciting. He said hello to a few of the keepers who were straggling in, but they all quickly disappeared into the bowels of the building to attend to their own assigned tasks, and he saw no more of them until the mystery presented itself.

It was as he was approaching one of the wooden suspension bridges over a moat and waterway that his day suddenly took on a most interesting and decidedly spooky turn. Concentrating as he was on the aspects of the cleaning, he almost washed the evidence away before he realized just what it was that he was seeing in front of him. There on the edge of the wooden bridge was the wet and dirty footprint of a male gorilla! There was no question about it. Even Jesse, about as far from a certified biologist as one can imagine, had no doubt that this was not a human print. For one thing, it was more in the shape of a hand than a foot with an opposable "thumb" that no human foot would have. For another it was about the size of a dessert plate, much broader than any human foot would be. And there was just one print. No other tracks presented themselves. Jesse took a few cautious steps to that side of the bridge and looked around. There was just open space for a considerable distance before the rock cliff of the gorilla enclosure rose up. The lighting inside that part of the Primate Center was quite low, and the overhanging vegetation, purposely designed that way by the builders, gave the impression that one was in the midst of an equatorial rain forest. There were long shadows everywhere. It didn't take much imagination to conjure up the menacing bulk of a malevolent ape lurking somewhere in one of those black spaces. Reason told him that even if one of the great beasts was out in the public area the odds of being attacked were extremely low. Most likely any wandering beast would want to avoid him at least as much as he would want to avoid it. Still, he had seen what an angry gorilla could do in terms of physical destruction, and he had no illusions that he could stand up to such force. He put down his power washer and took up his walkie-talkie.

In a matter of minutes there were several keepers gathered around the footprint gesturing and talking excitedly. Speculation as to what had happened there in the hours that the zoo was closed ran rampant. There was no question in anyone's mind that one of the gorillas had managed to get out of the enclosure and trespass on the public space, potentially a very dangerous situation. Like most modern zoos the Franklin Park prided itself on "natural" enclosures that didn't appear like real cages at all but rather large open spaces that separated the animals on exhibit from the public with moats, waterways, or large panels of bulletproof glass. In the case of the gorilla exhibit, there were also strategically placed electrical wires and mesh fencing that were designed to keep the wildlife from the human beings. These devices were as unobtrusive as they could be engineered and still do the job. In this instance the job had not been done. Following protocol, a quick and complete census of the gorilla population was completed. All of the animals were accounted for. None showed any sign of having been outside the designated enclosure. None of the gorillas were talking.

The Primate Center at the Franklin Park Zoo in Boston, Massachusetts had been constructed in the early 80's as a consequence of the major renovation project that had been undertaken at that time. Prior to this there had been no great ape presence at the zoo for many years. In fact, there were no gorillas at all in Boston then. The only gorilla presence was at the Stone Zoo in Stoneham, Mass. where a few of the large creatures were being kept in a relatively tiny enclosure that was out of date from the aspect of space alone. By means of a fundraising project and with the major assistance of one Robert Beal, a primate loving philanthropist, the 15 or so million dollars that were required to build a modern primate exhibition area were obtained and the Stone Zoo animals were transferred to the Franklin Park. Several more animals were obtained from other zoos across the country. Of course, the building also housed a number of other exhibits including mandrills, tapirs, a pygmy hippo and a number of flighted birds that had free rein of the entire gorilla enclosure, but there was no question that the gorillas, massive and human-like that they were, were the stars of this particular show. Up to now, there had been no untoward gorilla incidents of any kind. There had been some internecine gorilla violence involving isolated animals that couldn't get along with one another, but this concerned only the gorillas and the keepers and had nothing to do with the paying public. This matter of the mysterious footprint, however, was another story.

In the ensuing weeks and months, a team was assembled to evaluate the situation and certain recommendations were made as to how to increase the security in the Primate Center. Mesh fencing in the area of the wooden suspension bridge was reinforced and added to and the electrical wiring was also repositioned and enhanced. The zoo administration was satisfied that the problem had been addressed and that the exhibit remained a safe one. However, the administration did not speak with a united voice, and several of the keepers evidenced strong reservations about this conclusion. Jesse Calderone, the janitor, was also in this latter group. The problem as he saw it was that no one really knew that the situation had been rectified for one simple reason. No one really knew what had happened. The footprint was real enough. A gorilla had unquestionably breached the security. The problem was that no one knew how.

MEETING OF THE MINDS

"Love looks not with the eyes, but with the mind, and there is wing'd Cupid painted blind."

Shakespeare

There occurred a long pause in the proceedings when nothing at all appeared to be happening in regard to the lawsuit.

Somewhere over the horizon the minions of evil were marshaling their forces, making their plans, sharpening their swords, constructing their great siege engines, and forging their unholy alliances, but we in the castle were largely ignorant of these preparations. Life went on as before, almost as if the unpleasantness did not exist. Occasionally, I would awaken prematurely in the dark hours of the early morning with a vague feeling of dread, but these times were rare; and, since I felt that I had done what I could in terms of the record review and early preparation of the defenses, there was little over which to obsess.

We did get some personal news of great import from our older daughter, Alexandra. She and the young man with whom she had been living in Boston, Zechariah Harvey, were planning to get married in September of the next year, a little over a year from the time of their announcement. This did not exactly take us by surprise as they were already doing everything that a married couple does for the most part, and they might just as well make it official from the perspective of their parents. Like most thoughtless offspring, however, they did not seem to take our perspective into perspective. Cassie and Alexandra immediately began making all sorts of plans to which I was only tangentially privy. I was, after all, the father of the bride and, as such, deserved some minimal consideration. The operative word, of course, was "minimal" and so it would come to pass that I heard almost as little about the wedding plans as I was hearing about the legal plans.

The story of just how Alexandra and Zac got together is an interesting one, though not a particularly unusual one these days. In high school, Alexandra had been an intelligent over achiever, applying herself to her studies diligently, and participating in multiple extracurricular activities from the school musical to the student council. Her junior year she had been elected class president, but she was defeated by a narrow margin in her senior year and had to settle for class secretary. She did no dating in high school though she had many friends of both sexes.

Her hard work paid off when she was accepted into Smith College in Northampton, a fine school with an excellent reputation and interestingly enough, the same college that Cassie had attended those many years ago. Although her grades were excellent and her SAT scores were very good, she did not receive any financial aid. Still, Cassie and I were quite pleased.

In her freshman year at Smith, as was the custom of students of her era, Alexandra spent a lot of time on the Internet, mostly researching papers and the like, but also communicating widely with friends, family and others. Online, she met this fellow named Zac Harvey, a 25-year-old graduate of Penn State who was attending the Wharton School of Business in the MBA program. At that time, Zac was living with a couple of male roommates, sharing the rent and utilities in a small three-bedroom apartment near the school. Sight unseen, he and Alexandra found common ground and before long were planning to meet. Ultimately, they

decided that he would come to our house for a few days that summer between Alexandra's freshman and sophomore years. And so,
it was the first notice that her mother and I had of this budding
romance was that a stranger, not only to us but to our daughter
as well to our way of thinking, would be coming to our home out
of nowhere! Okay, out of Pennsylvania, if the truth be told, but
still, this was a bit scary. Cassie immediately began to conjure up
visions of us all being murdered in our beds. I, myself, was more
than a bit apprehensive. But then I took the other point of view.
Here was this 25-year-old man taking a long train voyage to the
home of some people that he had never seen before, or with whom
he had never even had any contact except through their daughter.
When looked at from that angle, it was a very courageous and enterprising move, and it said a lot for the potential relationship of
these two young people.

And, indeed, it came about that the mental rapport that
Alexandra and Zac had developed over the ether extended itself to
a physical attraction, and they fell in love. Alexandra drove alone
to meet him at the train station and brought him back to the house
to introduce him to us. When I first saw him, I thought he looked
remarkably like Clark Kent, Superman's alter ego in the com-
ic strip. He wore thick, black glasses which made him look a bit
like a nerd, but his build was mesomorphic and athletic. I would
guess that he was about six feet and four inches tall and weighed
around one hundred and ninety-five pounds. He had broad shoulders and walked with that panther-like bounce that athletes affect.
His handshake was firm and, when he offered his hand, his eyes
locked onto mine with laser-like intensity. We later learned that,
belying his outward appearance, with the exception of the thick
glasses, that Zac was not involved in athletic pursuits and, in fact,
had led almost purely an existence of the mind. In high school, he
was a member of the science club and the chess club, played cello
in the school orchestra and was a finalist in the National Merit
Scholarship contest. In college, he mostly studied and read prodi-
giously outside of his course work as well. And, of course, he was
deeply into computers and the Internet. After college, he decided

to go to business school; and, as an undergraduate, he majored in economics with that plan in mind. He was one of five students to graduate summa cum laude from Penn State that year and pretty much had his pick of business schools. Since Wharton was close by and a great school, it was a good choice, and he decided to go there. At the time we met, he told us that he was thinking of going into international banking or doing something related to financial markets in the United States. To me this was all deadly dull and did not augur well for the ultimate happiness of my first born; but as we got to know Zac better, we found that he had a great sense of humor which his keen intelligence and probing intellect served to maximize and that he was most of all a considerate and caring person who would do right by our daughter. And, of course, there was that overriding and most compelling argument, the fact that they loved one another and would come together regardless of how we felt about it.

The fact was that from her sophomore year on, Alexandra lived with Zac more than she lived with us. When he graduated from Wharton, he got a job in Boston working for BankNorth doing something with numbers that made no sense to us but earned him a considerable salary at the entry level. He got a nice apartment there on the Fenway and, as soon as her summer vacation began, Alex moved in with him. It was also convenient that she was able to get really good summer jobs in Boston as well. One summer she worked with the penguins at the Boston Aquarium, and one summer she worked as the caretaker for the animals at the Boston Museum of Science. These jobs would stand her in good stead after she graduated and was looking for a zoo job of some sort. Her ultimate goal was to be a zoo curator, at least of a large aviary section and, hopefully, an entire zoo. To this end, she had majored in philosophy and minored in biology. We joked that she would be able to carry on a most sophisticated conversation with her parrots.

The plan, then, was for Alexandra to graduate and to get

some sort of zoo related job around the Boston area. Then she and Zac would get married that fall and live happily ever after. She would have the job of her dreams, which wouldn't be very lucrative, but which would bemost fascinating and stimulating and Zac would largely support them both with his number crunching and his mathematical theorizing.

And, indeed, the initial aspect of the plan came to fruition exactly as they had imagined it. Alexandra did get precisely the job that she wanted the summer after graduation. She was offered the position of aviculturist at the Franklin Park Zoo and snapped it up. We told her that "aviculturist" simply meant "bird woman" and that this meant she was merely a colleague of those little old ladies who feed the pigeons in the park but nothing we could say would dull the obvious pleasure that this new position held for her. She settled into the new job with great enthusiasm and preparations for the wedding went on apace.

'TIS THE SEASON

"See, Winter comes to rule the varied year, sullen and sad."

James Thomson

F all fell gently into winter that year; and, while we got our usual share of snow, winter was a bit more forgiving than that to which we had been accustomed. There never was an extended period of very cold weather which, where we are, would be greater than twenty degrees below zero Fahrenheit. By late December Lake Champlain had still not frozen over, and the heating bills had not yet gone through the roof. Other than an occasional listing of fees for "record review" and "back-ground investigation," there was still no word from the lawyers pro or con. The two insurance companies were fighting over the right to not represent me in court, each claiming, of course, that the other was responsible. This meant that I was paying all of the bills up front and, if nothing else, was in their favor in regard to money paid out and interest accrued. Since they undoubtedly had lawyers on their payroll on a regular basis, this cost them nothing more in legal fees than the usual price of doing business and they could hang onto their funds for that much longer. As a private citizen, I had no such options and was required to take out further loans and live more frugally.

The Christmas season had always been a big deal for us as a family. Cassie started decorating the house more than a month before the holiday and we always had at least one large Christmas party to which we invited two hundred or so people. Not that I am anything like a social butterfly (Moth would be more like it), but I did have plenty of colleagues; and Cassie, working in a big school, had also many co- workers as well as friends. Alexandra and Tatiana would both be home for the holiday as well as Zac and both sets of our parents, Cassie's and mine, would also be there. As usual, Cassie spent an inordinate amount of time making sure that the house was ready to entertain various and sundry visitors. Whatever worries and anxieties were plaguing her from the pending court case were replaced by the particular concerns of just what ornaments went where and what decorations needed to be cleaned and updated. She was frazzled but since she had been doing this regularly was good at it, she worked efficiently and quickly. Still, it took over a week of concentrated effort on her part just to complete the decorating. We had two trees, one large artificial one from Neiman Marcus which was ten feet tall and came pre-lit with multicolored lights, and one natural balsam that wasn't much smaller which Cassie said we needed to "make the house smell like Christmas." I, of course, being the insensitive male, remarked that a good pine scented room could serve the same purpose at far less cost and effort but, as usual, my input was given as much weight as one of the origami paper ornaments on the tree. The house was filled with Christmas dolls, Christmas wreaths, Christmas candles, Christmas lights, Christmas stockings. Well, you get the picture. Cassie pretty much did it all herself with minimal input from me. And, to my great relief, she did it flawlessly. Again, she seemed anxious and preoccupied, but that was only natural. The big party came off without a hitch. There was one little glitch when Cassie couldn't remember the name of one of her fellow teachers with whom she had been working on a regular basis, but this was one isolated event and didn't alarm me or anyone else for that matter. There was, after all, a large punch bowl of eggnog, as is customary at these affairs, and both Cassie and I had our share. We had crackling fires going in two downstairs fireplaces and one upstairs fireplace. Poor Orion was restricted to the mud room in the back of the house where he couldn't bother any of the guests. He did whine for a short period of time, but, when no one took pity on him out there in the dark, he gave up pretty quickly and went to sleep. Several of the guests were fellow physicians and local lawyers who had some knowledge of the case pending against me and expressed condolences and assurances that I would surely prevail in the end. I accepted these predictions gracefully but was not sure in my own mind that they would come to pass. It was a small town, and many more than I would have liked were aware of the case, but none had access to any of the details, and so their prognostications were essentially without foundation (other than that of my own spotless character, of course). It seemed to me that a good time was had by all; and when the party wound down about midnight, Cassie appeared content that we had once again achieved social success and satori. We left the cleaning up for the next day and went to bed in a pleasant state of early alcohol poisoning.

The family Christmas was even more pleasant as it was less hectic and more personal. Everyone, including the two sets of grandparents, was in good health. No one was terribly stressed out, as the semester had ended for Tatiana and she had no exams or papers; I had taken the week off as a vacation since I luckily did not have any coverage days scheduled for that week for a change, Cassie had the week off between Christmas and New Years as she usually did as a school librarian, the grandparents were retired and Zac also had been able to take a few days off around Christmas Day itself. We ate large meals, went running, skiing and snowshoeing, played board games together, caught up on each other's lives and managed not to get on one another's nerves too much. The girls were pleased that they actually were able to win some of the word games that we played, as Cassie usually won them all. That Christmas she did not dominate as she traditionally had. Even I won a few of these contests, and, when we divided up into teams, Alexandra and Zac ran roughshod over the rest of us. I could see that Cassie was frustrated, but she took it with good grace and there were no pyrotechnics. It was only later that I realized that, not only had she not won, by far, the majority of the word games, she had not won a single one. I put it down to the pressures of the court case and the unusually heavy pressures of the holidays. The dog was in his glory as all who were present scratched and patted him almost continuously and allowed him, as usual, to put his head in their laps or on their stomachs as he stretched out on the couch. The snow was so deep that he had to swim through it, and it made for a great workout for him when we went out on the skis or snowshoes. As we glided or floated above the snow, he was forced to mush through it. This gave him a tremendous amount of exercise and ensured that he slept well at night whether before the fire, on the couch or in his cage. All in all, it was one of the best family Christmases that I can remember. When the family dispersed once again to our individual lives and occupations, it was with no little regret that such moments come only too infrequently in our separate and busy lives.

By the end of February, when cabin fever just begins to rear its ugly head, the temperatures had already started to moderate, and there was every indication that spring would follow closely. From the lawyers, there had not been a single blemish to mar the polished mirror of the holiday season, and there was still no fallout whatsoever from the impending trial at that point. At that time, I made a big decision regarding my medical career which, besides the obvious ramifications of its effects on my professional life, also turned out to have some unexpected and unpleasant effects on my personal life.

CHANGES

"Nothing endures but change."

Heraclitus

F or the nine years previous, I had been the medical director of the Richford Health Center, a small clinic in the town of Richford, Vermont up along the Canadian border. This had come about in the following way. Several members of that community had been searching for a physician to oversee the medical care in the town and to make the clinic viable. One of those members was a tiny lady named Moira Stem. Five feet nothing in her stocking feet, Moira was anything but small in her ambitions or her character. She had been a concert pianist in her own right and, while married to George, her career Navy husband, who had been the captain of a nuclear submarine, had managed to raise seven children and generally to take care of business while her husband was at sea. In the case of a nuclear submarine officer, this meant extended periods of time indeed.

It was not surprising, therefore, that Moira Stem was well versed in the day-to-day management and planning of just about anything that life could send her way. When George had retired and decided to move back to his boyhood hometown of Richford, there was a long list of community problems and deficiencies that quickly came to Moira's attention, and she proceeded, in her inimitable style, to try to fix just about all of them. One of those things was the delivery of medical care.

Because of her piano playing talents, Moira was soon much sought after locally, and she took on several positions involving the provision of piano accompaniment. Among these was the job of accompanist for the Champlain Chorus, a group of largely amateur singers who got together once a week to sing all kinds of music, mostly classical works, and gave three or four concerts a year in one of the local churches. As happenstance would have it, one of the members of the bass section was Jon Ziebaska, local internist and bagpiper. And one of the sopranos was Gail Caspersen, widowed trucker's wife and nursing home manager. Moira slowly began to insinuate the idea of Richford's needing a doctor into the conversations that she and I occasionally had during the breaks at the chorus rehearsals. At first, she simply asked my opinion as to just what directions the community might explore to find a physician who might be willing to aid them in their quest. I provided the names of several colleagues who were either living or practicing in towns fairly close by and suggested that these would be the best people to contact. As time went by and it became clear that none of these folks would work out for one reason or another, it somehow became understood that perhaps I myself might be the person for this job.

Initially, I rejected the idea out of hand as I already had a busy practice in St. Albans with no dearth of patients to be seen or work to be done. I also had a physical presence in that city with an office that was fully staffed with people who, of course, had to be paid regularly no matter where I was or what I was doing. Moira ever so gently averred that these were obstacles that might be overcome but no specifics were forthcoming in this regard; and I, myself, could see no practical way of doing so.

It was, as has often been the case in my business experience, my office manager, Rachel Cobb, who came up with the answer that could solve all of these problems. When she had heard my outline of the dilemma, she thought only a few moments before responding, "You know, Dr. Z., we could actually use some time here with you out of the office. We have so much darned paperwork what with the referrals and billing and all that, the time could be put to good use. As it is, we get so far behind doing the daily work of seeing patients that the cash flow is affected, and that, as we all know, is a very bad thing."

I raised the usual objections as to overhead, salaries and another block of time where I wouldn't be available to my patients in St. Albans, but Rachel had an answer for that as well.

"If you could get them to agree to pay you by the hour a regular salary that would cover all of the overhead and salaries in this office while you worked up there, it could work. As for the patients, it would be true that you wouldn't be available for emergencies on the day that you went up to Richford, but we could probably book you more fully during the other days to take care of the routine appointments in a timely manner, and the ER could certainly handle any true emergencies until the evening when you got back."

"Well," I said, "I'll think about it."

And I did. Over the next several days I mulled this idea over in my head. The more I thought about it, the more it seemed like a workable plan. I talked it over with Cassie who wasn't exactly enthusiastic about it, but did agree that it was at least worth exploring, provided of course that Moira could get the Richford folks on board with the financial details. The next time I saw Moira, I informed her that I would consider taking the job.

The very next day, she called on the phone at my office and told me that the board would be happy to go ahead with my proposal if only I might come down some on the hourly fee that I had demanded. Financial negotiations have never been my forte, and, after some more mulling, I agreed to their offer. And so, it came about that I was the medical director of the Richford Health Center The Center, thanks to the hard work of its Board members who did all of the considerable paperwork required, would soon become a federally qualified rural health care clinic.

With this official designation, they were able to get increased reimbursement from the government in regard to Medicare and Medicaid patients, and so were not only able to keep the clinic going but also to pay my princely salary as well.

Initially, it was just me and Joan Pressner, a good natured and extremely competent woman who worked as secretary, file clerk, nurse and lab assistant all at the same time. I did all of the EKGs myself until I taught Joan to do them, and I drew all of the blood for the lab work as well. We then began a search for a physician's assistant or a nurse practitioner who could man the clinic for the other four days a week when I wasn't there. This took quite a while before we found the right person, and a few people came and went before we settled on the perfect someone to fill the slot. Eventually, we did find that individual and were able to hire a physician's assistant named Rosaire Archambault. He became a tremendous asset for the clinic and was able to keep things running quite smoothly when I wasn't there. In fact, Rosaire pretty much was the medical provider for the town of Richford, and I functioned in largely an advisory capacity as far as outpatient medicine there was concerned. "Dr." Rosaire, as most of his patients came to call him, was the real presence in the town. This arrangement worked well; the clinic prospered and many improvements were made in the years that followed.

In the meantime, the local hospital, seeing what a success the Richford Health Center had made of itself, attempted to establish several other rural health clinics in the surrounding communities. They built beautiful state of the art physical plants in three northern Vermont towns, staffed them with physicians and tried to make a go of it. Unfortunately, there were several problems from the very beginning that assured failure in this enterprise. This was a hospital production and not a community production as had been the case in Richford. The groundswell of community support was thus not as great and solid as it had been in Richford, and the use of the clinics was not very great. Also, the clinics, being owned by the hospital, were unable to get the rural health clinic designation that meant so much in terms of reimbursement. Adding to this was the fact that the salaries of the doctors needed to staff the clinics were considerably higher than those of mid-level providers such as physician's assistants. And lastly, hospitals are notoriously bad at running medical practices. This is not what they do and they are generally very bad at it when they try. The three northern health centers soon began hemorrhaging money, and they continued to hemorrhage money for as long as they existed in that format. In desperation, the hospital began looking for a way out. Ultimately, the managers of the hospital asked the Richford Health Center if they would take on the job of managing the three other health centers; and, after a great deal of soul searching and evaluating, Moira Stern and her compatriots agreed to accept this challenge. Immediately, they asked me if I would be the medical director of this building conglomerate.

Just as immediately, and in no uncertain terms, I told them that I most certainly would not. It was not my life's plan to be an administrator of any kind. My experience with administrators, although not entirely negative, convinced me that I did not wish to become one. I went to medical school to take care of patients and that's what I intended to continue to do. But, of course, "the best laid plans of mice and men. . ."

I continued to function in my capacity as a medical director of the Richford Health Center as well as running my private practice in St. Albans. The Richford Management Group, as they now called themselves, continued to look for a medical director for the three other clinics and attempted to keep all of the clinics staffed with a hodgepodge of physicians and ancillary personnel. Many of these physicians felt that they could see the handwriting on the wall, and most of them moved on, leaving yet another vacancy in the hierarchy. Patients, seeing that their doctors were leaving, also left. The continuity of care suffered, and the situation worsened.

Periodically, various folks, including Moira and her companions in arms, would ask offhandedly if I might reconsider taking on the post of medical director. I would reiterate my usual objections of just not wanting to be an administrator to begin with and then raised the further objection that I had an entire practice in St. Albans that I wasn't about to leave in the lurch. I had employees there that were loyal to me and had become good friends, and I have patients there that might feel, quite rightly, that I was deserting them. We left it at that.

And then one day, Pam Perry, one of the more active board members along with Moira, who had taken on the position of CEO of the health center conglomerate, made the suggestion that I might consider moving my entire St. Albans practice to Swanton, the town immediately north of St. Albans, and one of the towns which, coincidentally, house one of the clinics. The light bulb went on. This could be a way to, in large part, retain my original practice, fulfill what I considered my obligations to my patients and my employees and serve as the medical director as well. Of course, I still would have to go over to the dark side and become an administrator.

I ran this idea past Rachel, who was enthusiastic and supportive. She actually lived in the town of Swanton herself so this would make commuting to work easier for her. (Though she would ultimately discover that this was a mixed blessing as she would be the one who would be relied upon to get to the clinic in bad snow storms or other emergencies and would be the one that patients tended to call at home if they had after hours problems that should properly be handled by the physician on call or by the emergency room.) Naturally, she had questions about salary, vacation schedules, retirement plans, job description, etc., etc. We eventually decided that if she and the other office personnel could get at least an equal situation as the one that they currently had in my office that they would be willing to make the deal.

In the evening on that day, after we had eaten our dinner,

I took up the subject of this proposed change in my professional position. I was still seated at the table and Cassie was at the sink rinsing dishes. As soon as the basic idea was out of my mouth, her face was instantly transformed from a pleasant calm to a bizarre fury. Her eyes widened in terror and, seemingly out of nowhere, she actually began screaming.

"No, no, no, Jon." She shouted. "You can't do it. I simply won't allow you to do it." Her face contorted maniacally and took on an expression of ferocity and apprehension that I had never seen before on that usual calm and beautiful visage. Those previous episodes of emotional outburst that had taken place over the last many months rose to the surface of my mind. A frightening pattern was developing. Orion, who had been lying on the kitchen floor calmly and half asleep, was roused from his torpor by Cassie's yelling. Uncertain as to what was happening but convinced that it was something bad, he added his voice to the din and began to bark loudly and uncontrollably. I was unable to say anything more until I had removed him to his run outside the house. Even there, he continued to bark continuously until Cassie herself had quieted down, but at least his barking was now at a distance.

"What do you mean, Cass?" I asked bewilderedly. "This would be a perfect solution for the clinics and would be a chance for us to get out of the day to day hassles of running the medical practice. We could sell the office and never have other stuff. When I eventually retire, I could just walk away."

She stood rigid at the sink. It was as if she hadn't even heard my words, or if she had, they didn't register.

"My God, Jon." She continued, "You know how precarious those clinics are. What if they go belly up? You'd be left without a job, and we could never pay our bills on my salary. We wouldn't have any funds to start a new practice, and we would probably have to sell our home and leave the area. I just couldn't take it!"

This was beginning to sound more and more like the incident when I had first told Cassie about the pending malpractice suit. Some of the themes were familiar, particularly the bit about losing our home and having to move. The level of anxiety, though increased exponentially, also was similar. Still, at least this most recent argument was partially grounded in reality and could be addressed rationally, or so I thought.

"With me as the medical director, the situation will be different." I rejoined. "The clinics should be viable entities, particularly the one in Swanton which will benefit from my entire patient base when they move there. Also, Moira has assured me that they will shortly be receiving the designation of FQHC, or Federally Qualified Health Centers, which will mean that the reimbursement schedules will be even better than what the Richford Health Center has now. Besides that, the Richford clinic will still be financially independent of the other three clinics so that if they do fail it will remain the going concern that it has been and I will still have the job there." These seemed to me to be good points and to address the fears that she had raised. Once again, however, her demeanor did not soften and, in fact, the volume of her voice actually went up a notch as she raged on.

"No, no, no!" she shouted. "It's just too risky. You can't do it. I won't stand for it. If you do this, I … I … I'll leave you. Yes, I'll leave you. That's just what I'll do." And she folded her arms over her chest and glared at me balefully.

She was such a picture of furious anger that I couldn't take it seriously and almost made the fatal mistake of laughing at her at that point. Needless to say, that would not have been a good idea. All of our married lives Cassie had been the most supportive of companions, and she had never, ever, balked at any of the career moves that I had made in the past. If she did have objections, she had always raised them quietly, and we have talked them out to both our satisfactions. This is not to say that she was a milksop or subservient wife. She had her own desires, plans and ambitions and was not hesitant about voicing her opinions and, I must admit, though I had been raised in a traditional household when the male parent ruled the roost (at least on the surface), I admire my wife greatly for this and wouldn't have it other way. This-over-the-top emotional performance with attached ultimatum was not the Cassie that I knew at all.

Stunned and reeling, I continued to try to calm her down and to answer any of the objections she raised, but this proved to be impossible. I tried to approach her and to take her in my arms but she physically fended me off and; to my horror and amazement, actually struck out at me a couple of times. She continued to rant and rave nonstop for literally hours before we went to bed, and even after that, remained awake for some time assuring me that her threats were not empty ones, and that she would do just what she had promised if I went ahead with any job changes. Neither one of us had a very restful night.

By the next morning, she had burned herself out and spoke no more of it. However, not only did she not speak of it, but she wouldn't allow me to do so either so any further discussion of the subject became impossible I attempted on multiple occasions to bring it up again, but she had erected an impenetrable barrier between us in this regard, and I was unable to do so. Ultimately, I was left to make a decision alone.

I agreed to take a position if salary, vacations, working conditions etc. could all be finalized to the satisfaction of myself and all of my original St, Albans people, and notified Moira of my decision. Once again, she took the news with disconcerting equanimity as if she knew this would happen all along; and after discussing the situation with the board of directors, she officially offered me the job. We agreed that I would be given a transition period of three months so that I could sell the building in which I was practicing, make the physical move and tidy up all of my affairs in St. Albans. Notices were sent out to all of my patients and ads were placed in all of the local newspapers informing people of what was happening.

In the following days, I was energized and expectant, what with making plans and working out the details of the move. Cassie reacted to this by withdrawing from me more and more. The more excited I became, the more unresponsive and withdrawn she acted as if she were a negative mirror of my emotions. As much as I tried, I could not engage her. Though we still shared the same house and the same bed, we spoke less and less and interacted less and less often. I would come home from work to find her lying on the couch, seemingly engrossed and in whatever program was on the television at the moment, staring vacantly off into space and barely acknowledging the fact that I had appeared. More alarmingly, she also started to withdraw from other aspects of her life in general. For example, Cassie had always had a very active mental life; and being an English major in college and working as a school librarian, she was always interested in wordplay and in crossword puzzles and other word puzzles. She religiously did the daily crossword in the newspaper and often bought other puzzle books to work out as well. She also had several word games installed on our computer that she would play periodically for an hour or two. As time went by, she engaged in these activities less and less and, by the time I made the move to the Swanton office, she was no longer doing any of these things at all.

Initially, I had thought that Cassie was falling prey to a depression due to the big change in my professional circumstances and our personal disagreement in regard to our future plans, but, as time went by and these other more disturbing symptoms developed, it became clear that the problem was even more serious than that.

One day I was called at work by Cassie's assistant in the library who told me that she had found her standing and crying in front of the bookshelves, holding a book in her hand and seemingly unsure of just what she should do with it. When her assistant gently asked what the problem was, she would only respond, "I don't know what to do with this. I can't remember where this goes." She proceeded to cry all the more and had to be led back to her desk where she dazedly began to stamp overdue books as if in a trance. In a short while she became her normal self, and she actually was able to drive herself home that day, but it was becoming more and more evident that Cassie was just not Cassie, at least not the Cassie that I knew. Luckily, the school year ended soon there-after and any problems that she had with work could be postponed until September.

This had its downside, however, for I continued to keep my head in the sand; and, in spite of this event, I did nothing to inter-vene until our younger daughter, Tatiana, forced me to realize that I had to. In retrospect, I'm not sure if this was because I was a phy-sician and felt that I should be able to handle things myself. Most likely it was some combination of the two. In any event, my hand was forced by a young girl who was concerned about her mother. Tatiana, who, like her older sister before her, was going to Smith College, had come home for the summer in late May. She had a summer job scooping ice cream at the Big Scoop in Swanton and sort of stayed with us. I say "sort of" because she was usually on a tennis court somewhere, or out with friends doing something or other and was rarely home. She mostly didn't eat with us and spent a little time with us but she did talk to her mother enough to real-ize that there was a problem. In fact, she did a better job than her dad, who was on the scene for much longer periods and suppos-edly was intimately involved in the situation. In my defense, I can only conclude that I was too close to things or too afraid of things to make a diagnosis or to force the issue. One evening in early summer, she came to me with a worried look on her face.

"Dad," she said, "I think that there's really something wrong with mom."

"Yeah, I know." I replied. "She's really been upset about the lawsuit and about the new job. I think all of the stress has gotten to her and that she's depressed. I was thinking that she probably needs to go to her doctor and get started on an antidepressant and some counseling."

"No, Dad," Tatiana reiterated, "you don't understand. I think that there is something really wrong with Mom. I don't mean just a depression. Not that that wouldn't be serious. But I mean that there's something else going on. Something worse."

Time stopped. Tatiana had given voice to my greatest fears. For some months I had been worried that the changes in my wife's behavior had gone past worry and anxiety but I had not had the courage to put a name to them. It was as if I had been engaging in primitive behavior myself, pretending that if I did not give voice to them they would not exist. But now, they had been given voice. The words had been spoken aloud and could not be ignored. Out of the mouths of babes. . . "What do you mean?" I asked."

"I think Mom's getting Alzheimer's Disease." She responded. "She keeps telling me the same things over and over as if she hasn't said them to me already. She's forgetting the simplest things and just not acting right. The other day she brought me a bowl of soup and the lid from the can was still in the bowl. It's not just the one thing, either. Every day it's something."

So there it was. The words had been spoken. The elephant in the room had been given a name.

DIAGNOSES

"My only hope lies in my despair."

Racine

L ike some forlorn and fragile space angel, Cassie lay suspended in the middle of the huge metal ring that was the heart of the magnetic imaging scanner. She was dressed in a johnny, one of those gowns that was more like a free flowing robe than pajamas and only added to the illusion of vulnerability and otherworldliness. Periodically, muffled clanking noises would echo through the cavernous room as the machine performed its task. Cassie was immobile and unreactive. Apparently the ten milligrams of Valium that I had given her about an hour ago was performing its function well.

I was seated in the antechamber alongside the technician who was running the machine and initially evaluating the images for clarity and completeness before the radiologist would officially read them. Although I was a practicing physician and not unfamiliar with the MRI, the technology never ceased to amaze me. Appearing before us on the flat LCD screen were image after image of Cassie's brain, precise cross section after cross section of anatomic exactness that, even to my professional eye, looked for all the world like actual physical slices of that organ. These were the same images that I could recall from my course in neuroanatomy when the professor had used thin slices of donated human brain to illustrate his points. Those slices had been fixed and mounted in plastic to preserve them but, in terms of structural detail, they were no more or less exact than the virtual images that, like magic, now appeared and disappeared in sequence on the screen in front of us as the scanner moved over its field of view. To my relatively untrained eye, these detailed pictures of Cassie's brain were disappointingly normal. Though I knew that it was a long shot, I had been fervently hoping that some theoretically correctable cause of her behavior would manifest itself. A benign meningioma that could be easily removed would be nice. Or unlikely as it was, far better to have a slowly growing tumor in some relatively silent area of the brain like the frontal lobe region rather than the more insidious and diffuse changes of Alzheimer's Disease. Ironically and most frustratingly, the latter would most likely not even leave a telltale signature even in the exquisitely detailed pictures that the MRI was producing. For the fact was that senile dementia of the Alzheimer's type could only be ultimately diagnosed by a brain biopsy which would demonstrate the microscopic neurofibrillary tangles that were the hallmark of the disease. Clinically, the news had been bad. In fact, the news was the worst that it could be. But still, there is always that thin thread of hope until it has been stretched to the point of breaking.

That day I had awakened Cassie early. We had an appointment at the "Memory Center" in Burlington, a multi-specialty clinic that specialized in the diagnosis and treatment of Alzheimer's Disease and other related illnesses of the central nervous system. Cassie had already been seen and evaluated by Marie Stokes, her personal physician and an internist who worked in my coverage group and was a colleague of mine. After the history taking and a brief physical exam that was mostly concentrated on the neurological exam and the mental status exam, Marie had told me what I, unfortunately, was already all too prepared to hear. Like my tennis playing daughter, Marie's preliminary diagnoses had been presenile dementia or Alzheimer's Disease, an illness that was both implacably progressive, albeit at a variable rate, and, most awful, without any know cause or cure. At this point Marie advised three things. First, a battery of blood tests to rule out any possible metabolic causes such as vitamin deficiencies, hypothyroidism, electrolyte imbalances, etc., etc. Second, a referral to the Memory Center to get the input of some experts in the disease. Third, starting treatment presumptively with Aricept, a drug that had been shown to be somewhat successful in early Alzheimer's in terms of slowing down the progression of the disease. We put this plan into action or at least as much of it as we were able. The lab studies, of course, all returned "within normal limits" so there was nothing there that was easily correctable. Unfortunately, Cassie couldn't tolerate the Aricept even at the lowest doses and developed debilitating abdominal cramps and diarrhea when she took it. This was a well-known potential side effect of the drug, but it was most discouraging even so. We tried a second drug, Reminyl, with similar results.

The referral to the Memory Center had been made the day of our office visit with Marie, but these tertiary referral centers are always booked up far in advance and, even though I was a fellow physician, this did little to move Cassie up in the queue. Marie had expressed some surprise at the degree of impairment that Cassie had demonstrated on these initial screening neurological tests as she was still functioning on a fairly high level and was still managing to do her job at the school. I, too, was surprised and bewildered that Cassie had been able to progress to this degree of illness without being more cognizant of it. In my own defense, I guess that I was too close to her to note the changes and had been concentrating on too many other things, such as the eminent changes in my own professional life, to be attentive enough to pick up on the, in retrospect, not so subtle cues that my wife had been presenting to me. Also, Cassie was an extremely intelligent woman to begin with, a quality that had attracted me to her in the first place and a quality that allowed her to mask and hide her slowly developing mental disabilities with other compensatory mechanisms. Up until that point, she hadn't gotten lost driving to and from work; and despite the fact that her job required use of short and medium term memory all the time in the shelving of books and the retrieval of information, her co-workers had not yet come to find her incompetent although there had been some touchy moments, such as the crying episode that one of her assistants had related to me. Mostly, her dysfunction had expressed itself as a slow acceleration and intensity of anxiety which, until prodded by Tatiana, I had rationalized away as a consequence of her insecurity in regard to what she had considered our uncertain financial prospects. In any event, by the time the actual day of the Memory Center appointment had arrived, Cassie had already had a trial of the two drugs that I previously mentioned.

The memory clinic was one of those modern one story buildings with clean architectural lines that consisted of a huge circular waiting room where the corridors all branched off like the spokes of a wheel leading off somewhere into the bowels of the building and the mysterious world of diagnostic medical testing. At that point, Cassie had not been sedated as she needed to be as clear headed as possible to have an accurate evaluation. Needless to say, her already baseline state of apprehension had been turned up another several degrees. It was all I could do to keep her in one place and to shepherd her in turn from one appointment to another. The staff there, however, was obviously used to this sort of thing and several young men and women were very helpful in calming her down and getting her from one place to another within the center. Cassie was seen in turn by a psychologist, a neurologist and yet another internist. She had several diagnostic studies including more of the same bloodwork, a series of mental status examinations and the aforementioned MRI. The valium had been provided an hour before the MRI was begun, and we had spent the time in the well-appointed and capacious waiting room at the hub of the spokes, I reading and Cassie mostly staring off into space. At the end of all this poking and prodding, both she and I were physically and mentally exhausted, I from the endless waiting and she from the endless testing and performing.

At the end of the morning, both of us were ushered into a plush office that was elaborately yet tastefully furnished and featured not one but three wall mounted salt water aquariums in which the most brilliantly colored of fishes cruised slowly about in rainbow display. There we were reintroduced to Norman Levy, the neurologist who had examined Cassie earlier that day and who was now privy to all of the results from the morning's testing. After this brief introduction, Dr. Levy got right to the point.

"Dr. Ziebaska," he said, "it is, I'm afraid, quite apparent that your wife is in the moderate stages of Alzheimer's Disease."

This really was not news to me. I was a professional and had seen it coming for months. Actually, the diagnosis had already been made by Marie Stokes and this was but a confirmation of her previous diagnosis and what I had suspected for some time. So why did I suddenly become fixated on one of the bright yellow parrot fishes in the tank on the wall behind Dr. Levy? And why was I unable to utter a word at that point? I could only nod my head dumbly. No words were spoken by either Cassie or myself.

"That is bad news." Dr. Levy went on. "But there is some good news. As you may know, there has just come out another anti-dementia drug that has been found to be of some use, a drug called Namenda. It has been helpful in cases of moderate to severe Alzheimer's. Up to now it's only been meant to be used in conjunction with the Aricept that your wife hasn't been able to tolerate but, theoretically, as you know, the progression of the disease is quite variable and it may take a long time before she is much more severely debilitated. We'll keep our fingers crossed in that regard. Otherwise, as I'm sure you also are aware, there is little that we can do other than supportive care, ensuring that Cassie is safe, well fed and cared for appropriately. You might consider looking into alternative living arrangements even at this early date as you have no idea how long she will remain viable in her current living situation at home."

As Dr. Levy had uttered these last words, I looked quickly at Cassie to see if she had understood the import of what he had just said. It seemed rather insensitive of him to have said such a thing in her presence, and I wasn't too impressed with his empathetic abilities at that point. In fact, I was more than a little angry that he had voiced such thoughts after this brief period of evaluation. I judiciously held my tongue. Luckily, whether it was the Valium, her underlying illness, denial or simply general fatigue, Cassie appeared not to have heard or notice and I could detect no response from her.

Dr. Levy provided us with prescription for the Namenda along the usual package insert with the list of potential side effects, detailed instructions for taking the medication and the usual disclaimer that said basically that the pharmaceutical company that made the drug was not to be held responsible for anything that happened to anyone while using the drug or, indeed, anything that happened within one hundred miles or so of anyone who had ever used the drug any time. He assured us that Dr. Stokes would get a copy of his notes and all diagnostic studies that had been done that morning; and then, politely and efficiently, he dismissed us. I took care of some more of the endless paperwork involved in any medical insurance plan at the front desk while Cassie fidgeted nervously. Then we were on our way.

As we drove home from the clinic, neither one of us said much. In fact, we said nothing at all for a good long time. Periodically as I drove, I would glance over at Cassie to see how she was doing. Each time she would be staring far off into space with a blank expression on her face. I could only imagine what she was thinking, this formidably intelligent woman with whom I had shared my life, who now faced the bleak prospect of a slow and unpreventable psychic dissolution. I thought to myself how terrible it would be to have pieces of your intelligence periodically breaking off from the central floe and drifting silently away, melting into the vastness of the surrounding sea, like the HAL9000 in "2001: A Space Odyssey," when its memory chips are removed one by one. Then, one time when I looked over, I found her looking back at me. Her eyes were bright and focused, and I had the overwhelming feeling that, just for that moment, the old Cassie, the real Cassie was manifesting herself.

"Jon," she said. "Please don't forget me. I couldn't bear it. Say that you won't ever forget me."

"Of course I won't forget you, Bug. Ever." I replied. "How could I possibly forget you? For over thirty years you have been my best friend, my best love. We've raised two fine daughters together and spent the longest and best parts of our lives together. It just couldn't happen. As long as I'm alive I'll remember you, I promise."

At that point, I could see that her soft brown eyes were misting over, and I just lost it. My ears started to ring, a powerful constriction climbed up into my throat, and a rising tide of emotion swept inexorably over me and smashed me down. I tried very hard to keep it in, but could not. Hot tears sprang unbidden from my eyes and my vision blurred. I slowed the car down and drifted into the breakdown lane where I put on the four-way flashers and stopped the engine. Then I turned to Cassie and took her in my arms. We both wept uncontrollably until all of our tears were gone. Then I started the engine and drove home.

That night, Cassie and I made love for the last time in our lives. We didn't know at the time that this would be our last, but things just worked out the way. Having spent the whole day with her, I felt particularly close to my wife that night; and when she came out of the bathroom wearing nothing but a coquettish smile, I was instantly and intensely aroused. By then it had been many months since we had last been intimate, and we came together fiercely, holding on to one another as if, indeed, we might lose one another if we dared to relax or grips. Initially, I saw Cassie smile with pleasure as I entered her, and this served to intensify the height of my passion. I lost myself in the moment, thrusting wildly and without control until I was spent. In that moment of ecstasy, I turned to see the face of my beloved. To my horror, she had gone somewhere else. Her face was empty and her eyes were vacant. There was no outward sign of emotion, no recognition, no acknowledgement of any kind. It was as if I had no existence beside her. Suddenly, in my own bed, with my own wife, I was ashamed.

Someone had turned off a switch and I felt like a necrophiliac, sating my desires on the hollow vessel of my demented wife. I looked again for some spark, some response, some hope. There was none. Her eyes were polished mirrors reflecting back on the dim light of the bedside alarm clock. It was a horrible thing.

SCHOOL'S OUT

"Time bears away all things, even our minds."

Racine

T he terrible events at the Memory Center, previously described, had taken place only shortly after the school year had ended. It had become obvious that Cassie would not be able to return to work that following September. Once the preliminary diagnosis had been made by Marie, it was as if this were a catalyst to speed the reaction of decline in Cassie's mental state. Just in those few weeks between the initial diagnosis and the confirmation of the diagnosis, she slipped tremendously. I theorized that she was only managing to hold on to her faculties by a great strength of will and that, once someone in a suitable position of expertise had given a name to the horror, this provided her with the permission to let go and to stop struggling against the inchoate monster that was eating her intelligence.

As Dr. Levy had said, the progression of the disease can be incredibly variable. I myself had known patients who went on for many years in a very mild state of dysfunction and didn't become completely dependent for some time. On the other hand, there were others who leapt headlong into babbling idiocy before the ink had dried on the consultant's letter of opinion. Just in that relatively short period between Marie's diagnosis and Dr. Levy's, I had to start driving Cassie to and from the school to be sure that she got where she needed to be. Her assistant in the library, Natalie Gagne, was kind enough to cover for her when she had problems with shelving books, checking books in and out or any of the other duties of a full time school librarian. Strangely enough, despite these other noticeable and serious declines, her reading abilities had remained to a large degree intact right up to the time that the school year had finished and she was still able to read just about any book to the children until the last working day. Her usual colorful delivery where she would put on various accents, use sound effects and take on some aspect of the character involved was understandably a bit muted, but only those of us who really knew what was going on could tell the difference. In any event, no one complained about her job performance right up to the end. Still, it was clear to me that changes were coming quickly and that they were not going to be good ones.

Already my own life was becoming more and more circumscribed as I had to make concessions to the encroaching illness. The weekly bagpipe sessions and my weekly duplicate bridge games became things of the past. I was unable to leave Cassie alone and ensure her safety. Not that this was a problem in itself. Cassie and I had long been best friends and had had no problem at all spending time with one another, even very long periods of unbroken time. We were not one of those couples who must have their breaks from one another in order to keep sanity in the relationship. Both of us were secure enough in our own heads to find individual activities which could be sitting reading in the same room for hours quite comfortably. With her not so slow descent into dementia, however, Cassie's sphere of activity became smaller and smaller. Ultimately, it would reach the point where she did nothing but sit in front of the television or, conversely, would pace up and down the living room and the hall ceaselessly for hours at a time. Orion would often get up and pace back and forth alongside her in these desperate walks to nowhere. It didn't seem to bother him that there was no destination to reach. It became impossible for me to go out for a run as I was always concerned that Cassie might go out and get lost, would leave the water running, would set the house on fire, etc. etc. In those black moments, I found myself thinking that there should be a way of designing a backyard run for human beings like the one Orion had to keep him out of trouble yet provide some much needed exercise. My existence became an existence of the mind almost solely. I would read fiction and medical journals, would use the computer to play various games, would use the Internet to write emails to friends and relatives and would get my bridge fix by playing online.

Due to the miracles of modern technology I was even able to play matches with my regular partner on one of the Internet bridge servers that had been dedicated to the task. All of these activities could be done in the same room in which Cassie sat, impassively, in front of the television screen, seemingly unaware of what I was doing or what else was transpiring in the wild world outside of her. Basically then, my life was the office, the hospital and home. It hadn't been particularly easy taking my wife to and from her workplace in those last days of the school year, but that was infinitely preferable to having her always at home where I had to monitor her activities continuously. Initially, I was forced to take some time off until I could make other arrangements. Relief came in the form of Sadie Lumbra, a matronly aunt of Rachel's who was widowed and retired and so had some time that she could use in this fashion. I paid her, of course, but no some of money was worth the peace of mind that I received by knowing that Sadie was at home with Cassie when I was at work or had to go out. There were nights when I was also on call for my group at the local hospital. There was absolutely no way to predict what would happen on those nights. I might be called in to admit patients or to handle in-house emergencies. It became clear that Cassie could no longer safely remain alone at home even in the middle of the night. (Who knows just when she might take it upon herself to get up to go to the bathroom and then become totally lost and terrified on the way up the hall?) I prevailed upon Sadie to sleep over in our house on these nights and weekends that I had the call. Sadie was a real gem. She slept in Alexandra's old room when she had to be at the house; and she was always very good with Cassie, reassuring her when it was called for and guiding her into her familiar paths of behavior so that she wouldn't panic or decompensate. The other evenings and the other weekends were mine.

Soon, however, there came more respite. Our younger daughter, Tatiana, came home from Smith College. She was between her junior and senior years and had intended that summer to run the Big Scoop, a local ice cream parlor which was only open in the summer. In past summers she had worked there as one of the scoopers and had a great deal of experience setting up the operations and closing up at night. She was looking forward to being the boss and to taking on the extra responsibilities of setting up the work schedules, doing the payroll, ordering supplies, etc., that would go with running the whole show. In her off hours, as usual, she intended to work on her tennis game with various professionals in the area and several of the male players at the university nearby. She didn't seem particularly pleased when I suggested that she babysit her mom for the summer instead but, after a short interval of grumbling and mumbling, she stepped into the breach and agreed that she would do it. We decided that I would pay her a salary to stay with Cassie during the times that I was at work and that she would also be available on those nights and weekends that I was on call. This would give Sadie the summer off, and she could resume in the fall when Tatiana went back to school. I would largely continue to be the caretaker at all of the other times when I wasn't working, but, with Tatiana there, I would at least be able to get out for a run or some other activity every once in a while.

Tatiana, as with many sibling situations, was far different from her sister. Where Alexandra was studying, Tatiana was partying. While Alexandra was curled up with a good book, Tatiana was out on the mountain tearing up the ski trails. This is not to say that Alexandra was physically inept or that Tatiana was unintelligent, it is simply that they either chose or were drawn to different aspects of life to a much greater degree. Alexandra became interested in the biology of birds and Tatiana became interested in tennis. Strangely enough, these disparate interests lead them both to the same college. By her senior year in high school, Tatiana was a nationally ranked junior tennis player and was actually offered scholarships at a few good schools with competitive women's tennis programs. Smith College, where Alexandra was studying biology and philosophy, had a very good tennis team; and, while they didn't offer her any money, the thought of going to the same school that her older sister had sweated bullets to get into was just too much for Tatiana to pass up. Besides, the "Quad" where many of the freshman dorms were located at Smith was notorious for its party atmosphere, and Jordan House where Tatiana had been promised a freshman residence was the "Leader of the Quad." This was an offer that she was unable to refuse.

During her first three years there, Tatiana had made the most of Smith. She played a lot of tennis and played it very well. There was much talk of her going into the professional ranks when she graduated. She did a lot of partying as promised and had a lot of fun. In between the parties and the tennis, she actually did a fair amount of studying and managed to really do quite well in regard to her academic standing, though, much to her competitive chagrin, not as well as her sister. The only problem was that she could not decide what she would do with her life, other than the tennis that is. In the three years that she had been there, she had changed her academic major six times, an average of twice a year. The most recent choice was history with the thought of doing some work as a museum curator but none of us were holding our breaths. In any event, I was just happy to have her home for the summer and especially to have someone to share the burden of being caretaker to a large child who, day by day and very slowly (though not slowly enough) was becoming more and more debilitated.

Despite her original reluctance, Tatiana proved to be the best possible caretaker for her mother. Her patience was inexhaustible, and her ability to orient and to calm Cassie was unique. I more than once found my eyes misting over as I watched mother and daughter walking hand in hand together on the beach outside our house or gazing raptly at yet another gorgeous sunset over the mountains across the lake. Tatiana was also terrific at doing those little interpersonal things such as brushing her mother's hair or painting her fingernails. I could see that this was hard on her, however. She had always been a very sensitive child, and the close proximity to a failing parent for such long periods of time was a strain. Several times that summer I would catch the tears falling silently down her cheeks as she gently tended to Cassie.

WEDDING BELLS

"One's tootings at the wedding of the soul. Occur as they occur."

Wallace Stevens

T hat summer was actually a pretty good one as far as I was concerned. With Tatiana home to take care of her mother during office hours and at those times when I was on call, the burden of constantly trying to schedule someone to stay with Cassie was lifted if only temporarily. Tatiana and her mom got along quite well and didn't need to be constantly in one another's hair to ensure that Cassie was kept safe and that Tatiana was kept sane. If Tatiana had to run errands during the day, she would have Cassie come along with her in the car riding shotgun. The same would be true for me if I had things that I had to do outside our property in the evenings or on weekends. For the day to day activities of yard work, lawn mowing, etc., Tatiana was able to provide me some extra time on occasion, and Cassie even got involved with some of the gardening chores herself. Also, Cassie's parents, though in their eighties, were still very much alive and were not only in good mental health but were in good physical health as well. They would drive up from Massachusetts to see us, and would spend a large amount of time entertaining and taking care of their only daughter. The sight of Cassie being coached to perform some simple task or other by her own elderly mother was heartbreaking for all of us, but at the same time was extremely helpful in the overall scheme of things. Also, the extra attention that Tatiana and her grandparents lavished on Cassie actually appeared to slow her deterioration to some extent. Or maybe it was the Namenda. Over those twelve weeks or so of summer, I could detect no appreciable worsening.

I had already decided that Cassie would go on sick leave for the next academic year and would then resign her position. In all her years of working at the school, she had never had to take any time off because of illness and consequently had accumulated over a year's worth of sick time. This would prove to be a godsend as we could use that sick leave as a buffer now to continue to pay bills such as college tuition and other outstanding loans which we had. Also, we were able to use her school insurance to help pay doctors' bills and medical expenses. At the end of the year, she would have to retire, of course. Still, she had been working long enough that a small pension would be coming to her and that, coupled with social security disability, would continue to bolster our financial situation.

With Tatiana's help and support, I was also able to resume something of a social life and could attend some bagpipe practices and performances, some duplicate bridge sessions and the occasional run. This went a long way toward restoring my morale.

Still, all good things must come to their natural end; and when the summer ended, Tatiana had to return to college, and the search to find regular caretakers was on again. Mrs. Lumbra, as before, was very helpful and an overall wonder, but she was unable to fill all of the time slots that were needed and I ended up hiring two other women on a part time basis to stay with Cassie when Sadie wasn't available. They were also good women, reliable and conscientious, and they did their best to not only care for Cassie but also befriend her. There never was the connection that she had developed with Sadie, not to mention that which she said had with Tatiana, however; and, whether or not it was the dementia or simply Cassie herself, she just never was as calm or as comfortable with these other caretakers. Part of the problem, no doubt, was that I tried to use them as infrequently as possible; and so, in a way it was a self-fulfilling prophecy. They never got to know Cassie that well because they weren't that involved with her care and, because they didn't get the chance to know her, I didn't involve them so much in her care. Needless to say, this wasn't the best situation, but it was the best I could do at the time.

Meanwhile, it was as if the lawsuit didn't exist. I heard nothing from any of the lawyers. No one had asked me for a deposition or any other opinion on the case. This was just fine with me. I simply went forward as if there were no case and no doubt hoped within my heart of hearts that it would simply go away. After all, it had always seemed from my perspective that there was no case in the first place so it would not be so strange then if everyone had come to their senses at last and it had disappeared as time went by. It developed, of course, that this was rather a naive hope on my part and that any delays were a matter of the incredible slowness of the legal system and the backlog of civil cases that exists in our suit-riddled society. At the time, however, ignorance was bliss.

On a more positive note, the wedding of Zac and Alexandra was fast approaching and the preparations for the great event were ongoing. Initially, Cassie had been very involved with the planning, picking out dress styles, flowers and music, deciding upon those who would be invited and those who would not, making preparations for a bridal shower and sending out those invitations as well. With her illness, however, she became less and less involved in these matters and her own mother and Alexandra herself took on most of these chores. In some ways this was actually a good thing as, for example, Alexandra was perfectly happy to make all of these decisions concerning her own wedding. Naturally, the mundane tasks of sending out all of the invitations, hiring the caterers, finding the musicians and arranging their contracts, etc., was not so much fun. There were a few awkward moments when certain arrangements that had been made by Cassie earlier were inadvertently changed by Alexandra because no one except Cassie had been aware that such arrangements had been made in the first place. Luckily, these were very few. Also, her grandmother helped considerably; and the preparations moved along very nice-ly.

And so it came to pass that in late September of that year on what turned out to be a fine fall day our elder daughter was married to Zac, her betrothed. The wedding was held in a small church in Highgate, just about nine miles north of our house; and the reception took place in a large Victorian mansion that was lo-cated just across a small green from that church. Cassie and I both gave Alexandra away. Alex had wanted it that way, and I certain-ly had no objection. Her mother and I had both raised her; and, truth be told, a mother often plays a much larger role in the bring-ing up of children, particularly female children, than the father does. This was most certainly the case in our family. Why then shouldn't Mom be allowed to share the spotlight at the ceremony? Also, of course, there was the subtext of Cassie's illness, and it was just as well that she be at my side where I could watch over her and comfort her as needed. Although I did watch her very closely during the ceremony, I couldn't be certain how much, if anything, she understood about what was happening. Did she understand that her first child was getting married, was embarking on life's great adventure, leaving the nest for good and all? She said noth-ing that might answer the question. But she did smile brilliantly throughout, and I was hopeful that, if nothing else, the general happy tone of the occasion had impressed itself upon her.

At the end of ceremony, the bride and groom got into a horse drawn carriage and were piped across to the Highgate Man-or led by a solitary bagpiper (yours truly) playing "Raabe's Wed-ding." Strangely enough, this was not my idea. Zac and Alexandra had approached me to do the piping for the wedding, much to my surprise. I was enough of a ham to be quite pleased to do so and enjoyed doing it very much. The weather, though the day had not started out very auspiciously with a thick overcast and even some sprinkles of rain, had cooperated nicely by clearing off the cloud cover about noon; and by the time the ceremony had begun, the skies were bright blue and clear as they often are here in the fall of the year.

The manor was a large, ornate building that in former years had served as a tourist hotel for those who were "taking the waters." At Highgate Springs, natural mineral springs in the area had a high sulfur content and were prized for their medicinal qualities. After this form of treatment had fallen into disrepute. The Manor had fallen into disrepair and for many years after was considered a dive where bikers and lowlifes gathered to drink and experience other forms of chemical entertainment. In recent years, however, that had changed after a young couple had purchased the property and refurbished it. At the time of the wedding, the building was newly renovated and painted and the grounds were ablaze with flowers and flowering shrubs. In keeping with the color scheme of the new bride, a profusion of yellow and burgundy chrysanthemums lined the paths and sat in pots along the walls and the edges of the porches. This, coupled with the usual fall foliage and the bright autumnal sunlight which emphasized the multiple colors, turned the entire area into a rainbow extravaganza and set off the stark white of the bride's wedding dress to full effect. In keeping with my bagpipe playing duties, I was dressed in full kilted regalia wearing the green, brown and black of the Thomson hunting tartan. (My maternal grandfather, Archibald Thomson, was the family connection to my Scottish heritage. He had died when my mother was in her teens. I had never met him, but I could still use her surname to gain entry into certain ethnic organizations.) Not only was this regalia appropriate for piping but, in true penurious Scottish stereotype, it had also saved me the price of renting a tuxedo.

At the Manor, we initially had a solo harpist play classical music for the half hour or so that it took people to cross over from the church and go through the receiving line and then "Jimmy D", a local disc jockey took over, spinning CDs for the dancing. There was an open bar and hors d'oeuvres before the dinner and all of the guests were loosened up and in a good mood before the dancing began. The dinner itself was preceded by the usual toasts and speeches. Tatiana, who was his sister's maid of honor, gave a nice little speech about growing up with Alexandra and intermittently chasing her around the house with sharp objects in a typical sibling expression of affection. All told, there were about eighty people at the wedding, mostly immediate family and friends of the bride and groom. I had also invited Rachel and Peg and other people in my office who had now been working with me for over twenty five years. By this time we were all good friends as well as coworkers. It seemed to me that everyone was having a good time. In the middle of all of these festivities, I came upon an interesting piece of information. I was talking to Cassie's Uncle Edward, a man of impeccable taste in clothing who was well dressed even in comparison to the male members of the wedding party who were all wearing tuxes, when, for some reason we got onto the subject of travel. It was probably Uncle Ed who brought it up in the first place as he and Cassie's Aunt Joyce were known in the family as world travelers. I remembered at that moment that the two of them had been in England a few years ago and asked Uncle Ed if he had a recollection of obtaining a book while he was there.

"Sure." He responded promptly. "Joyce bought one of those "Rumpole of the Bailey" books from a woman at one of the bed and breakfasts that we stayed at. I remember she was quite full of herself because the book hadn't even been officially published yet. This woman apparently was the publicist for the guy who wrote the books. Didn't Joyce lend you guys that book? I thought that she did."

Another mystery solved. I hadn't been losing my mind after all. But this gave me little satisfaction in view of what had transpired with Cassie subsequently. I could hardly crow over my petty triumph of being right in that argument. Better that she had been correct. Uncle Ed and I spoke some more about their travels in England and then I excused myself as the dancing began.

When the dancing started, everyone but a few of the elderly aunts managed to make an appearance on the dance floor. Tatiana and I had great fun imitating the disco dancers of the 60s with our take on the Saturday Night Fever moves of John Travolta in the movie. The music was as electric as the guests, with Polish polkas alternating with rock, classic tunes from the 70s, a few waltzes and even some classic music and a tango thrown in. As the father of the bride, I moved from table to table trying my best to play the gracious host, attempting to see that everyone had a good time and that no one felt neglected.

The traditional dance for the bride and her father was announced and Alexandra and I took to the floor to the sound of Billy Joel's "Lullaby." The emotional impact of dancing with my daughter at her wedding caught me by surprise, and I actually found myself tearing up as the lyrics of the song played out. I had read of this as a significant life event and thought that I had already played it out in my head to the point where it wouldn't affect me too greatly; but, as usual, the theory and the reality were not the same. This was my firstborn, my oldest child, my Alexandra. She was all grown up and leaving us to formally begin her new life, her new existence as a married woman apart from the original family group. All of the old feelings of tenderness and the desire to keep one's child happy and safe came to a crescendo in that one moment. The sensation was at the same time one of exquisite happiness with an underlying sadness accompanied by a further undercurrent of what I could only describe as a true pain. The jumble of emotions left me bemused and unfocused as the dance ended and I returned to my table in a pleasant haze.

Next, as is tradition, Zac and his mother danced together. I took this time to pay some attention to my wife who was sitting beside me. Cassie had been fairly unreactive throughout the whole affair, seemingly uninvolved in the ceremony or in the festivities that followed. She sat at our table with flatness of affect, responding only briefly to the many guests who addressed themselves to her as the mother of the bride. Most of them, though not all, were well aware of her medical problems and did their best to keep the conversation light and pleasant. I couldn't tell if she recognized anyone as she gave little outward indication that she did so though she remained cordial and polite throughout the whole ordeal, eventually summoning up a fixed smile. She said little to me as well, and I was unable to determine whether or not she was aware of what was going on. Once again I wondered whether she understood the significance of the day's events. Did she understand that this was Alexandra's wedding day? Did she realize that our little girl was now at the milestone in her life and that this was the ceremony that would mark that seminal age? I had no idea.

The band, or rather the CDs, played on. Tatiana and a group of her young friends from school started a line dance and gyrated around the hall in uproarious good humor. Uncle George danced a mean tango with cousin Sylvia who was less than half of his age. Aunt Jean, who had trouble keeping up with George even in the flower of her youth, looked on with good humored bemusement. We had placed disposable cameras at each of the individual tables, and people amused themselves by taking pictures of folks at the other table in candid (read embarrassing) poses. A couple of guests imbibed a bit too much and made good natured fools of themselves but nobody cared. A good time was had by all.

At the end of the evening, a minor miracle occurred. The disc jockey announced the last dance of the evening, a slow dance designed for those spouses and partners who had come together in the ceremony to celebrate the establishment of this new partnership. Just as the music started, Cassie appeared in front of me, her arms open wide and a sparkle in her eyes. I was floored. Every once in a while through the course of her illness, Cassie had shown these isolated times when she seemed to be peering out from the fog of her dementia with her old personality. As time went by, however, these episodes became more and more infrequent and, lately, I had just about given up on ever seeing the woman that I loved again. Here then, at this singular moment and significant time in our lives, was another such manifestation. How did it come about? I didn't pretend to know. Somewhere down there in the middle of those neurofibrillary tangles there was a spark and connection; and, against all odds, the essential spirit of Cassie had resurrected herself. At this already emotional time, this was the crowning touch I took her in my arms, and we danced this last dance with tenderness and grace. She moved her body against mine lightly and artfully and we moved together seamlessly to the strains of a romantic ballad. All too soon, the music rang its final note and the dance ended. Everyone said their goodbyes and we went home.

INTERMEZZO AND THE NOT SO GREAT ESCAPE

"I love to wander by the stream that dances in the sun,
so joyously it calls to me, Come, Join my happy song!"

The Happy Wanderer

L ater in the fall as time turned back, so did my life turn back to its previous patterns. Once again, I was prisoner to Cassie's care, unable to maintain any sort of social life outside of our increasingly one way relationship. As before, the underpinnings of our previous life ensured that this was not entirely a bad thing as she and I had always had that close relationship that two people who care deeply for one another develop a second skin. The trouble was that Cassie was no longer Cassie or, at any rate, not the Cassie that I knew. Those brief times of "normalcy," like the incident at Alexandra's wedding, slowly flickered lower and lower until they finally went out altogether. Whereas in the past I might look up from the book that I was reading, catch Cassie's eye and smile, and have the smile returned or even elicit a short exchange of conversation, in this new grey world I couldn't get my wife to acknowledge that there was anyone in the room. Orion, puzzled and confused about the whole affair, would do his best to cuddle up to her; but, other than a desultory pat or two, he also was largely ignored. This caused him to whine unhappily and continuously until he got on my nerves and I had to put him out of the house. The poor beast knew that something was wrong, but couldn't understand why he had to suffer for it. More and more, I was alone together with my wife.

Zac and Alexandra had honeymooned in Costa Rica, the bird watchers' paradise. This was the perfect place for her to be with her interest in the lives of birds, but, unfortunately while they were there, it rained almost constantly, a dirty trick when they would not get a chance to go back for many years afterward. Alex told me that they knew that they were in trouble when they appeared at the dock of the hotel at which they would be staying and the dock was nowhere to be seen, being at that time already over a foot under water. In the time that they were there, this dock submerged another foot under water. In spite of the inclement weather, however, their spirits were not dampened; and they both insisted that they had a great time. They donned slickers and boots and tramped into the hills of Costa Rica looking for exotic birds in all shapes, sizes and colors. Each evening they returned to their hotel room exhilarated by what they had seen and tired to the bone. Sleep came easily and deeply (in between the usual honeymoon activities that are never discussed by daughters and their dads). I received several postcards addressed to Cassie and me and, indeed, "wished that I was there." Like all great times, it ended all too soon, and they were both back at work in Boston before either of them would have liked.

Several weeks later, in the early evening, I received a telephone call from Alexandra.

"Hey, Dad, guess what? She excitedly asked. "One of the gorillas got out of its enclosure in the Primate Center. No one was hurt. It was after hours and he didn't even get out of the building but he was out there walking where the visitors walk for quite a while."

"You're kidding me." I exclaimed. "How did he get out"

"Well, that's the thing." She replied. "Nobody knows exactly. No one saw him actually get out, but one of the janitors did see him while he was out so there is no question that he did get out. It reminded me of the guy whose wife is suing you who told us about at Christmas. No one saw him get out of the house or over the wall but he did it on multiple occasions. Same way with Little Joe. Joe's an adolescent male who stands about five feet tall and weighs 300 pounds. That isn't very much for a gorilla, far less than an adult male. It means that he is able to get around better than the big adults and is still large enough to have a long reach. We figure that he somehow was able to swing out over the edge of the moat and get to the other side. Luckily, as I said, it was after hours, and there were no visitors to interact with, frighten or injure so there was no harm done. Joe walked around a little, visited chimpanzees, was spotted by the janitor and then, before any of us keepers could even appear on the scene, he apparently got bored and went back into the gorilla enclosure of his own accord. No one saw how he did that either."

"Terrific." I said. "Now you have an escaping gorilla but you have no idea how he made his escape. What are they going to do about it?"

"We had a big meeting today to kick around some ideas. The primate Center will have to close a few days, at least the inside part. Visitors can still see the animals from the outside, and the animals can go out as usual. Meanwhile, on the inside we are going to ramp up the security and make some physical changes in the enclosure. Mostly, this will mean adding electrical fencing along the edges of the moat where the wall and the moat come together. Although no one saw Joe actually get out that way, it seems most likely."

"I hope you're right." I replied. "It won't go over too well with the viewing public if they had to contend with an escaped gorilla, adolescent or not. In the middle of the city, wild things better remain in the cages, especially big, strong wild things."

"No kidding, Dad," remonstrated my older daughter. (I could see her rolling her eyes in my mind.) "It is disconcerting not really knowing how he got out or whether or not we're actually fixing the problem by doing what we're doing. But what else can we do? The gorillas are a major attraction at the zoo, and we don't want to limit anyone's zoo experience if we can possibly help it. I really can't imagine any other way he could have gotten out. Gorillas can't fly, you know."

"Neither can human beings." I rejoined. "But Martin Wennar went over the wall enough times to drive his wife to hire 24/7 personal caretakers. Maybe that's what you people should do with Little Joe."

"Very funny, Dad," she retorted." I can just see some poor sap sitting all night by the gorilla enclosure waiting for something interesting to happen. Probably get so bored that he'd let the gorillas out himself just to relieve the monotony."

"Yeah, you've got a point there. Not the most interesting of assignments watching gorillas sleep. Still, you could do other things. Set up alarms, use closed circuit television, put tab alerts on the gorillas."

"You're a bundle of laughs, today, Dad, but I don't think a gorilla would tolerate a tab alert. You may have something there, though. I know that they have little bar code tabs that can be injected beneath the skin of dogs and other pets as a theft deterrent. We could put something like that on all of the primates and have it trigger an alarm if any of them gets out of the cage. Then, if one did get out, that would be a good way to track it. I think I'll suggest that at the next meeting."

"See, your dad can have some good ideas after all. Just come to me with whatever zoo problems you have and I'll be happy to render an opinion."

"I'm sure you will. By the way, how's Mom doing?"

The tenor of the conversation became a great deal more somber at this point as there was not much good news on the Cassie front. I described how she was becoming more nonreactive and recounted how even the dog was getting upset with the way Cassie was treating him. Alex commiserated at some length but there was little that she could do but offer her moral support. Not that I wasn't grateful for that but it, of course, did little to remedy the situation. We talked a bit longer about this and that, nothing much of any consequence, and she hung up.

Tatiana had gone back to Smith, as we had planned and

was having a good but hectic time there with her school work, her tennis and her multiple social obligations, not, unfortunately, in that order. I heard from her infrequently to begin with and then even less as the academic year went on. Still, she did call me every once in a while to keep me up to date on how things were going in her life, and I was thankful for that. One nice but also sad benefit from Cassie's deterioration was that I was becoming closer to our daughters. In the past, they had always preferred to talk to their mother, and at times I would merely get to answer the phone before they would ask that I "put Mom on." Now they would talk to me at some length as I was the default connection to the homestead and their mother was unable to carry on any sort of reasonable conversation. A few times, I actually found myself feeling pleased that this was the case and basked in the delight of sharing their lives more actively, but these thoughts almost immediately brought up such horrible feelings of guilt that I repressed them as quickly as they surfaced. Certainly I wouldn't have hesitated if I could have traded this closer bond with my daughters for the opportunity to have Cassie back. Some choices we just don't get.

Whenever I did speak to our daughters, I would immediately relate the conversation to Cassie as close as I could recall it word for word. There were times when she seemed to understand what I was telling her; and that fall right up until about Christmas she did sometimes respond verbally and ask questions about the girls that, for the most part, were appropriate. I would always answer her at some length, hoping and pretending that she was comprehending what I was saying. It was frustrating and depressing when she would respond with some odd non sequitur or would not respond at all even to what I would consider the most interesting of news. Those times became more and more frequent.

THE BEGINNING

"Cry 'Havoc' and let slip the dogs of war."

Shakespeare

The family was together on the major holidays and, bereft of any social interaction as I was at that time, I looked forward to those days with anticipation. Of necessity, there was sadness as well as joy associated with those times as the contrast between our lives then and our previous holidays with Cassie were brought into contrast. Cassie had always taken charge during those times of celebration, taking on the organization of activities, doing the decorations, buying and preparing the food, cleaning the house and in general setting the whole tone. Her guiding spirit no longer manifested itself and those chores, which for her had been labors of love, were now largely left to me. This meant that they were not necessarily done to begin with or that they were done ineptly. Still, the girls did help tremendously and ungrudgingly when they were home and Zac pitched in like the member of the family that he had become. Alexandra even developed some interest in cooking, and for Thanksgiving, she pretty much did the whole meal in advance at her apartment and she and Zac trucked it up from Boston the day before Thanksgiving Day. Despite my domestic shortcomings, I did swing a mean credit card and was able to bring together all of the side dishes and incidentals like pickles, olives, cranberry sauce, wine, cider, fruit salad, etc., so the holiday feast did not lack much. Cassie had always traditionally prepared a Waldorf salad complete with walnuts for the day. This was Tatiana's favorite, and she was quick to point out that this item was missing from the table when we sat down to eat. At first, I put her criticism down to petty grumbling; but, when I actually noticed the tears in her eyes, I realized that her disappointment and consternation had more to do with the fact her mother was no longer able to function in that capacity than the bare fact that her favorite side dish was missing from the lineup. This did cast a pall over the proceedings, but we all forged ahead. Cassie could actually be enlisted to perform some simple tasks at that time such as peeling potatoes or vacuuming floors. We could place the appropriate implements in her hands, and she would sometimes continue to bend to these tasks for hours even to a state of exhaustion. On the other hand, at other times, she might simply smile or stare off into the distance without any apparent understanding of the work at hand. Even so, we made the most of things.

By its more elaborate nature, Christmas was more problematic. The usual big party was out of the question with Cassie's illness. I was not up to decorating, or going to the local tree farms and cutting a fresh balsam fir to stand in the living room, but this tree was merely a tiny replica of our past efforts and was nowhere near as lavishly decorated as past tradition would dictate. Nonetheless, the whole family was once again together for the holiday week, this time including my parents and Cassie's. In fact, and much to my embarrassment as the putative host, the older folks did all the cooking and preparation of the holiday meals and the younger folks did all of the cleaning up. Orion, a year older and a little more settled in his ways, joined in the festivities and did his part in the cleaning up as well. This mostly involved eating a lot of leftovers at which he excelled.

It would be wonderful to be able to say that a good time was had by all, but Cassie's largely unreactive presence served to mute a great deal of the "sounding joy." For me, the worst part of it was the word and board games at which my lovely wife, with her formidable vocabulary and incisive mind, had always been the champion. I couldn't help but note the expression of bewilderment and confusion that clouded her face as we chose teams for one of the contests and she wasn't included. Her reaction went no farther than that, but that was enough to put all of us off; and by an unexpressed but mutual consent, we sadly agreed among ourselves that we would forgo this part of the festivities, and with heavy hearts we packed up the games and put them away. Instead of these games, we talked together, watched television, listened to Christmas carols and read quietly. As usual those days, the television was left on at all times so that Cassie could "watch" it. It was not clear that she understood anything that was happening on the screen, but it seemed to sooth and calm her, and the rest of us could treat it as background noise and ignore it for the most part. In spite of this, it was a fine thing to have this close family in the house, and we managed to have some pretty good days together as a family. Those days were all too brief. Work was interesting and busy. The four clinics kept me on the go and the hospital patients that came out of the four practices dramatically increased my day to day census at the hospital. Often I would come into the hospital in the morning and find several patients who had been admitted by one of my colleagues the night before. Since I had literally moved my entire practice to the Swanton clinic, that clinic was immediately up and running and was in the black in a matter of weeks. Rachel and Peg were taken aback at times with the new situation and the unavoidable changes in administrative interaction now that they were working for the Richford Management Group and not for me, but they were adaptable and these problems were not insurmountable. The Richford Health Center itself had been a going concern for many years already, thanks to Rosaire; and it continued to do well.

The other two clinics were also seeing more and more patients every week and were operating at a small profit. I had the gratification of knowing that I was part of a good system and that not only were we doing good work but also we were making a living doing it. Naturally, there were some problems at times, both administrative and personal, but none of these was too significant, and none would stop the clinics from rolling on.

Gail Casperson and I would see each other not infrequently at the nursing home. She would always ask about Cassie, and we would pass the time of day in mutually enjoyable conversation. Gail always seemed pleased to see me in any event, and I surely was pleased to see her. Frequently I would find myself going out of my way to knock on the door to her office and make small talk. Often I would get a feeling that we could take the relationship to a different level, but I couldn't bring myself to do this. I was, after all, still a married man, and I did love my wife. As the days followed on into weeks and months however, the bonds of that love began to loosen, and I could sense a change in my relationship to both of these women. I was like a small world orbiting between two suns, one of which was slowly burning out while the other shone more brilliantly each day. Another spring, another summer, and fall came round again, the full passing of an entire year since the marriage of Alexandra and Zac. I still clung to the thought of who Cassie used to be and what we meant to one another. With this passage of time, however, I became more and more aware of feelings and desires that could not be ignored forever. I knew that there would have to come a change.

As for the lawsuit, it was as if it didn't exist. I heard nothing at all from my lawyer or indeed anyone at all who was connected with the case for that entire year. This seemed strange to me, but I was ignorant of the mechanics of the law and put it down to the normal snail-like workings of the legal process. Besides, denial is the most primitive defense, and it was just as well for the health of my psych to pretend as long as possible that the lawsuit didn't exist. For all the news I heard of it, it might just as well not have. On the other hand, there was no announcement that the case against either me or the nursing home was being dropped so I had to assume that something was happening somewhere. Nonetheless, this prolonged silence was disconcerting.

I did see the plaintiff from a distance on one occasion. She and I happened to attend the same social function, a presentation of scholarships to selected high school students who would be going into the medical field. It so happened that I was a member of the scholarship committee, those who chose the scholarship recipients, so that I was somewhat obligated to attend this affair. I was able to get a sitter for Cassie and did go. Arriving late, I hurried into the main ballroom where the crowd was mingling and imbibing pre-meal cocktails. Most of the attendees were connected to the hospital or the medical profession in some way so that I knew many of them. There were, however, a number of folks who were simply the more privileged of St. Albans society who for one reason or another, disposable funds, charitable inclinations, or merely the desire to see and be seen, chose to participate in the affair. Of these, there were a substantial number that I didn't know. Kathy Wennar fell into this latter category. Of course, it was impossible not to recognize her. Her physical beauty was an overwhelming presence in any room, even a large function room such as this, and it wasn't more than a few moments before I realized that my erstwhile legal nemesis was lurking close by. Of course the word "lurking" might not exactly be appropriate when one is describing a gorgeous woman in a designer dress surrounded by a crowd of fawning men. I had been warned at some length by my legal counsel to keep my distance from the plaintiff so I followed this advice to the letter and made my way to the other side of the room where I spent the rest of the time waiting for the event to begin. When it came time to be seated, I made sure that my table was as far away from Ms. Wennar's as I could get. I did notice that she was attended that evening by one of the local attorneys, no one involved in my case, a good looking gentleman several years older than her and, no doubt, very well off financially, as he was the founding partner in the biggest legal firm in town. He was also a widower, and I couldn't help but hope that Kathy might hook up with him on a permanent basis and decide to forgo any future legal actions as irrelevant to her wonderful life. Not likely...

WEDDING BELLS

"One's tootings at the wedding of the soul. Occur as they occur."

Wallace Stevens

T

t was now the fall of 2003; and as far as I was aware, there was still nothing happening in regard to the lawsuit. Behind the scenes, lawyers were briefing expert witnesses. Or so I imagined. There wasn't so much as a bill from my own attorney to provide me with some information. I did think it strange that no one was involving me in any of this since I was the one who was intimately familiar with the medical aspects of the case and felt that I could be invaluable in helping lawyers, my own lawyers in particular, understand the nuances of the medical problems and the care that had been rendered. Somewhere out there, the Damoclean sword was hanging menacingly; but out of sight out of mind, and since no one was taking care to keep me in the loop, I simply went about my quotidian activities as usual.

Cassie continued her not so slow decline. Slipping month by month into the abyss; and she began to speak more and more infrequently. The long talks and discussions that had made up much of our lives together had gradually ceased to exist; and even the day to day pleasantries of, "How was your day?" and, "How are you doing?" rarely elicited a response any more; and even if there was one, it was never a coherent one. She still would answer "yes" and "no" fairly appropriately when I would try to get an idea of her needs and wants, but there was never anything more specificity forthcoming than that and there was no spontaneity of conversation on her part. The last expression of individuality I remembered was sometime in May of that year when a male cardinal had come to the feeder in our kitchen window (We have one of those bird feeders that sits in the window itself and has a one-way mirror as a back wall which allows us to see the birds up close but does not permit them to see us.), and Cassie had said," Look at the pretty red bird, Jon." Since I had never had an extensive social life or cultivated the interest or companionship of many friends, a huge aspect of the human condition was lost to me as my wife lost her ability to interact. More and more, I felt myself adrift, cut off from significant personal interaction, isolated and alone in the middle of my busy work schedule and the burgeoning responsibilities at home and on the job. At this, the beginning of her second year of not working as a school librarian, there could be no pretense that Cassie would ever work again, and there was no further sick leave to call upon. With this inevitable loss of her job would come the loss of her salary; and, coupled with the expense of full-time caretakers whenever I was on call or had to be out of town for any reason, finances were becoming a serious issue. Though Tatiana had graduated that spring, Smith is not an inexpensive school; and we still had several educational loans outstanding that required monthly payments. Just before Cassie had been diagnosed, we had embarked on a very expensive home improvement plan which had involved taking out a second mortgage on the house. Again, it was lucky that she had had that one-year cushion of accumulated sick leave on her job, but now that that was ending it would be a stretch just paying the bills and getting by. This was another reason that I wasn't entirely displeased that I hadn't gotten any recent bills from my lawyer. The common myth is that all physicians are very well off financially, and certainly most doctors don't have to worry about where their next meal is coming from.

However, Vermont is notorious for the low salaries that professionals of any kind command, and despite the fact that I had a thriving practice in terms of workload and patient census, I was not exactly rolling in the dough. Cassie and I had always joked that we could never move from the state because we could never afford to maintain an equivalent lifestyle anywhere else. Even so, monetary concerns were secondary in my life at that time to more basic concerns of emotional and physical survival. Essentially, my existence was reduced to work and taking care of my wife. The most terrible part of the situation was that she was unable to sympathize with me or to thank me or even to acknowledge my efforts. At times, I found myself awash in self pity, wishing that the disease had been cancer or multiple sclerosis or any one of hundreds of maladies that, while certainly no less devastating, at least allowed for communication and companionship between the involved parties. Damn it, at least I should get some recognition for my martyrdom. These were not good thoughts and I was ashamed to have them.

September 26, 2003. It was the first wedding anniversary for Zac and Alexandra. I had intended to call them and wish them a happy anniversary that evening, but shortly after six that evening, the telephone rang at my end and it was Zac.

"Hey, Jon, quick, turn on the TV to Channel 4, the Boston Station. Do it right now."

I put down the phone, grabbed the TV remote and did as he had instructed. As the picture resolved itself, it was a shot of a street in the Columbus Circle area of Boston taken from a helicopter. Walking down the middle of the sidewalk was a gorilla! Behind the gorilla, several people were running to catch up to it. Ahead of the animal, several people were running to get out of his way. The television voice-over became audible.

"...not clear at this time just how the gorilla escaped. We have preliminary reports that at least one person has been injured, and a spokesperson from the zoo reports that a capture team is headed for where the beast is now being tracked by our aerial camera."

The scene switched over to a studio shot where two announcers, a man and a woman, were seated at a desk facing the camera. The camera zoomed in on the face of the female announcer.

"We want to emphasize that this is a potentially dangerous animal and not a pet. Citizens are urged to stay off the streets and out of the way until the gorilla is captured. Do not attempt to get close to the animal or to interfere with it in any way. We will keep you updated as the efforts to recapture Little Joe." The next story was on the progress on the "Big Dig" the routing of I-93 under the streets of the city, in which I was only marginally interested. Besides, how can a longstanding construction project compete with an escaped gorilla?

"Wow!" I exclaimed to my son-in-law. "I was just about to call you guys to wish you a happy anniversary. What happened to Little Joe?"

"Somehow he escaped from the zoo grounds and was out roaming the streets of Boston. All zoo personnel were recruited to help track him down and recapture him."

"How did he get out?"

"I don't know anything more about it than what I've told you and what's been on the news. They said that he followed two young girls out the door of the Primate Center and had vaulted over the twelve foot fence surrounding the zoo with incredible ease. They also reported that, in darting past the two girls, he had knocked one of them down and had scratched the other one. I hope that no one was seriously injured or the zoo will be sued for sure."

I seconded the motion.

"Well, have a happy anniversary anyway. Have Alexandra call me as soon as she gets home so that she can give me the details."

He assured me that he would and we ended the conversation. When I got off the phone, I related the news of Little Joe's escape to Cassie but got no reaction there. I spent the next few hours after making sure that she was fed and settled, working on some new bagpipe tunes on the chanter, and then trying to catch up with a few medical journals. When the phone rang again, it was after ten. "Hi, Dad." Alexandra said wearily. "I just got in. Everything's OK. We managed to get Joe back and nobody got hurt, including him. The vet darted him with a tranquilizer gun and we got him loaded into one of the zoo's vans. Man, it took a person on each arm and each leg. Luckily he was out like a light."

"Where is he now?"

"We're not exactly sure. Remember I told you that he had gotten out last fall? You may recall that it wasn't clear then just how he had escaped. They made some changes and improvements in the security at that time but it obviously wasn't enough. Somehow Joe got out of the gorilla enclosure again. This time it was during regular zoo hours, though, and he was able to get out of the building. After that, it was easy for him to leave the grounds. A regular fence isn't much of a barrier to a gorilla."

"Zac said that he may have injured someone, a young girl?"

"Yeah, apparently he brushed by two girls on his way out the door and one of them was knocked to the ground. I don't think she was hurt much, if at all, but I don't really have the details. By the time we got Joe back to the zoo and settled into his cage, I was exhausted and just wanted to get home to a hot shower. I'll call you tomorrow with the details."

"Fine." I said. "You get some sleep. At least no one was seriously injured and Little Joe is back where he belongs. And, by the way, happy anniversary."

"Thanks." I don't think I'll forget this one."

"I'm sure you won't."

With that, we ended our conversation. Over the next several days, the facts of the great gorilla escapade revealed themselves. Subsequent news articles had made much of the interaction between Little Joe and the two girls, stating that the wild gorilla had "attacked and injured" two young girls and "had jumped on one of the girls after knocking her down." Now it defied common sense that the girl was not injured very severely after a three hundred pound gorilla had jumped on her stomach, but the press apparently felt obligated to convey some quality of sensationalism. After his "deadly attack" on these two girls, Little Joe had left the grounds of the Franklin Park Zoo and proceeded to roam freely through the streets of Boston. Luckily for Joe, the other citizens of the city and the zoo keepers, he had had no significant contacts with any other human beings during his subsequent sojourn. An enterprising photographer for the Boston Herald managed to get the picture of the year when he was able to take a photograph of the adolescent gorilla standing on a street corner and grasping with his right hand the pole of a sign that read "Bus Stop." Cassie's mother later sent me a copy of this picture through the mail.

As Alexandra had related, after a couple of hours of chasing the escaped gorilla around town, the keepers eventually managed to get close enough to him to use a tranquilizer gun to dart him and render him unconscious. They then transported him back to the zoo in one of the zoo's vans, and placed him in solitary confinement where he remained for a few weeks. I suggested to Alexandra that the zoo exhibit Joe in a separate cage of his own with all of the newspaper articles and photographs of his escape mounted on a sign in front of it. It seemed to me that this would be a prime attraction for the zoo and that they could make some badly needed money from Joe's recent notoriety. The administrations of the zoo did not take my suggestion.

Once again, it was never determined exactly how Little Joe had gotten out of the gorilla enclosure. After his great escape, a significant amount of time was devoted to trying to obtain an answer to that question. Experts from the zoos which had live gorilla exhibits were consulted at some length. One particular gorilla guru, after being presented with the particulars of the case and told that, in addition to the electrical fencing and high walls, there was a fifteen-foot dry moat that separated the gorillas from the outside world, opined that, "Fifteen feet should be adequate." The keepers, after a few seconds of stunned silence spent looking around questioningly at one another, had responded with the obvious fact that, while it may have been true in the mind of at least one expert consultant that fifteen feet should have been adequate, it hadn't been. To this, the renowned gorilla guru repeated his previous statement, " Fifteen feet should be adequate." And that was the best advice that they got that day.

There was some talk that the zoo or the city might be sued by the two girls who had been injured by Little Joe in his dash to freedom. But, whether the girls were not of sufficient litigious nature, whether their injuries were so minimal as to not allow for great sums of money as recompense or for some other reason that will forever remain unknown, no suit was brought. The keepers all breathed a collective sigh of relief.

Some months later, the zoo in Dallas, Texas, had one of their gorillas escape. That misadventure ended in tragedy when that gorilla injured a young child by biting her multiple times about the head and face and the gorilla was finally shot to death by the Dallas police. This got me to thinking about demented human beings and the possibility that they could injure those that they came upon in their unauthorized meanderings. I could only conclude that wandering around in our society had its problems, both for gorillas and for other primates.

THE BEGINNING

"Cry 'Havoc' and let slip the dogs of war."

Shakespeare

T s the depths of yet another Vermont winter closed around us the long dark nights echoed my own feelings of depression with Cassie dropping down ever further into the abyss of neurologic malfunction. On an early December morning, shortly after her 54th birthday, she reached another more terrible milestone in her life when I couldn't make her get up in the morning to go to the bathroom. She had become more and more unsteady on her feet lately and had taken to leaning on me whenever she went anywhere. I had thought that this was more out of anxiety and the fear of falling rather than any true physical limitation, but whatever the underlying reason, this infirmity added another aggravating dimension to her care. This particular morning, I awoke at six o'clock, took my shower and performed my usual start of day ablutions. When it came time for Cassie to do the same, however, I simply could not coax her out of the bed. She just refused to budge.

"Come on, Cass." I entreated. "It's time to get up. You have to go to the bathroom, brush your teeth and wash up." At this point, she had to have the brushing and washing done by me, but it wasn't helpful to point that out.

At first, she said nothing at all in response, just silently resisted me, staring straight up at the ceiling and failing to meet my gaze. I bent down to look her in the eyes and repeated myself.

"You have to get up, Bug. Sadie will be here any minute, and we have to meet her in the kitchen. Orion has to be walked, fed and watered before I leave for work. Come on, now. Get up." My tone was becoming more desperate as I realized that I wasn't making any progress.

At this point, she actually looked at me, and seemed to acknowledge that there was someone addressing her. Her eyes focused on my face for the first time during the "conversation." She spoke. Of late, she hadn't spoken very much at all, and, in my foolish optimism, I had a brief moment when I thought that this was a good sign.

"No. I can't, I won't." she said. And that was all. Any hope that I had that this was a good thing was immediately dashed into pieces. This turned out not to be a temporary aberration either.

From that morning on, Cassie no longer was ambulatory. Just like that. Again, it wasn't clear whether this was because she just didn't have the mental impetus to walk or was so anxious about losing her balance that she wouldn't try or because the actual neural connection between her brain and her feet was not functioning properly, but the end result was the same. And not walking meant not walking to the bathroom, which, in turn, meant incontinence, adult diapers and another whole level of caretaking that was increasingly difficult to bear, both by myself and by the paid caretakers whom I had hired. On top of that, she would no longer feed herself and meals turned into marathons of forking and spooning which went on forever. I put up with this because I felt I had no choice and Sadie, bless her kind heart, hung in there as well, but the other caretakers first demanded more money and then ultimately quit when even the monetary reward did not seem to make the effort worthwhile. I scrambled to find others and did after a while, but the time in between was hectic and anxiety filled.

The next set of caretakers were even more expensive and less personally involved with Cassie, never having known her when she was a real person, an individual in her own right with dreams and a personality. These were good people for the most part, and I was not dissatisfied with their efforts, but naturally there wasn't the same human contact between them and my poor wife which friends or relations could provide. The worst thing about all of this was that Cassie didn't seem to care. Whereas in the past she would definitely react positively to people whom she had known previously and was comfortable with, particularly myself, at this juncture she related to each and every caretaker in the same way, interchangeably. Having your wife treat you just the same as the young woman that you had hired to take care of her only yesterday was a humbling and frightening experience. Of course, I had to come to the realization that this was Cassie now. This was the way that she would be until the end. I began to have serious thoughts of nursing home placement for the first time.

Christmas, the third since the diagnosis had been made and the death sentence had been passed, was the worst holiday that I had ever known. I found myself becoming increasingly depressed and couldn't even get up the energy to decorate the house. When I would come home from work, the bare walls and the treeless living room would silently mock me. Alexandra was unable to get time off from her job to come home. Like doctors and farmers, the zookeepers, or at least some of them, must do their job every day of the year. Animals don't take holidays from eating. This year was her turn to do the duty. Coincidentally, I was also on call that year on both Christmas and New Year's Days. Just as well. Cassie's parents, still going strong in their eighties and mentally intact, came to spend the holidays and provide me some respite. There were some feelings of guilt and irony on my part with the elderly parents again taking care of their daughter in the twilight years of their own lives, but these feelings were quickly and easily suppressed out of necessity. The time around the holidays was busy in terms of medical emergencies and so at least kept my mind occupied and saved me from dwelling on my own self-pitying thoughts.

Tatiana also was able to get home that Christmas and did her part to share the work. It was wonderful to have her there though I could see that the strain of seeing her mother in that condition was almost too much for her to take. Several times I found her sobbing silently as she combed Cassie's hair or washed her face.

Once again, my younger daughter led the way in terms of coming to grips with reality and facing the situation as it had become. On the day before she left, while we were eating a light breakfast of cereal and juice, I looked up to find her looking at me with tears in her eyes once again.

"Dad, I know that this is hard for you. Mom's a lot worse than she has been. She doesn't even recognize me anymore. I don't think that she's realized that I've been here for even one second this entire week. I think you have to consider putting her in an institution."

I stared back at her in some surprise. Tatiana had always been the closer of our two daughters to her mother, and in the last few years had spent the most time with Cassie other than myself. She had in the past actually said that she would never entertain the thought of putting any of her relatives in a nursing home. In fact, this was yet another reason why I had been avoiding making that decision.

"I have thought about it some." I admitted. "But so far with the paid help we have been able to get by. I was thinking that as long as I can afford it I would carry on."

"I know you love Mom, Dad. But I can see that this is killing you too. You still have to live, you know. It's ripping me up seeing what it's doing to you and seeing Mom like this. It would be different if she were there. But she isn't. She just isn't. I try and try to talk to her, to get some human response, even a nonverbal one, but I can't. She's gone, Dad. We have to realize that and move on."

At this point, my vision also was blurred by tears. A great and painful lump rose into my throat and prevented me from saying anything else. Without further words, Tatiana and I rose from the table simultaneously and embraced. We held each other tightly and sobbed together for several minutes before we could collect ourselves enough to say our goodbyes. I told her that I would consider what she and her sister had said.   She seemed to be satisfied with this plan and made her departure. I was left with Cassie and the dog.

WEDDING BELLS

"One's tootings at the wedding of the soul. Occur as they occur."

Wallace Stevens

T n early January, finally and at long last, the game was afoot in the matter of this ever-ongoing lawsuit that had dragged on and on. The first rumble that occurred was again a surprise, and not a pleasant one. Out of the blue, or in this case out of the grey since, it was, after all, midwinter in Vermont, a time when the bleak days of little sunshine wrapped the earth in frozen bonds of ivory iron and the dull skies pressed down upon the human psyche like so many stones upon an accused witch's chest, I received a phone call at work from my erstwhile legal representative, the distinguished Beatrice Germanowski, whom I had never even had the pleasure of meeting face to face.

"Hello, Jon," she announced. "I am sorry to have to give you this news, but the tentative court date for your malpractice trial has come out, and I have a conflict.

"Now, before you get too upset, I can tell you that I've assigned one of my best colleagues to your case, a sharp young guy named Chauncy Winthrop who has already been doing most of the background review and planning the strategy for the case anyway. Chauncey is young but a real up and comer. I have the utmost confidence in him myself; and if you have any misgivings whatsoever, I can tell you that he'll have access to me and my advice at all times."

To say that this news had taken me aback was an understatement. Here I hadn't heard a peep from Beatrice in many months, and now she was telling me that she wasn't even going to be representing me personally but was sending a junior member of the firm in her stead.

This was my professional life at stake here and I wasn't too happy that she was sending a boy to do a woman's job. I said as much.

"I know this isn't what you had in mind; Jon, but, believe me, you will have no less of a defense than you would have had with me there. Chauncey is damn good. He was sharp when I hired him a few years ago and under my tutelage he's become a razor. Besides, I'm afraid that you have no choice. The trial date that the judge has set is for early April, and I find that I am already tied up with that Fletcher Allen thing for the entire month. There's no way that I can get out of it." I knew that she was right there. The "Fletcher Allen thing" to which she was referring was the biggest malpractice case that the state of Vermont had ever had up to this point. It involved a patient whose family was suing the big medical center hospital in Burlington for twenty seven million dollars. The patient had unsuccessfully attempted suicide while in jail for a minor crime, drug dealing, I believe. While he had been found hanging from the bars of his cell in time to save his life, he had already developed significant brain damage to the point where he was unable to breathe on his own. He ended up on a respirator in the intensive care unit. After several weeks of intensive care, when taken off the respirator, he had died. The problem was that he had never precisely met the criteria of brain death. The doctors who made the decision had relied upon the clinical judgment of the physician who had been assigned to the patient's care and a consulting neurologist. No EEG had been done, period, not to mention the usual two flatline EEGs at least forty eight hours apart that were the nationally accepted standard for determining brain death. In reality, the distinction was philosophical and, many would say, moot, for the patient had so little brain function at the time based upon the clinical exam that he would never have regained consciousness, never mind awareness or function. But these were strange times, and the voices of the "preserve any life at any cost" were loud and harsh upon the land. Worst of all, the family of this particular patient were wed to that philosophy and were determined that their point of view should and would prevail. Thus the notorious lawsuit to which Beatrice had alluded. As the most successful and best known malpractice defense attorney in the state, it was not surprising that she was selected to handle the defense. It was also not surprising that my case would finish a distant second in priority when push came to shove. Still, while I quickly understood this intellectually, in my gut it just didn't seem fair. After all, I had hired Beatrice some time before the Fletcher Allen case had even come to light. When I complained that this was the fact of the matter, however, she immediately demonstrated to me where the power lay. "Of course," she flatly stated, "you can always find another firm to represent you. That would be your prerogative."

Oh, sure, I thought. Now I could go out and get yet another lawyer and bring that person up to speed on the facts and nuances of my case. That sounds like a good plan. And while I'm at it, why not brew up a gallon or two of hemlock? There was a slight pause, no more than a millisecond, while I assessed the alternatives.

"No, no," I capitulated, "I think that this Chauncy will be fine especially if he has you to fall back upon. You people have researched the case and already know it to some degree. I sure don't want to have to go there to go over all of this with another lawyer. So, what do we do now?"

"You don't have to do anything. Don't panic and wait for us to contact you. We will do all of the remaining preparation and legwork. If we need you, we will call you. Again, Jon, I really am truly sorry that this situation has arisen, but I had no control over it, and we have to do the best that we can. Hang in there and try not to worry."

Ha! Easy for her to say. She goes on to star in the preeminent malpractice case of the day while I go on to face the sharks of Kathy Wennar with "Chauncey the Razor" as my sole protector. I said goodbye as graciously as I could under the circumstances and hung up the phone a bit more forcefully than usual. The only saving grace in all of this, if it could be called that at all, was the fact that I no longer had to worry about giving Cassie the bad news.

About a week later, just as I was finishing up the dictation on the most recent patient, Rachel appeared at my office door and announced without any other preamble that I would be speaking to my lawyer for the next hour or so. It was eleven in the morning and she had blocked off the hour just before lunch hour and we continued to review the case while we ate. She then ushered a tall, good looking man whom she introduced as Chauncey Winthrop, the famous "Razor" of whom Beatrice Germanowski had spoken. Chauncey Winthrop was not quite the same man as Jacques Parent, my initial knight in legal armor. Physically imposing, he was six feet four inches tall and two hundred and ten pounds in weight without a visible ounce of fat anywhere about him. He wore a pair of mirrored wrap-around sunglasses and was coated in, rather than dressed in, a steel grey suit that, at the risk of any lawyer-like stereotyping, could only be described as "sharkskin." When he moved, I swear that this suit shimmered and changed colors subtly as the light caught the cloth at different angles. He was as deeply tanned as a Florida lifeguard at the end of the season, and it was hard to imagine him closeted in some law library looking up legal precedents.

I stood and we shook hands. Chauncey looked me straight in the eye (At least I assumed that he did as he turned those silvered lenses of his in the direction of my face.) and gripped my hand in a firm lock that convinced me that if nothing else he was serious about the workouts in the gym.

"As you know, Beatrice couldn't make it." he said. "She's working her ass off on the Fletcher Allen case. But don't worry, I'm up to speed on your case. In fact, I've been doing most of the grunt work anyway and probably have a more basic grasp of the facts than she. I've reviewed all of the pertinent information and have a copy of all the records right here with me that you can have to go over at your leisure. Just give me a few."

Before I could protest that I had already reviewed the re-cords at some length, he turned abruptly and left the room. He must have had the records right outside the door as he returned within a few seconds bearing two large file boxes which when he handed them to me proved to be very heavy and for very good reason. They were both completely filled to bursting with medical records, primarily records from the nursing home but also some copies of my own office records and copies of hospital records. At this point, I did weakly protest that I had already reviewed the nursing home records, but it was apparent from the great bulk of material that he had brought that there were indeed yet other re-cords which I had not as yet seen.

"You need to go through these at your convenience, Jon." He advised. "But I can already tell you that there are some prob-lems here. Did you know, for example, that the plaintiff's lawyers are asking for six million dollars?"

"Actually, I did hear that figure." I responded. "But you have to be kidding me, right? There isn't even a case here to begin with. Six million dollars? The case isn't even worth six cents. Why? They should pay us money for the insult of taking us to court on such a ridiculous matter."

"Well, I agree with you there." said Chauncy. "I would guess that the case in reality is worth about two hundred and fifty thou-sand dollars. The plaintiff's lawyers always ask for a big number to start out with to shock and awe the opposition and to give them a starting point for the negotiations. But I do think that there is a case to be made here, and I'll tell you why."

He then went on to tell me that, first of all, my progress notes were too brief in general and did not always address prob-lems as they arose with the patient in question. I countered with my usual argument that the notes indeed were brief but only because there was no ongoing active medical problem when those notes were written and there was no sense in writing for writing's sake. I pointed out that when a problem did occur as reflected in other parts of the record such as the nurse's notes or notes of ancillary personnel and in contrast to what he had just alleged my notes did address that problem. At this point, he dropped the bomb that served to immediately change my perspective on the upcoming trial and actually had me seriously worried for the first time.

"Do you realize that you wrote one of these brief notes of which you speak after Mr. Wennar had already developed a pressure ulcer on his heel following the initial hip fracture and that you didn't even mention the ulcer in that progress note?"

"What? I don't believe it!" I was dumbfounded and more than a little shocked. How could this be? I knew what kind of doctor I was and that I never would have failed to address such a serious problem in any patient of mine. To my knowledge, I had never done so in the past, and I couldn't conceive of doing so in the future. It was beyond my comprehension, and I could not imagine that it could be true.

There had to be an alternative explanation.

"That just can't be, Chauncy." I said. "It's just not possible. We had better review the record more closely and see if there is some other explanation. There has to be. I'm sure of it."

"Well, that's why I brought all of this paper with me. You can sit down and wade through it at your leisure. But, I am telling you here today that there is no question from my own review of the record that the ulcer was present as memorialized in the nursing notes on the day that you went to that nursing home and wrote a note that said there were no ongoing medical problems other than the underlying dementia and the hip fracture that seemed to be healing properly. This is going to be a big problem for us at trial and we are going to have to find some way to deal with it."

The good news was that there were no other smoking guns that Chauncey unveiled during the rest of our hour together, and we were able to discuss the other aspects of the case with a good understanding and develop a reasonable plan of defense. As far as the two of us could determine, there where no other chinks in the armor. That one chink, however, that had come as such a surprise to me was more than enough. And before Chauncey left, he dropped another little incendiary.

"Oh, by the way, Jon," Chauncey said, eyeing me speculatively, "I'm pretty sure that I have a handle on why Kathy is bringing suit." This was news to me.

"Really, Great Seer," I sarcastically rejoined, "and how do you happen to come by this information, may I ask?"

"We of the legal profession do have our pipeline. You know that there is that thing called attorney-client privilege that's supposed to keep our mouths shut just as you have the doctor-patient privilege in medicine. Well, just as in medicine, sometimes that secrecy doesn't necessarily hold among professionals. When lawyers get together, we tend to talk shop the same way you doctors do, I imagine. At any rate, let's just say that I have my information from a good source." And this is the story that Chauncey Winthrop passed on to me that day.

Now, Martin Wennar was not a stupid man as one might imagine from the way he had built a business empire up from literally nothing. There is no question that he was besotted and bewitched by the lovely Katy but, even so, he still maintained some sense of balance where financial matters were concerned. Thus, he and his legal advisors concocted quite a Machiavellian prenuptial agreement and will. The thrust of it was as follows. If Kathy and Martin remained married, she would share equally in his fortune while he was alive though he, of course, would decide what "share equally" would mean. In the event that they divorced, she would get to keep a car, a lump sum of one hundred thousand dollars, and an allowance of the national poverty level for the rest of her life. If he predeceased her, Kathy would be allowed to live in the house for the rest of her life, would get to keep her vehicle and would again receive an allowance of the national poverty level for the rest of her life. Of course, she would be free to take any job within her qualifications that she wished and could therefore add that salary to the poverty level stipend at any time. The will also stipulated that, should Kathy wish to try to better herself, get a higher education or take some technical courses, the estate would pay for that. If there were any children arising from the marriage, Martin had arranged that they would inherit a share of his estate that would equal the shares that his two children by Mary would get when they reached the age of twenty one. Thus it could be seen that Kathy had some good reason to keep Martin alive at any cost and that, upon his death, she would suffer some financial reverses. "That would certainly explain why an elderly man with profound dementia was placed upon a respirator, tortured, and not allowed to die with any shred of dignity or common sense." I said. It's too bad someone couldn't sue Kathy for that. We live in a strange world. That certainly answers a lot of questions for me. Thanks for the information, Chauncey."

Looking well self-satisfied, Chauncey acknowledged my thanks with a princely wave of his hand and said that he had to get going. We again shook hands, and he was out the door. After Chauncey had breezed out, I sat back and reflected on what he had said. Once again, I could not fathom that what he had asserted could possibly be true, though he certainly had no reason to twist the facts. I vowed that I would carefully go over the record as soon as I had the time and certainly before I was deposed by the enemy so that I would have a good counter argument in hand if it came to that. Logically, one might think that I would immediately, that very night, delve into those records with a vengeance to vindicate myself. In reality, however, I didn't go near the huge pile of paper for several months. The main reason that I didn't was that I was never deposed.

Before he had left, Chauncy had told me that, as anticipated, the actual trial would begin sometime in late March or early April. That was the soonest that the Franklin County Superior Court would have an opening on the docket. It turned out that he was almost on the money, as the actual trial began in late April. Before that beginning, however, a few events of some magnitude would take place.

WEDDING BELLS

"One's tootings at the wedding of the soul. Occur as they occur."

Wallace Stevens

T
assie spent her days lying in a bed that we had brought downstairs from the attic expressly for that purpose. Although she was not physically a large person, it was just not possible to conveniently or safely carry her up and down the stairs with any regularity, and, since most of my time was spent downstairs watching television, working on the computer, or using the Internet, or just preparing meals, this was the logical place for her to be. There, in one of the front rooms, I was at least able to keep a vigilant eye on her and could attend to her needs if I could get an idea of just what they were at any given time. Also, when Orion was in the house, he loved to get up on the bed and cuddle with her as often as he could. Prior to her illness, he wasn't allowed to so much as put a paw up on the furniture so he actually thought that this was a good deal and, from his canine perspective, I suppose it was. Her diminished activity and reactivity didn't bother him too much as far as I could see. Home health nurses were coming in once a week at that point to give Cassie a bath and tend to other aspects of her hygiene, which was a big help. It was a sad time for all of us, particularly the two girls who, not living with their mother day to day,

were impacted all the more with the deterioration that would seem to geometrically multiply since the last time that they had seen her. Her verbal output had shrunken to the word "yes" which she now used at all times in response to all questions whether they seemed to require an affirmative or a negative answer. Much of the time, she simply said nothing, but when she did say something now, it was always "yes." I put this down to the fact that Cassie had always had a very positive personality and found some small comfort in the fact that the last word she would cling to was an affirmation rather than a negation. With some trepidation, I had steeled myself to broach the subject of putting their mother in a nursing home to the girls. Tatiana, of course, had been forewarned; and since it was she who had first raised the question to me, I knew that she would take the prospect reasonably in stride. Somewhat to my surprise and to my great relief, Alexandra also didn't even raise the slightest of objections. In fact, they both took it as a natural progression of the way things had to be. Alexandra did start to cry when I told her of my plans over the phone, which started me crying as well; and by the time we were done, even Zac was shedding a tear or two in the background. Tatiana again told me that she could see that her mother was gone in spirit and that she understood the great burden that she was placing upon me. Both she and Alex had seen for themselves what a time and energy commitment this undertaking required and had been a part of it for several days during the Christmas festivities, such as they were. I was heartened by the lack of recriminations and was touched and appreciative of their support and understanding.

So it came to pass that, in the middle of February in the year 2004, I was filling out paperwork at La Place D'Espere to commit my darling Cassie to a nursing home. And a mountain of paperwork there was. I met with social workers, physical therapists, a dietitian and, naturally, Gail Casperon, the manager of the home. In the meeting with Gail, the subject that I had dreaded came up for the first time. She raised the question in a perfectly straightforward manner without any circumlocution or equivocation.

"What's Cassie's code status?" Gail inquired.

There was a pause that stretched out to the point of being uncomfortable.

"She's a full code." I replied, and when Gail's eyebrows arched up, I quickly and defensively rushed on before she could say anything else. "Cassie and I discussed this on several occasions before she became ill and she always said that she wanted to be kept alive as long as possible no matter what the circumstances. I tried my best to persuade her otherwise, but I couldn't do it."

Now Gail was well aware of my feelings in this subject, feelings that came about in part directly from my experiences as a physician who often took on the responsibility of directing the care of people in exactly these same trying circumstances. It was my feeling that when the mind was gone that person was gone and to keep the empty shell alive not only served no purpose but was a cruel travesty of our earthly being. Though there are exceptions, I have found that people working in the medical field feel this way for the most part. We have all seen what happens when extraordinary measures have been used to prolong the lives of patients dying of cancer or other terminal illnesses and have witnessed the warehousing of demented patients who have had their meaningless lives extended by all sorts of medical interventions including cardiac bypass surgery, kidney dialysis and feeding tubes. To my mind, such misguided efforts were not only unethical, they bordered on the criminal. On a few occasions, I had actually asked the relatives of some patients to find another doctor to carry out their wishes when they insisted upon putting feeding gastrotomy tubes into end-stage dementia patients; patients who were just like Cassie the way she was now. How could it be then that I was sitting here telling Gail that my poor demented wife should be resuscitated if she should have a cardiac arrest? Well, perhaps I wasn't thinking clearly and was still feeling some guilt about this nursing home placement. That was only a human reaction, after all. Besides, I had made a promise, and I believe in keeping my promises even when they discomfort me.

I was grateful for the way Gail handled the situation. Instead of calling me to account or badgering me to change my mind then and there, she merely arched her eyebrows; and after gently asking me again if that was what I really wanted to do, she said that I could change my mind at any time and that, after thinking about it, could get back to her. I took that opportunity to make my escape.

From that day, it was as if a great weight had been lifted from my shoulders; and, in a very real sense I got a large part of my life back. Naturally, I felt guilty about that too. There remained that huge hole that used to be filled by Cassie but, then again, Cassie had been long gone anyway. Still, her physical presence alone had kept me company in some strange way; and no matter that we hadn't had a conversation in many months I found myself missing her all over again. However, I was now able to leave the house at any time. Orion could be put on his run and I could go out to rent a movie or eat a meal on a whim. It was a whole new lifestyle. I did continue to visit Cassie in the nursing home, usually making it out there at least twice a week, but I wasn't sure if I was going there to check on her or to see Gail with whom I was developing a deeper relationship eveyr time I was out there. On one of my frequent visits, there occurred an incident that marked a sea change in our relationship. Gail and I had been talking about one thing or another for several minutes in her office with the door closed. I can't even now recall what the conversation was about. What I do recall indelibly is that suddenly, without warning or premeditation, I simultaneously became very aware of the closeness of her and the attractiveness of her. Before I consciously realized what was happening, we were wrapped in each other's arms, Kissing hungrily and passionately. To this day I can't be sure which of us initiated this, whether I moved towards her or she towards me or if we both moved towards one another. Suffice it to say that I was holding her curvy softness tightly to me and that the flames of desire were exploding around us. The feel of her breasts and thighs against me was incendiary, melting and hardening me at the same time. From the depths of me, longing and want reared up and roared.

Down in the core of my mid-brain a primitive part of my being wanted nothing more than to rip off her clothes and ravish her right there in that office. I was drowning, drowning in that molten and volcanic sea.

The next thing I knew, I had raised my arms, disengaged myself and stumbled backwards. As I did so, I thought that I caught a look of shock and hurt in Gail's eyes.

"I'm sorry, Gail." I said. " I just can't do this. Not now. I just … I just …I'm not ready. I want to. I definitely want to. But I just can't. It's not that I don't like you or don't want you. You can see that I do. I love you. But I think I still love Cassie. I know that she's gone but she's still here, here in this very building. Please give me some more time."

That wounded look of hurt quickly disappeared, and she immediately became her usual vivacious self. A twinkle appeared in those eyes that I had only moments ago felt were about to become awash with tears.

"I understand, Jon. I really do. And it's okay. You're still grieving for Cassie. You haven't completely come to terms with what's happened to her, with what's happened to the both of you. I just want you to know that I'm here for you." She smiled. "But I don't intend to wait forever. Think about it." As if I could possibly do anything else from that moment on.

For the next several days, we tiptoed around each other, not quite sure of how we should act in one another's presence. But, as the days went by, we gradually resumed our old relationship of easy friendship, and things seemingly went on as they had before. Under that placid surface, however, the molten magma roiled and curled, groping blindly for some way through the ever thinning crust, silently striving for some means of breaking that barrier and erupting into the light.

Soon thereafter, I received notice from Chauncey Winthrop that the judge in the Wennar lawsuit had ordered a mandatory mediation session among the parties and that this mediation was to take place one week hence. This seemed like overly short notice to me and would require that my entire office schedule be changed for that one day but there was no choice in the matter, I couldn't see that there was anything to mediate. From my point of view, I was innocent of malpractice and wasn't about to give anyone anything in terms of money or anything else, so what was the point of mediation? Chauncey indicated that, as my lawyer, he would appreciate it if I put in an appearance nonetheless so I grudgingly agreed to do so. The next week on a Tuesday, I found myself driving to Burlington to the law offices of yet another firm, neutral ground where the mediation was to take place. A third lawyer, whom I had not previously met, was to function as the mediator.

Present at this meeting were the respective lawyers, Chauncey for myself, Jeff Peterson for the plaintiff, a tall black man named Dikembe Nkomo for the nursing home and the mediator, Bill Harshorn. Also there were Gail Casperon representing the nursing home, Kathy Wennar, a recording secretary and a second attorney who apparently was an assistant to Mr. Peterson. I was introduced to everyone but didn't catch the name of the assistant. Jeff Peterson was a short, rotund man with a full white beard that was cut long and a bald head. I calculated that he was approximately five feet six inches in height and weighed about two hundred and fifty pounds. His handshake was one of those limp "alright, if I really have to" handshakes which I hate, but he smiled avuncularly and seemed pleasant enough. I later came to think of him as a malignant Saint Nicholas.

Dikembe Nkomo was a real gentleman. He was thin and extremely tall, probably around six feet ten inches. I think he was genetically a member of the Dinka tribe in Africa which would explain his body habitus. He introduced himself to me gravely and asked if I were well. To this inquiry I responded that I was as well as could be expected considering the fact that I was being sued. He laughed gently and replied that he understood exactly how I felt.

We seemed to have an unspoken understanding about most of the aspects of the case just from this brief introduction.

Attorney Harshorn then asked if there was anyone present who wasn't familiar with the way these mediation hearings were conducted. Gail, Kathy and I all raised our hands. Bill went on to explain to us the mechanics of the mediation and spoke a bit about the philosophy behind mediation, attempting to free up the legal system, which already had a significant backlog, and saving all parties concerned the trauma and the time lost from productive work that going to trial would entail. He then told us that we would be meeting in separate rooms, the nursing home people in one room and my lawyer and I in another. His job would consist of going back and forth between these rooms to see if some common understanding could be achieved concerning all of the parties involved in terms of money or other interests (mostly money). To begin, the plaintiff and the nursing home representative and their respective lawyers would be closeted together, and Chauncey and I were shunted off to a small side room where we were told to await further developments. In contrast to the initial room in which we had convened, which was large and well appointed with plush wall-to-wall carpet, an enormous cherry wood table with carved wooden chairs, and hunting prints on the walls. This second room was spartan, with a small formica table, four plastic chairs and a coffee maker in one corner. There was one window which looked out over a tiny lawn to the curtained windows of the building across the way. The walls were unadorned with the exception of a calendar with a Vermont country theme that hung slightly askew on the wall opposite the single window. Obviously, William Harshon, Esquire, was not out to impress us.

Our entire involvement in that day's proceeding consisted of Bill Harshorn coming in to talk to us briefly on exactly two occasions. Both times, Chauncey reiterated that our position was unchanged, that Doctor Ziebaska had done nothing wrong and that our intention was to pay no money to anyone.

Chauncey and I got to know quite a bit about one another as we attempted to while away the time during which the nursing home and the plaintiff argued over their offers and counter offers. I learned that he had been a high powered attorney in Washington, D.C., where he had been involved with cases concerning industrial pollution and the environmental control board. He had been on the side of the polluters in all of these cases; but he assured me that they were simply small businessmen (and many not so small) who were just trying to get ahead and had inadvertently run afoul of one obscure environmental regulation or another. This sort of practice produced big bucks, but Chauncey's wife, a native Vermonter whom he had met in law school, did not appreciate the hectic big city life or the dog-eat-dog atmosphere of the large law firms there and, after their first child was born, issued an ultimatum that they move to a more relaxed and safer part of the country, preferably her home state of Vermont where child-rearing would be less stressful and the obligations of career less demanding. This proved to be an offer that Chauncey could not refuse, but he told me that he was chafing under the slow pace and bucolic atmosphere of his second home and his current job.

"It's driving me buggy, Jon. These shit kickers and tree huggers up here don't seem to care if the outside world is running farther ahead of them every day. Christ, I know a guy, a lawyer in Montpelier, who closes his office, just shuts things up tight, whenever there's a good snowfall or a bright sunny day in the winter and goes skiing. Just like that. No sense of responsibility. How'd you like it if I did that to you? Sorry, Jon, but I can't be with you in court today. The moguls at Jay Peak are calling my name. Ridiculous."

I averred that this would not be a very helpful attitude on his part, and he nodded in vigorous affirmation.

"Exactamundo!"

"Still," I countered, "You do have to stop and smell the roses occasionally. Like they say, no one ever wished that they had spent more time at the office."

"Yeah, yeah, that's what Marnie keeps telling me. On one level, I know that she's right. But a part of me still wants to rev up the old engine and go. I'd like to make partner in the firm in the next few years for example. But it's a one woman shop, and Bea keeps a pretty tight rein on all the best cases. I know it's her reputation and her baby, but I have to have some goals of my own. Meanwhile, I run these triathlons all over the state to stay in shape. "*Mens sana in corpore sano*" and all that."

"Hey, Chauncey, relax. You're still a young man and Bea's a good deal older. She'll have to retire sometime."

"Ha! Not likely. The only way that lady is going to stop taking cases is when she buys the farm." Here Chauncey became subdued as if contemplating the long and difficult road ahead of him in his quest for partnership in the law offices of Beatrice Germanowski. But then he quickly recovered himself.

"Of course she could die," he said hopefully.

"There is that possibility. As you say, she is a good deal older than I. No medical problems I'm aware of though." Again, he affected a look of resignation and sighed deeply. I laughed.

"You poor boy. Better be careful what you say. If Bea kicks off any time soon, I'll have to report this conversation to the authorities."

"Just kidding. Just kidding. What's a little death threat among friends, anyway?"

Chauncey then went on to tell me how he prepared for triathlons, swimming, biking, running and weight lifting every chance he got in his free time of which he bemoaned the fact once again that he had entirely too much. This accounted for his mean and lean physique, however. Chauncey and his wife, Marnie, had one child, a boy named Jason, the apple of his parent's eye, and to hear Chauncey tell it, the prince of all he surveyed. In fact, Jason was having his fifth birthday celebration that very day, and in spite of his previous protestations of too much leisure time Chauncey was hoping to get out of the mediation early so that he could put in an appearance at this affair. I got the deep sense that he was really involved with his family, and that no matter what work philosophy he espoused publicly, there was a good underlying reason why he had taken his wife's ultimatum to leave the pressures of D.C behind them.

Chauncey got to know a bit about me at this time as well. He learned that I played the bagpipes, ran regularly, did some duck hunting when the time would allow, sang in the Champlain Chorus, and once fought the State Department of Transportation successfully over my right to reconstruct an old stone wall in front of my house. He learned that I had two daughters, both of whom had attended Smith College but for very different reasons and that one of them was a zookeeper and the other a professional tennis player with aspirations of becoming a museum curator when her tennis career was ended. He learned that my wife had Alzheimer's Dementia and was currently in a nursing home, and so he was offering to settle, if anything. I, of course, held to the position that they shouldn't pay a red cent whereas Chauncey was quite sure that they would settle for two hundred to two hundred and fifty thousand dollars. The good part about this was if the nursing home did settle Chauncey was certain that the case against me, which was very weak in our opinion even taking in account the possibility of my missing the initial foot ulcer, would be dropped.

"The nursing home is the deep pocket here, Jon." Stated Chauncey. "Also, they know that you have to fight them to the bitter end to maintain your professional reputation. It's a lot easier for the nursing home to settle. Besides which, they also are insured so the money isn't even theirs."

"And they don't know the half of it." I interjected. "I wonder what they'd think if they knew that I'm not covered by malpractice insurance. Maybe we should leak that little fact to the opposition, and they would get off my back entirely."

"Don't count on it. They would still want to keep the pressure on you. Let's hope that they do settle and that we're out of it entirely. You know what they say about juries. Never know what they are going to do."

I had mixed emotions about how I would feel if the nursing home did settle. Naturally, it would be great to be off the hook, and my sense of exposure without insurance coverage was certainly high. Alternatively, I felt a sense of outrage that anyone should make any profit at all from a case that was as bogus as this.

In the end, Bill Harshorn came by a third and last time and told us that we might as well go home. The nursing home and the plaintiff had not come to an agreement; but since there was no negotiating to do on our part anyway, there was no point in our hanging around any longer. We left. I was more than a little perturbed that I had wasted a full day which could have been better spent seeing patients and doing some productive work. Later, I learned that the nursing home had not settled and that the lowest the plaintiff was willing to go was two hundred thousand dollars. This was a lot less than the original six million but was high enough that the nursing home was not willing to buy in. What this meant was that the case was going to trial.

THE BEGINNING

"Cry 'Havoc' and let slip the dogs of war."

Shakespeare

After the long periods of inactivity, events now were accelerating at frantic pace, and very shortly after the efforts at mediation had failed, a court date was firmly set, and the trial at last was on. The first step was to select the members of the jury. I personally saw no need to attend this event, but my lawyer told me that it would be a good idea for me to be there, both to provide some input and to put in an appearance to show that I cared and was taking the situation seriously. I'm not sure that I was doing either, but when one hires a specialist, I have always been of the opinion that one should take his advice. Thus, when the time came to interview prospective jurors, I was there, sitting alongside Chauncey Winthrop at the second defendant's table.

The venue for the trial was the Franklin County Superior Court building, an imposing brick and stone structure on Church Street, just across the street from Taylor Park, the large rectangular swath of grass and trees that broke up the concrete and mortar of downtown St. Albans. The court building sat between two churches as if to establish a secular base between the outposts of the faithful. In response to the events of 9/11, the court now sported a side entrance on the north that was both handicapped accessible and possessed of a metal detector flanked two burly security guards. The main entrance, a huge arching wooden door with large cast iron rings for handles, was no longer used and remained permanently locked. The courtroom itself was on the second floor, accessed by a stairway on the south side of the building that divided in two as it ascended and provided entry into the courtroom on two sides, presumably to keep litigants apart and to allow the jury to move in and out without fear of contacting any of the participants in a given case. A huge, cavernous space two stories high, the courtroom had two flanking tiered sections that could be used as jury boxes, one on either side, a large section for spectators in the rear or south end, an equally large area enclosed by a wooden rail that would provide space for all of the litigants and, at the north end, the imposing judge's bench raised to a significant height above the rest of the room and fronted by more heavy wood than might be used in the construction of a medium sized boat. On the right hand side of the judge's bench as one faced it was the witness box, also of dark heavy wood. To the left of that was a chair for the court reporter, and facing the judge's bench in the enclosed area were four massive tables which served as desks and seating areas for the plaintiffs, the defendants and whomever else might be unlucky enough to be part of the ongoing festivities.

On this right-hand side were Jeff Peterson, the same minion who had accompanied him to the mediation hearing, and a female paralegal who was relegated to the rear table on that side. On the left, sitting at the front table, were Gail Casperson as the nursing home's representative, and Dikembe Nkomo, the lawyer for the nursing home. Behind them at the rear table on that side and across from the enemy paralegal were Chauncey and myself. Chauncey, as usual, was extremely well dressed in one of those grey-black suits with a blood red silk tie and matching pocket handkerchief. His shirt was so dazzlingly white as to increase the candle power of illumination in the room and sported a pair of white cuffs that peeked out about an inch beyond the sleeves of the suit, just far enough to expose a pair of gold cufflinks that

caught the light from the chandeliers overhead and tossed it merrily around the room. As if in contrast, I was wearing my usual
grey herringbone suit coat over a pair of black Dockers and sported a blue tie that had little red anatomically correct hearts on it.
The tie was a concession to the courtroom environment as I never
wore a tie anymore either at the office or in the hospital. There was
some published evidence that ties were unsanitary and there was
a lot of anecdotal evidence that they were a pain in the butt. This
meant that I would use any excuse not to wear one. Luckily for me,
the opposing lawyers, Jeff Peterson and his associate, and Dikembe were all equally sartorially challenged and were wearing regular, off the rack, suits and ties. Not that I was jealous of Chuncey's
wardrobe. I had never been a believer in the old adage that "the
clothes make the man" and, in fact, had always been of the opinion
that "the man made the man." To my way of thinking, dressing
well merely took money and the inclination to do so. Some might
say that it also took some sense of style, but if you have the money,
you can always pay for someone else's sense of style. So the bottom
line was that it took money. We have all known and seen powerful
and intelligent men who dress like they picked their clothes off the
floor at the Salvation Army. In any event, and as usual, my lawyer
was the best dressed man in the house.

Far more pleasantly distracting for me than Chauncey's
fine raiment was the sight of Gail sitting at the table directly in
front of me. She was wearing a simple grey sheath dress of some
soft velour like material that draped closely over her body in a way
that I can only describe as voluptuous. Mostly, due to our relative
seating positions, I had a circumscribed rear view of this vision,
but that view alone was worth the price of admission. Her hair
was worn up in a French knot leaving her long neck exposed and
vulnerable. One tendril of fine, honey blond hair behind her right
ear had escaped and was gently curled down her neck, emphasizing the line and adding to a sense of intimacy and femininity. It
was all I could do at times not to reach over and softly reposition
that stray tendril; but thank the powers that be, we were seated just
far enough apart to make this impractical if not impossible. Still,

more times than I would like to admit, I found myself gazing at the back of Gail's neck and letting my thoughts drift pleasantly away from the matter at hand.

The judge, one Charles Prouder, entered the courtroom, and the wheels of justice began to turn at last. At the back of the room, in the spectator's section, was the jury pool, a large group of people from whom the actual jury members and the alternate jurors would be selected. The bailiff read out the names of fourteen people at random, and those folks would then move to the tiered section on the right side of the room. They would then be asked questions by the three lawyers who would decide in concert who would stay on as a jury member and who would not be selected for this particular trial. Each lawyer had a number of jurors whom he could eliminate for cause, an acceptable conflict of interest or an obvious bias for or against one of the parties involved in the case. St. Albans being a relatively small town, there were many of these people in the jury pool who had relatives, friends or acquaintances who worked in the nursing home, knew me or were patients of mine or were in some other way connected to one of the parties in the suit so this process stretched out for most of the day. It was difficult for me to maintain much interest in the proceedings over the long haul though Chauncey tried to involve me in the selection process on multiple occasions. I was of the general opinion that it didn't matter too much who was on the jury as long as they weren't mortal enemies of mine for some reason. I naively thought that truth would inevitably come to the surface and that justice would be done.

There was one interesting little occurrence that was somewhat unsettling, however. As Dikembe Nkomo first rose to interview a prospective juror, Chauncey passed me a note that read, "Do you think that the jury will have any problems with Dikembe?" I was a bit nonplussed. What did Chauncey mean by this question? Was he implying that Franklin County juries were racist and would hold the facts of his racial origins against the lawyer for the nursing home and so might find against them in regard to the case? Where would he get such an idea? Was he himself a racist? I wasn't sure what my attitude should be, so I took the humorous route in my response and wrote back, "Yes, I think he is going to make them all feel vertically challenged." At this, Chauncey laughed shortly and gave me a quizzical look. I was left to make the situation whatever I might.

At the end of a long and boring day, the three lawyers finally agreed on a panel of jurors that they felt could judge and record the case to their mutual satisfaction. For the record, it consisted of eight women and four men with one man and one woman as alternates. Most of them were over the age of fifty, and all of them were, or had been gainfully employed. To me, they appeared to be a cross section of the citizenry, and I saw no reason to think that they would not hear the evidence and deliver a fair and impartial verdict to the best of their ability. Chauncy was quite pleased with himself at the makeup of the jury and was in good spirits when we parted after court was adjourned. I could only hope that his optimism was well founded.

WEDDING BELLS

"One's tootings at the wedding of the soul. Occur as they occur."

Wallace Stevens

T

t was a fine Monday morning in April, and the sun for a change was shining brightly in a cloudless sky. Auspicious beginning for a malpractice trial. Inside the cavernous courtroom, the light was much more muted, and I sensed that I was not the only person present who would have much preferred to be someplace else. From the fourteen jurors (twelve jurors proper and two alternates) to the lawyers themselves, we were all in our assigned positions. Chauncey and I sat at the last table on the left-hand side behind Gail and Dikembe. We were within shouting distance but not so close as to allow easy conversation. Our opponents, the two lawyers and a paralegal, sat at the table on our right, closer to the jury and closer to the microphone where the lawyers stood to address the court and the witnesses. Chauncey was dressed to the nines in yet another expensive charcoal gray suit, this time with a lemon yellow silk tie and a matching handkerchief in the breast pocket As best I could tell, Dikembe, Jeff Peterson and I were all wearing the same suits that we had worn during the jury selection. I could have been wrong but they sure looked the same to me. Kathy Shepherd, also sitting with her legal team at that table on the right was, as always, radiant. That day she was wearing an off the shoulder black dress that accented the pristine whiteness of her skin. Gail, to my eyes, was just as beautiful if not more so than la dame Wennar. Gail was wearing a simple white dress which set off her light tan and made her look like a California beach girl who had taken a wrong turn in Pennsylvania and found herself in Vermont. The jurors all looked somewhat sleepy but appeared attentive enough.

At precisely 10 A.M., the bailiff ordered us all to rise, Judge Prouder entered and the games began. The first order of business was the opening statements by the opposing attorneys. Peterson for the plaintiff was first. The bad news was that he wasted no time in painting a horrendous picture of neglect to the point of criminality on the part of the nursing home and its employees. He made much of the fact that Martin Wennar was a known and well established fall risk even before he entered La Place D'Espere and that, after he had been there, he continued to fall in spite of what was done there to assure otherwise. He also emphasized the fact that when the first heel ulcer was discovered it was already a stage four ulcer and this, to him, obviously meant that no attention had been paid to stages one through three. He went on to say that he would be showing the jury members terrible pictures, "some of the worst examples of bodily neglect that (he) had ever seen" and that they should prepare themselves for these unsettling visions. By the time he was through, he had painted a one sided and altogether damning picture that, taken at face value, would convince any rational person that a terrible wrong had been done here and that someone should pay... a lot. The good news was that he only mentioned me briefly and in passing, noting that I was the Physician of record but literally saying nothing about any of my alleged bad conduct and substandard care. I began to hope that he had forgotten me, but it did seem very strange since I had been named as co-defendant in the suit.

Next came Dikembe who simply denied point by point all of the arguments Jeff had made and asserted that Martin Wennar had gotten the best care possible at all times and that there was simply no case here at all. He stated quite simply that he would present evidence during the trial to come that every and all interventions that were humanly possible had been used in the caretaking of Martin Wennar and that it was only providence and the natural deterioration of an elderly, demented man that led to Martin's downfall.

Chuancey's little speech was just that, as little as one could get and still make one. In one sentence he stated that Dr. Ziebaska had delivered not only acceptable medical care but the best possible care to Martin Wennar, and that this would be proven beyond the shadow of a doubt as the trial unfolded. With that, he sat down, and the trial proper began with the calling of the first witness.

Kathy Wennar, born Kathy Shepherd, is the most beautiful woman that I have ever seen in the whole wide world. Movie stars, television starlets, the girls from Ipanema that one passes while walking on the beach, the lovely women walking on the street you just can't take your eyes off have nothing on her. She weighs about one hundred and ten pounds and is five feet six inches tall with natural white blonde hair that is her own and a pair of cerulean blue eyes that are as wide and limitless as the morning sky in Montana. Her skin, translucent and flawless as alabaster, despite her two pack a day smoking habit and generally dissolute lifestyle, is subtly enhanced with expert make-up. Not that she needs make-up, but the make-up that she does use is sophisticated and appears professionally applied. Not for her the garishly overdone application that one might assume with a raw young woman who had worked on the assembly line of a paper products manufacturing company. She holds her generous and perfect body straight and regal as if born to royalty and great affairs (no pun intended). She is an angel with sex thrown in.

The first impulse of married women on meeting Kathy is to get their man away from her as soon and as quickly as possible. The first impulse of single women on meeting Kathy is to remove themselves from her presence as soon and as quickly as possible.

What is the point of playing a pale moon to Kathy's glorious sun? The first impulse of any heterosexual male, married or single, on meeting Kathy Wennar is to paw at the ground and bay at the moon. On the other hand Kathy's inner soul is as grasping and black as a neutron star and her perception of the truth is generally whatever is good for her alone. It would be the job of Dikembe to penetrate the shining crystal shell of her great beauty and expose the corruption within. I was interested to see how he would do this, or if indeed he could.

Jeff Peterson called Kathy Wennar to the stand as his first witness and to set the tone of his case. All eyes were on her as she flowed from the plaintiff's table to the witness box, some eyes more than others, but all eyes just the same. Men or women, none of us could take our eyes off her, and speaking for at least one of the men, why would we even want to? This was a perfect excuse to stare without embarrassment at a beautiful woman for an extended period of time. Jury duty was never so pleasurable.

Jeff began to take Kathy through her first meeting with Martin and the early days of their courtship and marriage. Almost immediately as she recalled those happy times, she began to cry.

Now a woman's tears, particularly a beautiful woman's tears, unquestionably can be very moving in and of themselves. Unfortunately for Kathy, she wasn't very practiced in the public use of this weapon because she could not use it selectively. Basically, she cried through her whole testimony, thus blunting any effect that a judicious use of her lacrimal glands might have produced. She cried when she recalled their wedding. She cried when he became ill. Hard. She cried when the diagnosis was made. She cried when he became hard to handle. She cried when he went into the nursing home. She cried. She cried. She cried.

Glancing ever at the jury, I could see that they weren't buying it after awhile if in fact they had been buying in the first place. The eyes of one of the woman jurors actually rolled back when

Kathy began to weep for about the fourth time. I took this as a good sign.

Kathy then went on about how she had religiously visited Martin in the custodial care home and then in the nursing home and how she had been appalled at the nursing home to find him often unclothed there, sometimes with dried food on his person and often alone and neglected. She related how she had initially pleaded with and then bullied the staff to provide her husband with decent treatment but to no avail. She told the story of the fall that broke his hip, the subsequent hospitalization, the return to the nursing home where the neglect only continued to the point where first the one leg was amputated and then the second leg became infected with the organism that ultimately caused his death. Through this entire recitation she wept. She ended her initial testimony by asserting that if only Martin had even adequate care at the nursing home he would still be alive today. So far, she hadn't even mentioned my name.

Dikembe Nkomo rose to his not inconsiderable height and approached the interviewing microphone. He spoke softly and precisely, his voice only rising and falling slightly throughout the questioning. He began by once again going over Kathy's testimony in regard to how often she had visited her husband in first, the custodial care home and then the nursing home. At no time did he challenge her assertions but simply got her on the record as stating her continued involvement with her husband's care. He then went on to sum up Martin Wennar's stay at Madonna of the Mountains in terms of the falls that he had taken there and the injuries that he had sustained.

At the end of this summation, he asked, "Mrs. Wennar, at any time did you question the care that your husband received at Madonna of the Mountain custodial care home?"

"No, I didn't." responded Kathy.

"At any time did you think of bringing a lawsuit against the custodial care home?"

"No."

"When your husband was at La Place D'Espere and sustained all of those falls, did you at any time think of taking him out of there?"

"Well, I did think about it several times."

"But you never acted on those thoughts, did you?"

"No."

"When it became clear that your husband continued to fall multiple times despite anything that the nursing home had done, why didn't you hire extra people to watch over him, to follow him around and to catch him when he fell? You had people employed in that capacity at your home when your husband was still there, didn't you?"

Kathy didn't miss a beat. It was as though she had been prepared for this question all along and it wouldn't have surprised me to learn that that was exactly what had happened.

"Well, I was relying on the people at the nursing home to take care of the situation. That is their job and what they do for a living. They are professionals. I counted on them to keep Martin safe. I thought they knew what they were doing." And, of course, it goes without saying that Kathy Wennar was crying even harder as she delivered this response. She looked over at the jury with her enormous blue teary eyes as if to implore them to understand the enormity of the nursing home's failure and betrayal of her trust. Dikembe left things hanging there.

And now it was my lawyer's turn to cross examine Kathy. As I have said, she hadn't even mentioned my name during her own lawyer's examination so I wasn't really sure in my own mind just what testimony Chauncey was going to rebut, but there he was up at the microphone in all his sartorial splendor. He spoke softly and gently as if reluctant to intrude on the plaintiff's grief.

"Mrs. Wennar, at any time during your husband's stay at the custodial care home or at the nursing home did you indicate to Dr. Ziebaska that you were not satisfied with his care?

"No."

"Did you make any complaints to Dr. Ziebaska regarding that care?"

"No, I didn't. As a matter of fact, I do not feel that Dr. Ziebaska did anything wrong."

What was this? I had a hard time believing what I had just heard. Here was the plaintiff in the case, a case in which I had been named as a co-defendant, a case which was billed as a medical malpractice case, stating on the first day of the trial that I had done nothing wrong! So why was I here?

When Chauncey had rejoined me at our table, I asked him exactly that. His response was a shrug of the shoulders, and at that point I got nothing more out of him. I resolved to follow up as soon as we got the chance to talk at more length.

There being nothing further for Kathy to speak to, she walked regally back to plaintiff's table, smiling bravely, but beautifully as always, through her tears. Jeff Peterson was there to pat her consolingly on the shoulder with a meaty hand, and there was a brief pause in the action while she composed herself. Then, onto business, Jeff called the next witness for prosecution, who, to my surprise, turned out to be Gail Casperson in her position of administrator of La Place D'Espere nursing home. I knew, of course, that she would provide testimony at some time during the trial, but I was surprised that she would be called as part of the plaintiff's case.

Though Kathy was a hard act to follow in terms of female pulchritude, to my way of thinking Gail was every bit her match in that department if not her outright superior. While Kathy's beauty was ethereal and otherworldly, too perfect to be real, Gail was in every way an honest to God human female with all of the attributes and attitudes that the description conveys. Where Kathy was artificial, she was genuine. Where Kathy wept for no apparent reason, she was composed and forthright. Where Kathy's testimony seemed rehearsed at times, Gail's was straightforward and gave a sense of honesty and integrity. In short, Gail was believable where Kathy was not. At least that was my take on it. Of course, I may have been biased.

Jeff spent some time having Gail go over her background, training and employment history so as to set the stage. He then asked her to describe the corporate hierarchy of the nursing home ostensibly to give the jury some idea of just what the decision making process was for policies at the facility and who would be responsible for making those policies. Several times he asked her to whom she would report to as the administrator on site. She responded that she was responsible for the corporate headquarters in New Haven, Connecticut, and would deal with a corporate vice president named Frank Fields. He then asked her whether or not Mr. Fields had a boss in turn. To this she responded that she assumed that he did, but she was not aware of the name of that person. She did know, ultimately, the name of the man who ran the corporation and she mentioned the name of the majority owner of the Boston Red Sox at that time. This was a name that most Americans would recognize, and it was clear that the members of the jury did so. It was difficult to tell what Jeff Peterson was getting at here but if his intent was to establish that the nursing home had deep pockets, he was succeeding. In reality, of course, the nursing home was insured, and no matter what the decision, the owners of the nursing home would have little to fear financially other than the probable relatively insignificant rise in their insurance premiums.

After establishing these financial matters and layers of the corporate bureaucracy, Jeff then went on to get Gail to enumerate the policies and procedures that the nursing home had in place to take care of patients in general and demented patients who were a fall risk in particular. Gail spoke about the various tab alerts and personal alarms that could be used (These are various devices that are actually attached to the patient and sound an alarm when the patient gets up while unsupervised.), different means of restraint, both physical and chemical, that might theoretically be employed (Again, she emphasized that La Place D'Espere, like all nursing homes in Vermont, was normally a "no restraint" facility) and various other tactics such as placing that particular patient's room near the nurses' station or making sure that the patient was near nursing home personnel even while sitting in a chair during the day.

Jeff then went on to try to get her to comment on the post operative care of the fractured hip, the care and monitoring of the pressure sores, and the evaluation of the peripheral circulation. To all of those questions, Gail responded that she was not a clinician and could not speak to them. After about the sixth question along these lines, it was apparent that Jeff was getting more than a bit frustrated at what he seemed to feel was the inadequacy of Gails's responses.

"Aren't you the administrator of this nursing home?" he then asked.

"I most certainly am," she replied.

"Then how can you not know the answers to these questions?" he fumed.

"It's quite simple," she responded. "I am just that, the administrator. I don't have specific knowledge of medical matters and must rely on my director of nursing and the people under her to make the decisions in that regard. It is analogous to the CEO of a computer company not necessarily knowing the nitty gritty of chip engineering. He must rely on his technical personnel for that. I am in a similar situation here."

"But didn't the nursing home set you up as the 'expert' when we sent you our interrogatories?"

"I have no idea," said Gail "I just came here to answer questions as I was instructed. I had no input in making that decision."

"Well, it would seem to me that a nursing home administrator should know more about nursing," said Jeff Peterson. There may have been a hint of a whine in his voice there.

At that point, Jeff was done with the witness. Gail remained on the stand only for another few minutes while Dikembe quickly ran her through a list of all the protocols that the nursing home had established for patient care with reference to demented patients, restraints, frequent falls, and the general nursing care plans. He then asked her if all of these protocols had been followed in the case of Martin Wennar, to which she responded that, to the best of her knowledge, they had been. And that was the end of it. Chauncey had no questions for her at all so she was dismissed as a witness. She remained sitting at the table in front of me for the remainder of the trial, however, as she was the human representative of the nursing home in the case. I can't say that this upset me.

It was now close to noon, and Judge Prouder announced that the court would recess for lunch to resume at one o'clock. Chauncey and I decided to eat lunch together so that we could discuss what had happened that morning and to make further battle plans. We got our coats and hopped into my little yellow Volkswagen New Beetle and drove out to Wendy's for a quick lunch and a short pow-wow.

WEDDING BELLS

"One's tootings at the wedding of the soul. Occur as they occur."

Wallace Stevens

T

s we sat down to gobble our fast food lunches, I turned to Chauncey with an incredulous expression.

"What just happened in there?" I expostulated. "Did I or did I not just hear Kathy Wennar say that she doesn't think that I did anything wrong? I don't get it."

"It is a bit baffling," rejoined Chauncey. "I can only conclude that they've decided not to go after you to any significant degree but are keeping you on the hook in order to use you as a weapon against the nursing home. They're the deep pockets in this case, and you remember from the mediation that they didn't really make an effort to deal with us at all."

"That's all well and good." I said. "But why do I have to sit through this trial if I'm not really a defendant? Can't you get the judge to dismiss the case against me now since the plaintiff herself says that I'm not at fault? If all they wanted was my testimony, they can call me as a witness anytime, and I can otherwise go about my business."

"Certainly, I'll try for a dismissal," said Chauncey. "But it's unlikely that the judge will grant it. Plaintiff's attorneys are given a lot of leeway in this matter. They can leave you swinging in the wind for a long time."

"Just great. Some of us have honest work to do, you know."

Chauncey just grinned back at me at this point and addressed himself to the cheeseburger that he was eating. There was a pause in the dialogue as we both chowed down. Looking around me as I ate, I noticed that the fast food restaurant had really filled up for the lunch hour. I saw a few people that I recognized, including one of the jurors who was sitting on the opposite side of the room, but as far as I could tell, no one else from the trial was within earshot.

I remarked at that point that I thought that Dikembe was doing a good job for the nursing home and that Gail had been great on the stand. Chancey gave me a bit of a sidewise glance and opened his mouth as if to say something but apparently thought better of it. After a pause, he appeared to have made a decision.

"Don't get too cozy with Dikembe," he said. "I don't trust the guy. I've worked with him on other cases, and he's quite capable of stabbing us in the back. You have to look out for your own interests here. Also, don't get the idea that you have to defend the actions of the nursing home. This is war, and it's every man for himself. You have to consider your own position first and defend that position to the fullest even if it means cutting yourself loose from the nursing home. They would do the same in your place; and in fact, they will do the same if given the slightest opportunity. Don't forget that."

"Okay, I hear you. But I also don't think that the nursing home should be hung out to dry. In my opinion they didn't do anything wrong either and they certainly don't deserve to have a lawsuit filed against them. I don't like the idea that Jeff Peterson thinks that he can get me to say bad things about the nursing home care to save my own skin."

"I understand. Just remember what I said. If it comes down to it, it's you and not the nursing home that I'm defending. Also, Jeff is actually a good guy. He may be our enemy here, but he's a straight shooter. I've had some experiences with him in other cases as well. If he says he will do something, he'll do it. You can be sure that any deal he makes will be honored."

I was surprised to hear this endorsement of the Plaintiff's lawyer coming from my lawyer, particularly since that wasn't my take on Jeff from what little contact I had with him to date. Of course, Chauncey had known him a lot longer and in other circumstances so I should probably defer to his judgment. Still, I was used to making up my own mind and resolved that I would reserve my own judgment in regard to both Dikembe and Jeff until I saw how the situation would play out.

Back in the courtroom, Judge Prouder called the court to order, and Jeff Peterson called his next witness, a man named Robert Villarosa, a nursing home administrator somewhere in Florida. Mr. Villarosa was a big man with a florid complexion and a deep tan. Like my own lawyer, he was dressed to the nines in an expensive looking charcoal gray suit with an electric blue silk tie, matching handkerchief and black loafers polished to a mirror finish. He and Chauncey, given the style and expense of their clothing, both looked like they were Hollywood movers and shakers from somewhere up on the social ladder of Lalaland though Mr. Villarosa was more like a meat cleaver to Chauncey's rapier or stiletto, considering he weighed over two hundred and fifty pounds and was just under six feet in height. When he smiled, his teeth were so white that the ambient lighting in the room went up by a few hundred watts. He smiled a lot.

Jeff took him through the usual introductions, establishing that he was there to testify as an expert against the nursing home. He himself was a nursing home administrator though he wasn't running a nursing home at this time. He had run several nursing homes in the past, the most recent being was three years ago. Interestingly, he hadn't stayed at one location for any extended period of time. He would run one home for a period of one to four years and would then move on to another. Mr. Villarosa then volunteered that he had actually been fired from one of his administrative positions because he "couldn't get along with others." Specifically, he stated that it was one person in particular, the head of nursing at one facility, with whom he couldn't get along. He ascribed this to a clash of personalities and stated that it had never happened again.

It seems odd and self-defeating for witnesses of any kind, especially expert witnesses, to bring up events that would affect them adversely or potentially diminish their credibility with a jury, but apparently this is a common strategy that lawyers adopt. If there are facts that might reflect badly on one's position, one should bring them out first and so steal the thunder of the opposition. Villarosa then went on to soundly criticize every move that the staff at La Place D'Espere had made concerning the care of Martin Wennar. He particularly was critical of the fact, as he saw it, that there was no written care plan in the chart. At one point he actually alluded to "an acute lack of care plan" as a major deficiency in Mr. Wennar's care. He opined that many times certain boxes in the chart had not been checked off, and that this obviously meant that this care had not been delivered. He stated that it was just atrocious that Mr. Wennar had been allowed to fall and break his hip since he was in the nursing home because of frequent falls to begin with. It was his firm opinion that the post-operative care provided to the patient was woefully inadequate, and in and of itself resulted in the development of pressure sores which, again because of bad care and neglect, became infected and caused the death of the patient. He stated that the fact that these pressure ulcers were first noted to be stage four ulcers (meaning ulcers down to the tendons or the bone) meant that the nurses hadn't been monitoring skin integrity to any degree and were also negligent in their duties. He also noted that the patient had lost considerable weight between the fall and the development of the fatal ulcer and that this indicated to him that close enough attention had not been paid to the nutritional needs of the patient. Ultimately, he said quite clearly that the care of Martin Wennar was not only negligent, in his opinion it was criminal.

As a physician, listening to this "expert" testimony it was was extremely frustrating. For one thing, the idea for treatment for stage four pressure ulcer was obviously not clearly understood by Villarosa. The fact is that the staging of these pressure ulcers is just that, staging. The stages have nothing to do with the development of the ulcers but are only descriptive terms to quantify the extent and the depth of the lesions. A stage one ulcer is merely a shallow opening in the dermis while a stage four ulcer is one that extends down to the bone or exposed tendons. It rarely happens that a pressure ulcer starts as a stage one ulcer and then progresses through stages two and three to eventually become a stage four ulcer. The necrosis or death of the tissue actually first may occur inside the overlying soft tissue down near the bone where the blood supply is compromised by pressure that collapses the feeding artery against the bone. This may then lead to a situation where significant tissue death has already occurred, but there is no obvious outward indication that this is the case. On the surface, the skin appears normal at this point. An astute observer might be able to appreciate a "spongy" feeling of the tissue overlying the area, but this is a subtle finding. Then, in a period of only a few hours, the ulcer will quickly show itself as a stage four ulcer from the very beginning! This medical fact was obviously not appreciated by the plaintiff's attorneys, not surprisingly since they hadn't deposed anyone with a significant medical background. Most astonishing, however, was the fact that their "expert" witness didn't seem to have a grasp of this medical fact either.

Dikembe Nkomo began his cross examination of Roberrt Villarosa by asking him if he was being paid for his testimony. When Villarosa responded in the affirmative, Dikembe followed up by asking just how much he was getting. The nursing home administrator admitted that he was being paid two hundred and fifty dollars an hour to review charts and three hundred and fifty dollars an hour to testify in court. This three hundred and fifty dollars an hour was "portal to portal." As soon as Mr. Villarosa stepped out of his door to go to the airport, the clock started ticking and it didn't stop ticking until he stepped back in the door. Also, all expenses, airfare, meals, and lodging were paid over and above the hourly fee. One look at the faces of the jurors as these princely sums were revealed gave evidence that the Dikembe was making some points here.

Dikembe then extracted from our expert witness that not only had he not been functioning as a nursing home administrator for the last three years, but what he had been doing was either testifying in suits against nursing homes or participating in the giving of seminars to lawyers on the subject of suing nursing homes. Apparently, there was a huge industry that specialized in just these types of suits. Because of the vast number of federal regulations to which they were subject, nursing homes had proven to be particularly vulnerable to these suits. The lawyers could almost always find one or two regulations that weren't followed to the letter, and would base their suits on these infractions.

Next, Dikembe asked the expert what he had done to prepare for his testimony in this case. The response was that he had reviewed the nursing home records. Had he done anything else to prepare? The answer was no. Had he talked to any of the people who were involved in the care of the patient, the nurses, the dietician, the social workers, the physical therapists? Again, the answer was no. Sitting in my seat and hearing this, I was astounded. I turned to Chauncey.

"What kind of a case is this, anyway?" I said. "It's a nursing home case." He answered.

"How can anyone give an informed opinion of a patient's care if he doesn't speak to the people who provide that care? It just isn't possible."

To this, Chauncey repeated his original answer. It was a nursing home case.

Dikembe then asked the expert if he had ever had problems with pressure ulcers at any of the nursing homes where he had worked in the past. Mr. Villarosa responded that he had never, in all of his years as a nursing home administrator, ever had a patient with a stage four pressure ulcer. To let things get to that level would be criminal in his opinion.

Dikembe then showed him an article from the New England Journal of Medicine, a highly respected medical publication, that reported in 2001, even with the best in hospital medical care 60% of patients over the age of 60 who had fractured their hips subsequently went on to develop pressure ulcers, many of these are stage four. To this, our expert witness had no rejoinder other than to reiterate that in his (vast) experience this was not the case.

At this point, court was adjourned for the day. In talking to Dikembe later, he assured me that he didn't deliberately drag out his cross examination to ensure that Mr. Villarosa would have to stay overnight so that plaintiff's attorneys would be paying their three hundred and fifty dollars through the night while he slept. I swear that as he said this, however, I caught a twinkle in his eye.

The first day ended in this fashion. I drove home, ran my five miles, showered, ate, watched a little television and went to bed. Tomorrow would be another day.

THE BEGINNING

"Cry 'Havoc' and let slip the dogs of war."

Shakespeare

T t rained on the second day of the trial. As it turned out, it was the only day of the trial that it did rain. Each day before the trial started,I started my hospital rounds early in the morning so that I could be free for the trial that day. Life and death went on apace, my legal difficulties notwithstanding. It was not unusual therefore that I would have patients in the hospital, some of whom would have been admitted the night before while one of the members of my coverage group was on call in my stead. We averaged one night a week on call, and it so happened that I was scheduled to be on call on Thursday night of that week. I had traded that Thursday for the next Thursday with Mike Nicholson, one of my on call partners so that I wouldn't have to concern myself with the ongoing trial and being on-call at the same time, a situation that would have been untenable. On only one occasion that week was I late to court, and it turns out nothing of any import took place during the time I wasn't there.

Several of those mornings, the judge and the lawyers were closeted "in chambers," meaning that they were having some sort of legal wrangling in the judge's private suite of rooms out of sight and earshot of the nonlawyers, the jury, plaintiff and defendant. These meetings were all apparently top secret, and though Chauncey did loosely keep me apprised of what went on in them, I never did find out exactly what took place.

On this Tuesday morning, I thought that Chauncey would be bringing his motion for dismissal before the judge, and quite naturally I was very interested in how that would turn out. In the meantime, however, it was just plain boring waiting for something to happen. Whenever the lawyers were in chambers, the jury was taken out of the room so that left me, Gail, the bailiff and the court reporter to amuse ourselves the best that we could. This morning, Robert Villarosa was also in the courtroom, sitting at the back and waiting to conclude his testimony. Much of the time Gail and I would talk to one another, discuss the trial and how it was going so far, theorize about the secret goings on, and catch up with what was happening in our own busy lives in regard to Cassie and our respective children. That morning I congratulated her on her performance the day before. She was concerned that she had come off something of an ignorant fool because she hadn't been very familiar with the medical terms or the specific methods of care that were employed to treat pressure sores, but I assured her that the jury wouldn't have seen things that way and that I certainly hadn't. She appeared relieved, and we both proceeded to make fun of the so-called expert nursing home administrator who had testified that day. Since he was sitting at the back of the room at the time, we had to do this in whispered conversation; but that didn't detract from the amusing aspects of our discussion. We managed to keep ourselves occupied for the duration.

Unfortunately, the lawyers did eventually return as did the jury soon thereafter, and the open trial resumed. In the short gap between these events Chauncey informed me that the judge had not accepted his motion for dismissal although he had said some nicely negative things about how the plaintiff's case was going in regard to me. In large part, he felt that this was due to the fact that the main witness against me, one Howard Friedman, M.D., had not yet testified and that said testimony was the foundation of my involvement in the case. This testimony was next on the agenda after the nursing home administrator was finished so it would be coming up shortly. I couldn't wait to hear it.

Without further ado, Robert Villarosa retook the stand, and Dikembe resumed his cross examination. But really, there wasn't much more that he could get out of this witness. He had already gotten him to admit that he was practically a shill for the prosecution, and that all of his testimony was based on written records and most likely incomplete ones at that. He concluded by speculating that the witness would probably be willing to say just about anything for three hundred and fifty dollars an hour. Jeff Peterson was out of his chair objecting in mock outrage in a split second, but the damage was done. I could see that the jury hadn't thought much of Mr. Villarosa, and it didn't take much of a detective to see why. Since Villarosa had no criticisms to make of my medical care, Chauncey had no questions for him and he stepped down, presumably to fly back to Florida at three hundred and fifty dollars an hour.

Next on the hit parade was Dr. Howard Friedman, a gerontologist affiliated with the University of Pennsylvania Medical School, who was a specialist in the care of elderly nursing home patients. Doctor Friedman was providing all of his testimony by videotape. Apparently he was much too busy an individual to sacrifice any of his valuable time to testify at a trial where one of his peers was being pilloried for alleged substandard care. When I had heard that this would be the case, I initially was more than a little upset that I wouldn't be able to confront this man and to have some input in the rebuttal of his testimony. I wasn't at all sure that Chauncey understood the subtler aspects of the medical questions and would be able to ask all of the appropriate questions. It turned out that I was right in this, but overall it probably made no difference. Chauncey did have some ideas of his own that worked out quite well in the end.

First of all, Chauncey assured me that the jury would be completely bored by watching this doctor expound over a small television screen on long winded medical matters and, secondly, the impact of such testimony would be largely vitiated by doing it this way. It turned out that Dr. Friedman looked very much like the comedian, Woody Allen, even to the somewhat whiny voice, and his visual impact was poor even before he opened his mouth. Chauncey also had told me that he was able to represent our position well; and that, in his humble opinion, he had made the good doctor look like a fool in regard to several unwarranted assumptions that he had made concerning the case and my involvement in it.

As in the actual courtroom interviews, Jeff Peterson started by asking Dr. Friedman about his background and qualifications. It unfolded that he was a physician with a university research position who was, at the time of this trial, overseeing research work concerning the treatment of Alzheimer's Disease at a half dozen large nursing homes in the Pittsburgh area. He was, therefore, more of a theoretician than a hands-on physician, which meant that his sense of medical practice was not completely grounded in reality as far as I was concerned. This was brought home to me when he began to criticize my care of Martin Wennar in regard to measures that had been used to prevent his falls. He first criticized me for not trying the mattress at the side of the bed. Since he had only reviewed the records from the nursing home, he had no idea that had already been tried at the custodial care home. He then criticized me for not using other physical type restraints such as a merry walker or lap trays and seat belts. These measures are ineffective and in some cases downright dangerous. I doubt that Dr. Friedman would even have mentioned them if he had any real world experience with them.

He then went on to state that my involvement in Martin Wennars care was cursory at best and negligent at worst. He had come to this conclusion after reading the progress notes and the incident reports in the chart. Specifically, he noted that I had been informed on multiple occasions of falls that Mr. Wennar had taken in the nursing home, yet I had not responded to these reports and had not adjusted the care and treatment that the patient was getting at those times. Now Chauncey and I had gone over these incident reports with a fine toothed comb, and we knew quite well that the vast majority of them had not been signed by me but instead had been signed by Dr. Willian Zarabedian, the medical director of the nursing home, or, alternatively, by one of the other members of my on call group. By far the larger number had been signed by Dr. Zarabedian. In fact, the most crucial incident reports, dealing with the fall that had actually caused the hip fracture and another fall that had resulted in a large skin tear, had actually been signed at a time when I was out of town at a medical conference. Where I had signed an incident report, there was always a corresponding order to change the environment of the patient, increase vigilance or adjust schedules to attempt to prevent further falls.

Chauncey started out his cross examination by asking the witness how he knew that I personally had been informed of these adverse incidents. When Dr. Friedman replied that he had seen my signature on the incident reports, Chauncey simply pointed out to him after time that the signature on that particular report wasn't mine. There was in fact no evidence of any kind that I had been made aware of any of the incidents that Dr. Friedman was so concerned about. It was particularly embarrassing for the good doctor when Chauncey pointed out that I wasn't even in the same state when the most significant incidents were supposedly reported. In conclusion he asked Dr. Friedman if it wasn't his responsibility as an expert witness in the case, to establish that the criticisms that he made were directed to the proper physician. After a good deal of hemming and hawing and shuffling of papers, Dr. Friedman admitted that this was probably a reasonable idea. As far as I could determine, most of the jurors were still awake at the end of this performance in spite of its essentially boring nature, and I do believe that they got the point.

This accounted for the entire morning of the second day and it was again time for us to adjourn for lunch. In keeping with our newly established tradition, Chauncey and I adjourned to Wendy's to munch burgers and digest the morning's events. This time we took Chauncey's car, a new model black Mercedes Benz that, at rest, looked like a crouching panther and had a retractable sun roof that had probably not been retracted in many months. In the brief ride over to the fast food restaurant, I enjoyed the feel of the soft leather seats immensely. Even though the morning's cross examination had been on videotape, Chauncey was still adrenalized and couldn't stop talking about it. I assured him that he had done well which I felt that he most certainly had and that the jury had been impressed and convinced. I hoped that this was the reality of the situation. Chauncey spoke at some length about how he was determined to win this case and to maintain his excellent reputation at his firm so that he could get a partnership. He talked about his mother, a formidable women by his account who thought more about horses and their bloodlines than she did about her children and who; again by his account, counted up the successes and failures of her progeny on a large chalk board that she would constantly review before revising both her affections and her will. I had the feeling that Chauncey had some issues.

We both agreed that the case was going well. I wondered once again wether it was worthwhile exploring the idea of asking for a dismissal of the case since the expert witness against me had made no legitimate criticisms, and Chauncey agreed that it was worth another try. We finished our meals and headed back to court.

After another brief conference in chambers where, once again, our motion for dismissal was denied (From what I could understand, it was denied because Jeff Peterson had insisted that I was necessary to make his primary case though he wasn't required to say just why this was so.), the rest of that day was devoted to hearing testimony from one of the strangest looking people whom I have ever seen. Jeff Peterson called Rita Kilkenny to the stand.

Ms. Kilkenny proved to be a pixieish little woman who stood about five feet two inches tall and was, there is no other word for it, pointy all over. She had a pointed chin, a thin pointed nose and her ears were pointed at both ends. The tips of her ears were pointed in the manner of Mr. Spock on Star Trek and the lobes of her ears were also pointed. Accentuating this pointed physiognomy was a pair of earrings in the shape of an isosceles triangle with the long sides pointing down. The crowning glory was a short blonde hair-cut that was gelled upward into several protruding spikes. There were some titters in the jury box, quickly extinguished by a sharp look from the judge. It was all I could do to not give vent to a few titters myself.

When she spoke, it was evident that the only thing not pointy about Rita Kilkenny was her voice which was soft, well modulated, and imbued with a strong flavor of the deep South. Jeff went through the usual formalities of establishing her bona fides. She held a number of degrees including a PhD in nursing and was ostensibly an expert in the evaluation, prevention and care of de-cubitus ulcers or "pressure sores" as they were commonly called. At the time of this trial, she held a university position at the Virgin-ia Medical College and was writing a paper, the latest of many, on new nursing treatments for diabetic foot ulcers. She volunteered the information that she had not been spending as much time as she would have liked at the bedside of "her" patients as she was caught up in academic and judicial activities. She then proceeded to give a scathing indictment of the nursing care that had been administered to one Martin Wennar at La Place D'Espere nursing home.

Her first criticisms were directed to the means that had been used to try to keep him from falling, the gist of which was that they had obviously been inadequate since he had fallen, not once but multiple times and had the ultimate complication of a fractured hip. As anyone with any common sense could see, this automatically meant that the nursing home had not done a proper job and was negligent. Never mind that Mr. Wennar had fallen multiple times at home with round the clock help or that he had fallen at the custodial care home with all of their precautions in place. The nursing home was without question negligent, if not criminal.

She then went on to excoriate the nursing home staff for inadequately protecting Mr. Wennar's skin integrity, with emphasis on the skin of the lower extremities, stating that had proper nursing care and attention been given here, the patient would never have developed the complications that he had. Once again, to my incredulous surprise, she raised the issue of the stage four ulcer as an indicator that the nursing care had been inadequate. What was going on here? This was the second"expert" out of two that didn't seem to understand what the meaning of stage four was in this context. Once again there was this confusion between the staging of the ulcer, merely a descriptive term, and the development of the ulcer, the mechanism of its coming into existence. Could it be that these witnesses were deliberately distorting their testimony to place the nursing home care in a bad light, or were they really ignorant of the terminology that they were using? In the former instance, they would be directly contradicted when other experts would then explain to the jury the truth of the matter; and in the latter situation, they would be exposing themselves as ignorant in their area of expertise. It was baffling, frustrating and confusing. In any event, Ms. Kilkenny sailed merrily on with her testimony uncontradicted at this point. She, like Roberrt Villarosa before her, made note of the weight loss, the multiple skin tears and the terrible infection that led to the patient's death. All of these complications, in her expert opinion, could have been and should have been avoided if only the proper nursing care had been forthcoming. Jeff Peterson then thanked her profusely, looked meaningfully at the members of the jury and took his seat.

Dikembe, hunching over a bit to minimize the awesome height advantage that he enjoyed, took Peterson's place at the microphone, briefly introduced himself to the witness and, without further ado, launched into his cross examination. This proved to be almost a carbon copy of his examination of Villarosa and followed the same blueprint. First, he established that Rita Kilkenny was not much involved in patient care at all these days but spent most of her time and garnered most of her income by testifying as an expert witness in court cases. While she attempted to assert that she testified both for defendant and plaintiffs, he was easily able to glean that by far she testified for plaintiffs. In fact, Ms. Kilkenny was ultimately to admit that in the last three years she had testified for the defendant in a malpractice case on only one occasion. He then extracted from her the obscene amount of money that she was making by her involvement in this case which turned out to be one hundred and fifty dollars an hour for chart review and two hundred and fifty dollars an hour portal-to-portal for in court testimony. I couldn't help but notice that these figures were significantly lower than those that Mr. Villarosa had mentioned. Was this a result of gender inequality or the glass ceiling? Whatever the case, these numbers again would not sit well with the jury, a group of relatively ordinary hardworking folks who undoubtedly had never ever seen such money in all their working experience.

After this exploration and of background and salary, Dikembe then questioned the witness in regard to her preparation for the case. And once again, like Robert Villarosa before her, she admitted quite frankly that she had simply reviewed the nursing home records. She had not spoken at any time to any human being who had been involved in Martin Wennar's care! Dikembe expressed astonishment that this would be the case; and, indeed sitting in my seat at the defendant's table, I remained astonished as well. Chauncey had told me that not only had none of the nursing home personnel been spoken to by these experts but also that none of them had been deposed by Jeff Peterson. Once again, I had expressed my surprise, but Chauncey himself didn't seem to think that it was a big deal. I could only wonder what the jury members were thinking.

Having scored his points, Dikembe yielded the microphone to Chauncey. It wasn't clear to me why Chauncey was even cross examining this witness as she had not mentioned me by name or even referred to "the doctor" indirectly, but he assured me that it would become clear. He began by asking her some general questions about decubitus ulcers, questions that she had already answered in response to Jeff Peterson's examination. Then he asked a question that I felt was a big mistake on his part. He asked Rita Kilkenny, the expert witness on decubitus ulcers, what the arterial blood supply to the heel, the area where Martin Wennar had developed his pressure sore, was. I thought this was a big mistake because among medical personnel this was a very commonly known piece of information. Even a third-year medical student would be able to answer it correctly and with ease. Much was my astonishment when Ms. Kilkenny hesitated and appeared not to know the answer. Her little pointed jaw quivered briefly, and then, before she could say anything, Chauncey provided the correct response.

"Well, it's the posterior tibial artery isn't it?" he asserted

Quickly recovering her poise, she smiled and said, "Yes, that's right. Thank you."

Now, to give her the benefit of the doubt, she may have been momentarily caught off guard and just had a brief moment when the correct answer to a simple medical question did not instantly come to mind even though she knew the answer. On the other hand, regardless of the reason for her hesitation, this made her look very bad in the eyes of the jury and was a coup for Chauncey. I can't say that I was too unhappy about it either.

Later, when I expressed my misgivings to my lawyer about his asking the question in the first place, he told me that he really didn't care wether she answered the question correctly. In fact, he assumed that she would. He was merely laying the groundwork for the testimony of our expert witness and for my testimony in regard to the circulatory compromise in Martin Wennar's legs which specifically related to the pathology of that particular artery. The fact that she hadn't appeared to know the answer was just icing on the cake.

This ended the testimony of the plaintiff's third expert and the pointed lady promptly flounced out of the room, looking like some sort of upside-down exclamation point, pulling one of those suitcases on wheels behind her as she was obviously a busy woman who had planes to catch and other trials to go to. Court was adjourned for the day.

There then followed an incident that was very unpleasant but very interesting. With the adjournment and the judge and jury leaving the room, Chauncey and I spoke briefly about what had happened in court that day and what would be happening the next day. I then said my goodbyes to Gail and Dikembe and proceeded out of the court room. I had left my coat and boots in a small room at the top of the stairs where sometimes lawyers had private conferences with their clients or witnesses waited to be called. When I came to the room, I noticed that Ms. Kilkenny was sitting in there talking on her cell phone. As I entered, she hung up the phone, apologized for being there and offered to leave. I told her that she was welcome to stay as I was just getting my things. I then went on to speak to her in regard to her testimony that afternoon. Since she was purportedly an expert, I thought that it would be good idea for her to have some understanding of what the term "stage four decubitus ulcer" meant, and I went on to explain to her just why a stage four ulcer has nothing to say about how quickly it came about or the adequacy of care or monitoring before it appeared. Just as I was coming to the end of my little lesson, Jeff Peterson entered the room.

Upon seeing me there, Jeff became agitated and said, "You can't talk to her without your lawyer present. You had better leave now."

"What do you mean I can't talk to her? I'm a free American citizen and can talk to whomever I damn well please. Her part in the trial is over, and there is no question of anyone unduly influencing anyone else. It just seemed to me that as an expert she should have some understanding of just what it is she talking about."

Peterson's face turned a fine shade of purple.

"It's completely inappropriate I tell you. You had better leave." By this time, I had had it.

"Fine, I was leaving anyway. But it might be a good idea if the true facts came out in this case. Not that the truth has anything to do with what you're doing in this courtroom at the present time."

As soon as these words left my mouth, I was overcome with embarrassment. What a pompous and overbearing thing to say. Next thing you know I would be invoking justice and the American way of life. On the other hand, this was the truth of the matter; and if I got a little carried away there, what was the real harm? Before I could say anything more inflammatory or personally insulting in regard to Jeff Peterson, I made my exit.

THE BEGINNING

"Cry 'Havoc' and let slip the dogs of war."

Shakespeare

The first witness for the nursing home was a stroke of genius on Dikembe's part. Rather than choose a nurse or an administrator, he chose Renee Fortin, the young nurses' aide who usually worked the second shift at La Place D'Espere. Renee was a sweet young thing who, though she was in reality probably in her early twenties, looked like she was about fifteen. She was the picture of innocence and sincerity, and even before she said a word, I could see that the jury members would have a hard time thinking of her as a villain. Like those before her Renee began her testimony by providing background information as to who she was and what her job at the nursing home involved. She was led by Dikembe in a description of the techniques that caretakers were taught to use in regard to nursing home patients who were demented or otherwise had an altered mental status. The specific technique involved was called reapproachment. Renee went on to tell what she had been trained to do if a patient was combative or confused to the point where he wouldn't take simple instructions or allow basic caretaking activities such as feeding and dressing. Basically, the idea was to simply leave the patient alone for a brief period of a few minutes and then to approach him again. This was often just respite enough for the patient to react in a completely different manner and allow the previously resisted assistance to be accepted. If that didn't work, then a different employee might be asked to deal with the patient after another short interval. Patients in these circumstances would often react quite differently to a second, different person who was trying to complete the same task.

On the critical night in question, Renee had been on duty and was trying to get Martin Wennar fed and then dressed for bed. With some resistance and a great deal of help he had eaten the evening meal but then had refused to allow her to clean him up so that there was no residual food on his face. She decided that she would then get him dressed for bed before trying to clean him again, but he resisted this as well. When his clothes had been removed, he began striking out at her and would not allow her to put his pajamas on him. Following the established technique, she had covered him with a sheet and had left the room, intending to return in a few minutes to try again. It was at that very time that Kathy Wennar had entered her husband's room only to find him naked and with dried food on his face as he had promptly kicked the sheet off from himself. When poor Renee returned to the scene, Kathy went ballistic on her, screaming and cursing that the nursing home was a hellhole and that the people who worked there, Renee in particular, were sadistic morons. Renee, overwhelmed and outgunned, had burst into tears and ran from the room. She got the floor nurse to come and to try to explain just what was going on, but Mrs. Wennar would have none of it and continued to rant on. It was readily apparent that Renee had been quite upset and just recalling the incident brought tears to that innocent young face. Her distress was communicated very well to the jurors, and I was pretty sure that they all were thinking that anyone who would verbally abuse this young girl was an ogre of the first order. No doubt this is just what Dikembe had in mind to open his defense. Jeff Peterson had no questions on cross. He probably wanted to get Renee off the stand as soon as possible.

The next witness was one of the second shift nurses who was working on the floor where Martin Wennar had resided. After a short introduction, Dikembe asked her if she had ever seen Kathy Wennar before. The nurse responded that although she had worked quite regularly she had never seen Mrs. Wennar, the woman who faithfully visited her husband on a regular basis while he was in the nursing home, ever in her life and wouldn't have been able to recognize her. This nurse also spoke to the multiple interventions that had been tried to keep Martin Wennar from falling, everything from the tab alert tags to alarm bracelets and motion detectors to simply moving him nearer to the nurses' station and putting his chair closer to nursing home personnel when he was sitting in the day room. She also went into some detail about the many different measures that had been used to try to prevent pressure sores after the fractured hip had occurred. These consisted of multiple interventions from using an adductor pillow to prevent the patient from crossing his legs and thus put undo pressure on these extremities to special foot and heel protectors to keep the pressure of his own weight off of these areas. Dikembe showed a slide of Mr. Wennar sitting in a chair with an adductor pillow in place between his legs and large soft plastic air booties on his feet. In that picture, Martin Wennar was smiling and actually appeared to be enjoying himself in a sad parody of the demented patient. This nurse then described the many things that were done to treat the pressure ulcers that had, unfortunately, manifested themselves despite the good nursing care that she and her colleagues had provided. She emphasized time after time how difficult it was to care for a completely demented patient like Martin Wennar who not only would not cooperate in his care but also would constantly do things that would subvert that care and often do things that would render that care useless. In spite of this difficulty, she asserted that she and the rest of the staff had remained professional and had done a good and proper job.

After Dikembe had examined this witness, Jeff Peterson had only one question for her. He asked what shift she worked, and upon receiving the answer to that question, he then followed up by asking her if Kathy Wennar might very well have visited her husband at other times, such as on the day shift, when this nurse wasn't on duty. The nurse admitted that this could have been the case, and Jeff, looking very self satisfied, nodded knowingly to the jurors and ended his cross examination.

Wonder of wonders, the third defense witness turned out to be a day shift nurse, one Ingrid Staff, who, in essence corroborated the testimony of the first nurse and also stated unequivocally that although she also had worked regularly at the time Martin Wennar was at La Place D'Espere she had never seen Kathy Wennar there either. Dikembe had actually pointed to Kathy, sitting at the plaintiff's table, and asked Ingrid if she had ever seen her. When she responded in the negative although I may have imagined it, I could have sworn that there was a noticeable flinch on Kathy's part.

When Dikembe was done, Jeff jumped up quickly to the microphone and asked Mrs. Staff if there weren't in fact other entrances to that area of the nursing home other than those that led past the nurses' station. She responded that there was a fire door at the end of the corridor; but that as far as she knew, it was kept locked from the inside. Jeff then asked if it would surprise her to know that many times nursing home employees would go outside to smoke using that door and would often leave it unlocked when they did so. When she said that this would surprise her, Jeff got her to admit that it was at least possible. Once again, he acted as if this was a great coup and ended his cross examination.

There then appeared in quick succession a number of ancillary workers at the nursing home, each one of whom was there to counter the charges that had been made against that institution by the various experts who had testified for the plaintiff. A dietician described the special weight enhancing diet and foods that had been provided to Mr. Wennar to build him up in an attempt to heal his injuries and wounds. She also noted that the drastic weight loss that the opposing experts had touted as a measurement of the poor dietary care that the patient had been receiving, had coincidentally been related to the amputation that Martin had under-gone and the amount of weight was quite consistent with that of an amputated leg! A physical therapist detailed the special exercises and equipment that had been used to promote Mr. Wennar's mus-cular conditioning and to prevent pressure sores. A social worker, whose office just happened to be right off the front entrance of the nursing home, not only described the lack of interest that the lovely Mrs. Wennar expressed in regard to her husband's care (She hadn't even attended one of the care plan meetings though she had been there when the state ombudswoman had delivered her list of concerns and criticisms.) but also was able to testify that she had never seen Kathy come into the home to visit her husband. A third nurse testified that there was most certainly a care plan in place in spite of what the expert, Villarosa, had said, and she produced the written care plan and went over it for the edification of the jury members. The care plan detailed for every shift the specific activities and preventive measures that were employed to keep the patient safe in regard to falls, skin integrity, toileting and nutrition. Without exception, all the deficiencies that Ms. Kilkenny and Mr. Villarosa had mentioned were addressed. A nurse at Madonna of the Mountain custodial care home testified that the dementia ward where Martin Wennar had resided during his stay at that facility was locked at all times to prevent patients from wandering outside the building. There was no possibility that anyone could get in to visit him without getting someone to let that person in.

To this barrage of witness testimony, Jeff Peterson had no good answers on cross examination. Indeed, but for again getting the nurse from Madonna of the Mountain to admit that there was at least one other exit/entrance to the ward other than the locked door in the main corridor, he had no answers at all. To my un-trained legal eye, the performance of the plaintiff's attorney here was rather pathetic. But then, he didn't have much to work with af-ter all because there wasn't much of a case here to begin with. Once again, my lawyer didn't seem to share my view of the situation and; Chauncey, every time I did get a chance to talk to him between witnesses, maintained a mask of grave concern and averred that we still had a long way to go before we could rest easy. Still, I was feeling pretty good about the situation, and I was feeling particularly proud of all of the nursing home personnel who had testified. Their testimony was precise and professional and was a fine testament to the excellent care that La Place D'Espere was able to provide in spite of all the federal regulations and the tons of paperwork with which they were required to deal. I was even beginning to feel good about having patients in the nursing home, something that I had never felt good about in the past no matter how good the reputation of the nursing home involved. Dikembe had acquitted himself magnificently and had dealt masterfully with every single allegation that had been brought against his client up to this point. Chauncey had not had to say a word since no one, not any nursing home employee, not any lawyer, had even mentioned my name, not to mention accused me of anything. On this happy note, the third day of the trial came to what I considered a successful conclusion.

THE BEGINNING

"Cry 'Havoc' and let slip the dogs of war."

Shakespeare

After court had adjourned that day, I drove home, changed into my running clothes and ran a five mile loop to clear my head. The conditions were somewhat sloppy as there had been a new snowfall the night before; and most of it had melted off the roads by the end of the day, leaving slush and dirt to be kicked up by passing cars, but I was too adrenalized to pay much attention to getting wet and muddy. By the end of the run, however, even that hormonal anesthesia was not sufficient to keep me from feeling damp, sweaty and dirty so a nice long hot shower was the next item on the agenda.

Then, feeling refreshed and righteous from my completed exertions, I took Orion for a short walk, made myself some soup for dinner and dashed off to bagpipe practice which, as I said earlier, always took place on Wednesday nights. I went over the trial in my mind during the drive to and from practice; but, thankfully, the practice itself engaged my mind fully and put at least a momentary halt to that constant review of the previous court day and anticipation of the next court day. I got home around ten o'clock, watched an episode of Law and Order on the television (courtroom drama, just what I needed) and went to bed. For some reason, sleep came easily, and there were no dreams of lawyers or anxious witnesses to disturb my rest.

Chauncey had told me that Patrick O'Connor, a local orthopedic surgeon whom I knew very well, would be testifying the next day as an expert for the defense, and I was looking forward to that. Pat was an excellent surgeon, a good man, and, perhaps most important for the matter at hand, was articulate, knowledgeable and persuasive. More to the point, he was a doctor with a doctor's knowledge base and would at last provide some real medical facts upon which the jury might base a rational verdict. There might be some hope that truth would surface at all.

After rising early, I was able to finish hospital rounds in good order and so got to the court a bit early as well. The courtroom was empty but for Chauncey, the court bailiff and myself, and I remarked to Chauncey that I had thought that Dikembe had done a fine job up to this point with his defense. For once, my lawyer agreed with me; but still his assenting opinion seemed to lack a certain enthusiasm that I couldn't quite put my finger on.

"Yes," he said. "Dikembe is a smart guy and knows his stuff. No question. Just remember, he could just as easily be grilling you in that witness box. If it comes down to you or the nursing home, you have to know that you ain't his priority."

"Of course, I know that." I responded. But I couldn't help but think that I had nothing to fear from the tall black man who had been eviscerating Jeff Peterson's case so efficiently. What could he possibly use against me? Then I did recall that there was the matter of the progress note that didn't list the major problem as a problem, and my good mood went down a notch. But then, again, that hadn't come up yet either so there was a good chance at this point that it never would.

Gradually the courtroom filled. Pat O'Connor came in, and we re-introduced ourselves all around. Pat commiserated with me about the fact that I was even involved in such a bogus case, which certainly made me feel good, and we talked briefly about our families and what was happening at the hospital these days. Chauncey and Pat talked a very little bit about his upcoming testimony. They had already planned this at some length so there wasn't much, if anything, left to do, but Chauncey was ever the perfectionist in that regard and would always make use of whatever time he had to polish his presentation over and over again. Not a bad quality in your defense lawyer.

The jury came in and shortly thereafter the bailiff announced the entrance of the judge. Dr. Patrick O'Connor was called to the stand by Chauncey Winthrop, was duly sworn in and began his testimony. My every expectation was realized. Not only were Pat's credentials impeccable, but there were no asterisks or sidebars that would detract from them. He had never been dismissed from any position for any reason, had graduated from Harvard Medical School and had attended a fine orthopedic training program at Boston University Hospital. Most importantly, from there he had become a practicing orthopedist and was still working full time in that specialty at the local hospital in St. Albans. Although he did hold a part time faculty position at the University of Vermont, he was not some ivory tower physician who was not out and working in the real world. He saw patients and dealt with their orthopedic problems every day. It was readily apparent, at least to me, that Pat O'Connor lived up to the billing of "medical expert," in contrast to many of the so-called experts who had previously provided testimony in the case.

Chauncey then led Pat through the telling of how he had become involved with Martin Wennar as the orthopedic surgeon of record after Martin had fallen and fractured his hip. He related how he had first been concerned about Martin's peripheral circulation when he had noted on his original physical examination that Martin's peripheral pulses were not manually palpable. This indicated to him immediately that there would be a high risk of pressure ulcers after the original surgery to fix the hip. He then went into some detail as to the multiple measures that were used in an attempt to prevent the development of these sores and discussed at length the post-operative orders that he had written for ongoing care at the nursing home for that same purpose. He emphasized that, to his knowledge, these orders had been carried out to the letter. On those occasions that he had seen the patient, all of the appropriate devices and medications were being used. When the first ulcers had formed on the leg that had been broken, Pat described all of the treatments that had been used to attempt to heal them and related how they had ultimately proved unsuccessful and forced the amputation of the limb. He went into great detail about how he, personally, had discussed the situation with Kathy Wennar and how they had mutually come to an agreement that the amputation would be the best way to proceed at that time. Basically, he had told her that it was his clinical impression that her husband's circulation was so poor that there was no reason to consider stenting (opening the blocked arteries with a balloon and placing a metal lattice in that spot to maintain the opening in the arteries) or a bypass since the distal circulation was so poor that opening the proximal arteries would be of little help anyway. It was his professional opinion that if either of these preliminary measures were undertaken in an attempt to save the leg that the wounds and ulcers still would not heal and then the same situation would have to be faced with a patient that was now further stressed and debilitated. Also, there was the fact that this was a demented patient who was unable to co-operate in his care. Such a course would be incredibly risky even with the most co-operative of patients and would certainly be contraindicated here. After this explanation of the alternatives, Kathy had been completely in agreement with the amputation.

Once the amputation was done, and the pathology of the amputated leg was reviewed, it became obvious that Dr. O'Connor's clinical judgement was correct. The pathology had shown severe peripheral vascular disease with over ninety-five percent blockage of the posterior tibial artery and severe distal disease as well.

At this point in the testimony, Chauncey used an overhead projector to put up on the screen in front of the jury a page of Gray's Anatomy, one of the most well known and respected anatomical texts in medicine, which represented the arterial circulation of the lower extremity. Without any previous coaching or practice, Pat quickly and firmly pointed out and named all of the arterial branches going down into the foot including and particularly the Medical Calcaneal Branch of the Posterior Tibial Artery which supplied the heel with blood. These were the arteries that supplied the area of the foot where Martin Wenna's pressure ulcer had occurred. And, from the pathology, it was clear that these arteries were involved with severe and end-stage peripheral vascular disease that had no medical cure. Thus, even if Dr. O'Connor's professional opinion were to be doubted here, we now had the final arbiter, the pathologist, giving the ultimate opinion that Martin Wennar's circulation was terrible and that, no matter how excellent the medical care he was given, the final outcome would be the same.

Pat then went on to say that he had informed Kathy at that time that there was a very strong likelihood that the same process would occur in the other leg where the circulation was just as poor and that he was very afraid that the leg as well would ultimately come to amputation. He stated quite firmly that Kathy understood what he was telling her and appeared to accept the information. There was no question of getting a second opinion or of doing further testing to more precisely delineate the circulation. In Pat's opinion, that had not been necessary.

Chauncey then asked Pat about the timing of pressure ulcers and about how quickly they could develop. Without going into much more detail, Pat explained that they could and often did appear quite rapidly and that a stage four ulcer might appear in a matter of twelve hours. At that point, Chauncey raised several questions as to whether or not, in his professional opinion, Pat could say if first Martin Wennar's leg might have been saved and second if his life might have been saved if some other treatment had been provided. Pat answered that he was quite sure that no treatment of any kind would have made a difference and that his opinion, once again, was bolstered by the unforgiving pathology of the involved limbs.

Finally, Chauncey asked Pat to describe the separate roles of the primary care physician and the consulting specialist in such a case as this. He brought out the fact that all of the post-op orders were written by the surgeon and that, though the primary care physician was aware of the orders and would also sign off on them, they were generally considered the responsibility of the consultant and not that of the primary care doctor. Chauncey then asked Dr. O'Connor if any questions had arisen as to his care of the patient, Martin Wennar, or if he had been named in any lawsuit brought by Kathy Wennar.

Pat said simply, "No."

At this point, since Chauncey's direct examination was complete and it was obvious that the cross examination would go on into the lunch break, Judge Prouder decided to adjourn the proceedings so that Jeff Peterson could have an uninterrupted cross, and we were out for lunch.

As had become our custom, Chauncey and I adjourned to Wendy's where we indulged in the usual fast food fare. Once again, I did the driving in the little yellow bug, leaving Chauncey's black Mercedes crouching in the parking lot like some hungry predator with an appetite of its own. At the restaurant, we ran into Phil Corrigan, the administrator of one of the other nursing homes in town, and we had a brief discussion with him about the use or non use of the merry walker, the bedside mattress and other devices that might sometimes be used for patients who were considered to be at risk for falls. From this discussion we gleaned a few interesting facts and more than a few interesting opinions.

While we ate, Chauncey and I naturally reviewed the case and our part in it. I, once again, expressed the opinion that so far there was really no case against me at all and it didn't make much sense to me that I was still in court listening to all this nonsense. Once again, Chauncey tried to convince me that my optimism was premature. He then told a long joke about his fantasy of a final summation that he might use if, indeed, the case against any of his clients proved to be hopelessly weak. Apparently, he had first heard the tale on the television show, South Park. In this particular episode, the cook had been accused falsely of murder and had hired Johnny Cochran as his lawyer. After a Kafkaesque trial where no good evidence had come into play, it was time for the final arguments to the jury. Johnny Cochran had addressed the jury while standing next to a large photo of Chewbacca, the wookie sidekick of Han Solo in the "Star Wars" movies. The summation went something like this:

"Now you may ask yourselves, ladies and gentlemen of the jury," says Johnny "just what am I doing standing up here next to this uncouth, hairy creature? On the one hand you have Johnny Cochran, suave, sophisticated, debonair, intelligent, good looking, friend and councilor to the famous and the well to do. On the other hand, you have this hairy animal, dirty, ugly, smelly, loud and stupid. So, what are we doing up here together, ladies and gentlemen? Well, I'll tell you. It's like this case. IT MAKES NO SENSE!" "And that is the Chewbacca defense," concluded Chauncey. "I've always wanted to use it in one of my summations but so far I haven't had the guts."

"Well," I replied, "perhaps this case might be the one." "You never know," said Chauncey.

Back in the courtroom, Pat O'Connor took the stand again, and Jeff Peterson began his cross examination. He started by reviewing some of Pat's biographical information which was harmless enough. Then he asked some specific questions concerning the pathological findings. In particular, he was interested in just how long it would take for severe atherosclerotic plugging to develop in an artery, and he asked if it might occur in a matter of weeks or months. Pat responded that such plugging occurred over relatively long periods of time, generally years rather than months. Jeff then asked whether or not it was true that lack of use of the involved limb might accelerate the obstructive process, and Pat said that it certainly could. Jeff next asked him to speculate as to whether or not in this case the forced bed rest secondary to the fractured hip might have played a role in the worsening of the circulatory status. To this question, Pat initially answered in the negative, but when Jeff pushed him further he admitted that there might have been some small effect along those lines.

The last series of questions that Jeff asked had to do with the fall and the resultant fracture and the effects of this on Martin Wennar's future health. He first asked if it could be said that, had Martin Wennar not fractured his hip, he would not have lost his leg. After some pause, Pat said that, in view of the severe peripheral vascular disease both by physical exam and by the pathology, it was his professional opinion that the amputation of Martin Wennar's limbs, both of them, was inevitable. He was then asked whether if it weren't for the fall and the fracture Martin Wennar's leg would have had to have been amputated at that time. When Pat responded that it probably would not have been, Jeff made the mistake of asking the next question, which was whether or not Pat could put any sort of time frame on the event. To this question the answer was that it would probably have been sooner rather than later. And that ended Jeff's cross.

It was becoming apparent what the plaintiff's argument was. The pressure ulcers, the amputation, the further pressure ulcers, the infection and ultimately the death of Martin Wennar had all been the direct result of the fall and the hip fracture. The nursing home was negligent in not preventing the fall. Therefore, since the fall was the proximate cause of all of those subsequent events, the nursing home was responsible for all of those subsequent events as well. This was the cornerstone of Jeff Peterson's case. And that was the conclusion of Jeff's cross examination of Patrick O'Connor, MD.

Dikembe then got up and attempted to minimize any damage that Pat's testimony may have done to the nursing home. He again reviewed the pathology, both gross and microscopic, and got Pat to note and emphasize the horrendous nature of the vascular abnormalities. He then emphasized that because of this severe disease, the final outcome was probably inevitable, and that the fall and the fracture, while certainly not helpful in this regard, would not have accelerated matters to any great degree. Pat agreed that this was the case.

At the conclusion of Pat's testimony there still was a fair amount of time left of the afternoon. Chauncey, however, was reluctant to call his next and final witness (That would be me.) at that time, and he requested of the judge that there be a recess until the next morning so that his examination would not be fragmented. The judge, probably eager like most of us, to have an early end to this day, agreed; and court was adjourned.

Chauncey and I had agreed that we would meet at my house that evening and review the records again and go over my testimony for the next day. I had some beer and soft drinks in the refrigerator and planned to pick up a pizza on the way home so that we could have a working dinner. As I was listening to Pat's testimony about the orthopedic orders for Martin Wennar after the fracture, I began to get the glimmer of an idea of just what might have happened that adequately explained the problem of the progress note and I was eager to get another look at the records before Chauncey came over. As soon as I got to the house, I stuck the pizza in the oven to keep it warm and raced upstairs to where I was keeping the cardboard storage boxes that contained all of the copies of the voluminous records on the Wennar case that I had in my possession. It took a few minutes to find the pertinent notes but, eventually, I did find them. And there, in black and white upon the page, was the answer to my dilemma.

WEDDING BELLS

"One's tootings at the wedding of the soul. Occur as they occur."

Wallace Stevens

T hen I opened the door to Chauncey that evening, I was grinning like a fool and couldn't stop myself.

"I found the answer." I said. "I know now what happened and have the documentation to prove that it wasn't my fault and that there was no malpractice on my part. It's all right in the records."

Chauncey's face initially showed surprise and shock but, as the import of what I had said sunk in, this was quickly replaced by a look of pure pleasure.

"Fantastic, Jon," he replied. "Tell me all about it as we eat. I'm starving. Standing up in court all day is an appetite enhancing experience. I find that it dries me out, tires me out and makes me ravenous."

We moved into the living room where I had set up the pizza on the large coffee table surrounded by file boxes that I had placed there after moving them downstairs. Among these were the Doctor's Progress Notes and the Nurses' Notes, the particular records in which I was interested. On top of these two boxes were the pages that I had marked with yellow highlighting to indicate the pertinent passages. I obtained a couple of Labatt Blue beers from the refrigerator and joined Chauncey at the coffee table. He had already taken a slice of pizza and was digging in. As he gratefully accepted the drink that I offered, I began my tale.

"When Pat O'Connor was discussing the post-op orthopedic orders I recalled that picture that one of the nurses had shown earlier. You remember the one. The one where Martin Wennar is sitting in a recliner with an odd smile on his face and his legs are strapped to an adductor pillow with his feet enclosed in those venodyne booties to protect them and to help prevent blood clots? This got me thinking. I went back and looked through the nurses' notes that dealt with the day shift when I made my rounds and wrote that note. This is what I found." I read him the note that had been written by the nurse that went around with me on my visit that day. It said, among other things, "integument-intact, no redness, ulcers or skin lesions circulation- intact, all pulses two plus, adductor pillow and venodynes in place."

"You see here, the nurse who came with me was either new in general or hadn't cared for Mr. Wennar in a while. She apparently had no idea that he had developed a pressure sore and so didn't tell me about it. Since putting on and taking off all that protective equipment is difficult in the best of circumstances and all but impossible with a demented and uncooperative patient, there would have been no reason for me to remove any of it to look at his skin unless the nurse had informed me that something was wrong. This means that there was no error on my part."

Chauncey took the papers in question from my hand and took some time to read them carefully, comparing the dates and times as he did so. After a short while, he looked up at me and smiled wolfishly.

"By George, Jon, I think you've got it. This just about completely gets you off the hook. You must realize, however, that it doesn't help the nursing home. In fact, it makes them look bad. Now we have one of their employees failing to report a significant medical condition to the physician of record. This on top of the fact that the plaintiff's alleged negligence in the fall, the proximal cause of all of these problems to begin with, might suggest a pattern of substandard care."

"Maybe so," I rejoined, "but the fact is that even if I had been notified it wouldn't have made a bit of difference in regard to the way things happened. The nursing home personnel were doing everything that could be done to locally treat the pressure sore and to maintain Mr. Wennar's nutritional status. And, for that matter, even if they weren't, you heard what Pat said about the pathology of his arterial circulation. He would have had to have that amputation regardless. I thought that some harm had to be demonstrated as an effect of any negligent act in order to obtain any sort of monetary compensation."

"Technically, you're right." said Chauncey. "But juries can often make decisions on the basis of their sympathy for the plaintiff or at least a damned good looking one."

"Besides," I countered, "we don't even have to bring any of this to the attention of the jury or Jeff Peterson. They don't seem to know about it in the first place and we don't have to tell them. If they do manage to find out about it, then we can explain it away by the evidence that we have in hand. If they don't find out about it, the question is moot. I would hate to be the one to provide Jeff and his crew with any ammunition that might bolster their case against the nursing home." At this point, Chauncey favored me with a withering glance and began to lecture me once again about the obligations and duties that existed between a lawyer and his client.

"You remember what I said earlier about being an advocate for the nursing home, Jon?" he queried. "I know that you're sympathetic to the nursing home's position, that you work there at times, have patients there and have friends on the staff. But, I am telling you once again and hopefully for the last time that it isn't your job to go to bat for them. Your job in this trial is to look out for number one, you. And my job is to be sure that you do and that I prepare you as best I can to do exactly that. Do you think that Dikembe wouldn't throw you to the wolves in a New York minute if he could deflect some of the nursing home's guilt onto you? Believe me, I've had dealings with him before on other trials. He wouldn't even pause to apologize before he stuck the knife in your heart. I'm not about to let Jeff Peterson have the advantage of bringing up that progress note first as a means of linking you to any poor medical outcome in regard to Martin Wennar. I don't care if we have the best way in the world to explain it away. We are going to bring it out first and deal with it effectively before any one of those jurors even gets a hint of it."

I didn't really think that Peterson could now hurt me with the progress note at this point, but I acted properly, cowed, and assured Chauncey that I would, once again, take his advice and fall into line. We addressed ourselves to the beer and pizza and went on to discuss other aspects of my defense such as the explanations that I was planning to give for the use or the lack of use of certain restraints and medications, the exact mechanism of development of pressure ulcers, and the various incident reports that I had or had not seen. At one point when I was particularly involved with looking at a part of the record that dealt with Martin Wennar's bladder and bowel control, I looked up to find Chauncey looking at me with a most speculative look on his face.

"What?" I asked.

"You know, Jon," he responded. "I think that I might be able to make a deal right now with Jeff that would get you dismissed from the case even before it went to the jury. Really, in spite of his bulldog aura, Jeff is a good fellow and has been straight with me in the past. I know that I can trust him to do what he says he will."

To say that this surprised me would be an understatement. Here we had just found the piece of evidence that exonerated me completely, and my lawyer was talking about making some kind of deal with the enemy. Was this kosher? Was this ethical? Was this even legal? I expressed my concerns to Chauncey who quickly reassured me that there was nothing illegal about it (He never did address the ethical part.) and that opposing lawyers made such deals all the time.

"Well," I said, "just what would I have to do? I'm not sure that I could, in good faith, go along with any of Jeff's suggestions in this regard."

"Fair enough." agreed Chauncey. "I'll tell you what. Why don't I just call him right now and ask him if he has anything in mind."

I agreed that it couldn't hurt to talk and see what Peterson might have to offer, but I remained very skeptical that anything positive would come from such an inquiry. Still, one never knows, and Chauncey proceeded to pick up the phone and dial the number of a room at a local hotel where Jeff had set up his headquarters for the duration of the trial. In contrast, Chauncey was driving back and forth daily from his home in Burlington.

Chauncey and Jeff bantered back and forth for a while before getting down to the business at hand, but it was no more than a few minutes before Chauncey was able to relay to me a possible compromise that might get Jeff to dismiss the case against me the very next day. Jeff asked if I could say that Martin Wennar would not have lost his leg if he had not had the fall and the fracture. I balked at this, replying that the peripheral vascular disease was so bad and there was incontrovertible evidence that this was the case with the pathology available from the amputated limb that there was no question in my mind that he would have lost the leg sooner or later anyway. In fact, this is precisely what Dr. O'Connor had said when he testified. Jeff then asked if I could say that Martin Wennar would not have lost his leg at that time if he hadn't had the fall and the fracture. Now, keep in mind that Dr. O'Connor had already given that opinion and I felt quite comfortable with it as it was the truth as far as I could tell. I wasn't sure how much mileage Jeff Peterson could get out of this statement but that was his problem after all. I agreed that I would be willing to say this and Jeff agreed that if I did so on the stand the next day he would dismiss me from the case at the end of my testimony. Again, I wasn't sure just what value I was getting here as there was no case at all against me that I could see but the two lawyers, my lawyer in particular, convinced me that this was the way to go. We all gave verbal assurances that this would be the agreement. Chauncey hung up the phone and congratulated me about getting out of the case no matter what would happen the next day. Frankly, by this time, I was more than ready to testify and to tell the jury my side of the story as well as to explain to them some of the important medical issues that were relevant to the outcome of the case. After Chauncey left, I played some bridge on the Internet for a couple of hours and then went to bed. I didn't sleep well. Thoughts of my upcoming time on the witness stand kept intruding all night long, and I went over and over in my head the things that I would say and the answers that I might give to any conceivable question. Eventually, I must have slept because I remember getting up to the ringing of the alarm the next morning. Rather I felt energized and eager. It was time for me to tell my story.

WEDDING BELLS

"One's tootings at the wedding of the soul. Occur as they occur."

Wallace Stevens

T was sitting in the witness box looking out over a courtroom that was largely empty but for the players in the suits and the jurors. There was one lean middle-aged man sitting at the back of the room whom I didn't recognize and who, I'm sure, hadn't been there in the earlier days of the trial. For the next several minutes, my imagination ran rampant as I speculated on who this person might be. Was he a paid investigator for Jeff Peterson who had unearthed some heretofore unknown piece of evidence that would turn the trial on its head? Was he privy to some phone records that would prove that I had been notified multiple times by nursing home personnel regarding the falls of Martin Wennar? To my consternation, I actually started to sweat. At that point, I felt so guilty that I felt that I must be guilty of something. The truth, of course, was much more prosaic and had nothing whatsoever to do with my guilt or innocence. I was to learn later that this was a trial lawyer who had dropped by to observe the proceedings and to possibly pick up some tips on the proper way of going about the suing of nursing homes in the state of Vermont.

Apparently, this case was something of a test case for the state as the industry had largely made its reputation in larger states such as Florida where the nursing home population was much larger. In retrospect, I was glad that such a debacle for the prosecution was tagged as the test case for the state because this might mean that plaintiff's lawyers would be somewhat discouraged from bringing such cases in the future. I was, no doubt, overly optimistic in this regard. In any event, at the time of my testimony the identity of this spectator was unknown to me, and I could only speculate wildly as to just who he might be and what he was doing there.

Chauncey began my testimony in the casual manner with which I was quite comfortable by that time having sat through the testimony of many others. We went through my education, training, past and present employment, place of residence and some personal data such as whether or not I was married and how many children I had. Chauncey established the facts that I had a substantial geriatric practice and followed patients in all three of the nursing homes in St. Albans as well as the two custodial care homes in Richford. He emphasized that I was quite comfortable and familiar with caring for demented patients in similar circumstances as those of Martin Wennar and that I had been doing this for a considerable number of years. We also established that I had only one other malpractice suit brought against me and that was over fifteen years ago, and that I had been acquitted in a jury trial at that time. Chauncey then proceeded to question about Martin Wennar himself. We started at the very beginning when I had inherited him as a patient when he came to stay at Madonna of the Mountain, and traced his history from that time until his death in the hospital. Under Chauncey's guidance, I enumerated the various aspects of Mr. Wennar's care in each facility and in regard to every incident that was reported to me. I spoke of the various tests that had originally been done to assure that he had an irreversible dementing process and not some metabolic problem such as hypothyroidism or some other neurological problem such as a brain tumor. I described the urological studies that were done to be sure that the reason for Mr. Wennar's wandering in the night was not necessarily related to a need to go to the bathroom. We then moved on to describe all of the interventions that had been tried to prevent him from falling and to try to ensure that if he did fall he would not get hurt.

Under Chauncey's questioning, I explained to the jurors how Martin's dementia had altered the workings of his brain so that the higher brain centers could no longer prevent the lower brain centers from exerting their will on his body. This was a concept known as "disinhibition" where lower brain centers would take over and the patient would perform actions that he never would have if he were in his right mind. For example, the jury members would probably get an urge multiple times during the trial to get up and walk around, but their higher brain functions, knowing the serious business of sitting and listening carefully to the evidence, would not permit this activity. Mr. Wennar, in the same situation, would simply get up and walk around. This was a partial explanation of why he was always getting up in the nursing home situation.

I then went on to list and explain all of the interventions that had been tried to keep Martin Wennar from falling. For the first time, I established that the mattress at the side of the bed had been tried at Madonna of the Mountain long before he had gone to La Place D'Espere. Of course, it hadn't worked because Mr. Wennar's falls were not those of falling out of bed but rather falls that took place after he was up and walking. Actually, the mattress at the side of the bed was dangerous in this situation because it now functioned as a curb, a partial barrier over which the ambulating patient might very well trip and injure himself.

I then discussed the advantages and disadvantages of various sedative and tranquillizing medications, emphasizing that these had problems of their own in that they often "doped up" the patient so that he actually might be more prone to falls while taking them. Also, they might add to his confusion, diminish his appetite and interact adversely with other medications that he was taking. If the individual patient was, indeed, mostly falling out of bed at night or having the majority of his falls during the night time hours, cautious sedation might be successfully used since the patient was supposed to be sleeping at that time anyway. In the case of Martin Wennar, however, this did not apply.

At this juncture, I addressed myself directly to the specific interventions that Dr. Howard Friedman had suggested that I was negligent for not using. These included belt restraints, the use of lap tables and the merry walker, a device similar to that in which young children are often placed before they have learned to walk. The merry walker suspends the patient from a hip harness in the middle of a large plastic ring or doughnut which is mounted on wheels so that the patient may move about in a seated position but is unable to fall because he is in the middle of that plastic ring. I explained that this was part of the reason that enlightened nursing homes had the "no restraint" policy. These devices are all quite dangerous. The belt restraints and the lap tables can injure patients by putting pressure on inappropriate areas such as the neck if they slip down in their chairs, and it has happened that patients have hanged themselves in these devices. Also, the lap tables in particular are hard and unyielding, and patients can get bruises and skin tears from hitting themselves against them. The merry walker, a device that Dr. Friedman had specifically mentioned by name, is especially dangerous both to the patient and to any patients around him. Think about it. Here you have a confused demented individual now seated in a large mobile plastic doughnut that he can propel at some speed down the corridors of a nursing home where other elderly folk are attempting to walk with the aid of canes and walkers. When Chauncey and I had discussed this the night before, I had suggested that I might use the phrase "bowling for seniors" right about here, but Chauncey had assured me that this would be rather flip and inflammatory so I desisted. The jury got the idea even so.

Next came the discussion of the stage four ulcer, just what that meant and exactly how these ulcers were formed. I emphasized emphatically that there was no way even the most astute observer could detect that an ulcer was forming until it actually appeared and that the first appearance of the ulcer might quite easily be at stage four since the tissue had died from the inside out. Then the critical matter of the arterial supply in general and the specific tremendously compromised arterial supply as documented first by Dr. O'Connor's physical examination and clinical impression and then by the gross and microscopic pathology results of Martin Wennar was brought out. With this as background, I noted the fact that very little time would be involved in engendering a pressure ulcer in the heels of this particular patient. In fact, one might argue that an ulcer could theoretically occur in this patient with no outside pressure at all or even minimal pressure for only a few minutes because the baseline circulation was so poor. After all, if the artery was completely blocked from the inside the tissue it supplied, it would die whether or not there was any external pressure at all. I do believe that the jury members understood what I was getting at here as well.

Lastly, Chauncey and I went over all of the incident reports one by one and addressed each as it came up. The ones that I had not signed, we dismissed. All of the others we demonstrated that I had addressed appropriately and had initiated some plan of action. Without exception this proved to be the case. There was not one incident report that I had signed off on that I hadn't made some changes in treatment or ordered some tests to clarify the situation.

And now it was time for Chauncey to bring up the anomalous progress note, which he did, and for me to explain it away by reading the nurse's note for that shift, which I did. I elaborated on the situation by alluding to the photograph that the jury had previously seen and emphasizing the point that I had relied on the nurse to update me as to ongoing problems and that Mr. Wennar's protective armament had insured that I was unable to see for myself that there was a problem at all. It appeared that we had accounted for everything and that all the ground had been covered. Of course, we knew nothing of what evil lurked in the minds of Dikembe Nkomo and Jeff Peterson.

Dikembe's cross examination was actually quite benign. He concentrated on the incident reports and got me to admit that many of these were written during the day when I would naturally be in my office, and, unless I was on a vacation at those times, theoretically a nurse at the home should have been able to reach me by telephone. I could only respond that I had no recollection of such notification and that the signature on those reports was not mine. He expressed some exasperation at this answer which I suspect he considered an evasion, but the truth is that that's the way it was. There was actually little else that he could do, and, after some further attempt to cast doubt on my interpretation of the record, he gave up.

The end of the long ordeal was now in sight, and Jeff Peterson rose to conduct what I thought at that time would be the last cross examination in the case. He wasted little time on preliminaries and did not even bother to revisit any of the issues that I had already explained away in my initial testimony. In fact, the first question that he asked was the one that we had discussed and that I had agreed to answer in a specific way. But, wait one minute, that was not exactly what happened.

"Dr. Ziebaska," intoned the estimable Mr. Peterson, "would you say, in your professional opinion, and as Dr. O'Connor has already testified that, if Martin Wennar had not fallen and broken his hip that he would still have his leg and be alive today?"

There was a short pause as I tried to collect myself before answering. What was Peterson doing? He had asked not the second question, the one to which we had agreed, but the first question, the one that I had originally said that I could not answer in the affirmative because it was not supported by the anatomical evidence! Had he made a mistake and simply gotten confused in the heat of battle? Had he done this deliberately hoping that I wouldn't notice and would give him the answer that he wanted? And what would the jury think. They had heard the testimony of Dr. O'Connor and knew exactly what he had said. Or even if they didn't remember exactly, they could have the transcript read back to them and would certainly know them. Even if I had wanted to, which I didn't, I could not give an affirmative reply to Jeff Peterson's question. The jury would make me out to be either a fool or a liar. All of these thoughts rocketed quickly through my brain in that short interval of time, but I finally had to answer.

"That's not what Dr. O'Connor said." I replied.

For a moment, I thought that Jeff was going to fall on the floor. His face turned a sickly shade of white and his mouth opened and shut a few times like a bass thrown up on dry land. To give him credit, he recovered quickly and immediately posed the correct question.

"Would you say that had not Mr. Wennar fallen and broken his hip he would not have lost his leg at that time?"

To which question I was happy to say yes. That was it. Jeff Peterson was done. My part in the trial was over. I wasn't sure whether or not Peterson would live up to his agreement and dismiss me from the case since the agreement hadn't exactly come to fruition the way it was anticipated, but I was confident that I had told the truth and that I had done my best to explain that truth to the twelve citizens who were sitting in judgment. The rest was out of my hands.

Court was adjourned for lunch at that point, and as I came down from the witness stand I passed the plaintiff's table where Jeff was sitting. He scowled at me and said something to the effect that he had asked the question exactly as we had agreed, but I couldn't understand even that part of it precisely, and the rest of what he said was lost in the noise of the departing jurors. I decided that whatever it was that he had said or thought, I wasn't going to let it worry me. He had asked the wrong question, and he had received what he considered to be the wrong answer. To my way of thinking, he had gotten just what he deserved. I said as much to Chauncey when I reached my seat. He appeared to be upset, but at least he did agree with me that I had no choice in the way that I had reacted on the stand. He too wasn't sure what would transpire in regard to the agreement, but he said that he would talk to Jeff and try to make some sense of it all. He then left the courtroom leaving me to find a different partner for lunch. I would have been more than happy to eat lunch with Gail, but she had already left with Dikembe, the two of them in earnest conversation, and hadn't even acknowledged my presence as she passed so that opportunity was lost. As it happened, I went to lunch alone that day.

When I returned, earlier than usual because I had no one to talk to, the courtroom was empty but for Chauncey who had apparently been waiting for me. He motioned me into one of the side rooms and closed the door.

"Jeff was really pissed." he said. "He seems to think that he asked the right question, the one that you both agreed to, and that you gave him the wrong answer."

"Bullshit." I replied. "Not only did he ask the wrong question, he related it to a previous answer that Pat O'Connor gave that wasn't the right answer either. Is he incompetent or just plain stupid? Does he think that the jury members are stupid? Why all they would have to do is to review the transcript of Pat's testimony to see that he didn't say what Jeff said he did, and then they would think that both Jeff and I were stupid or incompetent. He can't blame me for this. It's his own damn fault."

"Okay, okay, I'll try to see what I can do to remedy the situation. Maybe we can arrange it so that Jeff can ask you some further questions and we can do some damage control."

"What do you mean by that, Chaunce? I thought I was done here.

What further questions would you have in mind?"

"Well, I talked to Jeff at some length during the lunch recess, and he says that, if you could truthfully say that, in your opinion, you couldn't say for sure whether or not Wennar would still have his leg today if he hadn't had the fall he would dismiss the case against you."

At that point, I was getting more than a little hot under the collar, and I could hear my voice beginning to rise.

"Wait a minute now. My job here is to tell the truth as I see it, not to shade the truth to favor the plaintiff or the nursing home. You're starting to piss me off here, Chaunce."

"Okay, I'll tell you what. Just agree to throw in that little bit of doubt, that you really can't say for sure if Wennar would still have his leg, and I think I can get the deal back. Do you think you could do that?"

I thought about it for a few minutes and then came to the conclusion that it wouldn't be dishonest to admit to some degree of uncertainty in almost any medical matter.

"I guess I could do that. But you be sure that Jeff knows that it was his fault that things didn't work out here initially and that he's the one who screwed up. Try to reason with him on that point. He may be less aggravated if he comes to that realization."

"I'll work on it." said Chauncey. "Let's go."

With that, he opened the door, and we stepped out into the courtroom. Sitting at the front desk on the left hand side of the room was Dikembe Nkomo who turned towards us and addressed himself to Chauncey.

"We have to go and see Judge Prouder right now." he said.

"What do you mean?" asked Chauncey.

"Just what I said." replied Dikembe. "We have to go and see Judge Prouder and talk to him about the possibility of undue influence in regard to Dr. Ziebaska's testimony in this case. Come on."

"Okay." said Chauncey. And without further ado, both of them walked quickly to the door at the front of the room and disappeared through it. Neither one of them had said a word to me. Soon thereafter, Jeff Peterson came walking in one of the back doors of the courtroom and also disappeared into the Judge's chambers. He also did not so much as glance in my direction.

Now what? All sorts of ideas were going through my head at this point. Was what Chauncey and Jeff were doing illegal? Had they simply lied to me and taken advantage of my lack of legal knowledge to embroil me in their illegal activities? What did this mean in terms of the trial? Would the judge declare a mistrial? That would be nothing short of a disaster for me as it would mean yet another week spent in a courtroom not only wasting more valuable time but also producing a whole new measure of anxiety and aggravation. To say the least, I was concerned, very concerned.

As is usual when one is waiting for an important decision, time took a holiday, stretching out lazily and endlessly as the lawyers and the judge participated in their arcane and secret ceremonies behind the huge wooden chamber door. The jury remained out as they would only be called in when the situation had been resolved. Gail came back from lunch, and the two of us spent some more time together which might have been pleasant enough had I not been on tenterhooks. Since she knew even less than I did about what was going on and I didn't think that I would have enough time to fill her in, we talked about other things than the trial. I hadn't been out to visit Cassie in a few days, and Gail was able to bring me up to date in that regard. Actually, Cassie was status quo so there wasn't much to say in that respect either. Erin, Gail's daughter, had just recently gotten her learner's permit so we commiserated on the dangers of teenage drivers especially when they are piloting their parent's vehicles. I related the sad but true tale of one of the women against whom I sometimes played duplicate bridge. This lady had five children, and every one of the five, without exception, had totaled the family car as they grew up and began to drive. Five children and five vehicles totaled. Amazingly, none of the five had been seriously injured so the tale wasn't nearly as sad as it might have been. Still, that's a lot of insurance premiums there. After a while, we ran out of things to talk about so we just sat there in companionable silence waiting for the trial to start again.

And eventually, it did start again. The chamber doors opened abruptly, and the lawyers strode out briskly as if they had someplace to go. As Chauncey came to our table, he gave me a wink and said that everything was going to be fine. The judge had agreed that Jeff could call another witness even though his case had already been presented. I assumed from what Chauncey had said that that witness would be me and that I would be asked the question about the proximate cause of the amputation yet again. It turned out that I was wrong.

Jeff Peterson did, in fact, rise to call another witness to the stand, but it was not me that he named. Instead, he recalled Kathy Wennar! Kathy, more beautiful and luminous than ever, today wearing yet another little black dress (She had worn a different one every day of the trial. Each was simple, elegant and expensive, and each showed her off to best advantage, though I am not sure that she could look bad in, or out for that matter, of any dress.), walked proudly to the front of the courtroom and again took her seat in the witness box. She smiled brilliantly and prepared herself to answer Jeff's questions. There would be no tears today.

To my amazement, Jeff asked Kathy about the social work-er whose office was off from the front lobby of the nursing home, and who had testified that she had never ever seen Kathy come in and visit her husband. Kathy stated that she knew this social worker quite well and, in fact, was very good friends with her. She related that she and the social worker would often go down togeth-er to visit Martin in his room. She said that the social worker had told her many times that she would always be there for her and that she could count on her. It was all the more devastating when that person had actually testified against her in court.

I was absolutely astounded when I heard this testimony from Kathy. Who would believe such a thing? It was just too bi-zarre. What did Peterson think that he was doing? I wondered if the judge had told him that he had to deliberately put Kathy in a bad light to ensure that he lost the case. Could he be serious? It seemed unbelievable to me, but he did look serious enough. Still, I couldn't imagine the jury buying this.

Jeff then asked Kathy what possible motive the social worker might have to lie to the court in her sworn testimony. To this question, Kathy responded that the social worker had a good job at the nursing home and no doubt wanted to keep it. Again, I was floored. Here was the plaintiff flat out claiming that one of the witnesses who had put her in a bad light was manufacturing her testimony to keep her job. If Jeff had wanted to lose the case, I don't think he could have found a better way than this.

And that was the last testimony that was heard in the case of Kathy Wennar vs. La Place D'Espere Nursing Home and Jon Ziebaska, M.D. Neither Chauncey nor Dikembe had any questions on cross examination and why should they? The plaintiff's case had already self destructed. There was no need to kick it while it was down. The judge said that closing arguments would be set for Monday and that the case would then go to the jury. He then adjourned the court for the day and the weekend.

That evening I received a call from Chauncey who informed me that the case against me had been dismissed with prejudice which meant that not only was I off the hook but that this lawsuit could never be brought against me again. The nursing home, however, was still in it, and the fate of La Place D'Espere would be decided by the jury, one way or another. Without doubt I was thankful and relieved, but I was also puzzled, angry and sympathetic to the nursing home and the people who worked there. I asked Chauncey if there was any possibility that I could sue the plaintiff's lawyers for wrongful prosecution since they had brought me to court for no good reason that I could see, other than to attempt to use me as a weapon against the nursing home and they had kept me there for an entire week even though their client had admitted on the very first day that she thought that I "had done nothing wrong." And all of this had been done without even hearing my side of the story, without deposing me. Chauncey informed me that it would be useless to sue the lawyers because they had the perfect defense. Since they were only lawyers, ignorant of medical matters, they had to rely on qualified "experts" to tell them whether or not a physician had committed an act of malpractice. If the expert opined that the physician had done so, the lawyer could then bring the suit in good faith having relied upon that expert opinion. Thus, the lawyer himself would now be immune to charges of malicious prosecution, and there could be no remedy for the defendant under the law. It seemed like a dirty deal to me, but it appeared that there would be no satisfaction other than that of getting off. I told Chauncey that I guess I would have to live with that, thanked him for his efforts on my behalf, wished him well in the future, and was almost in the process of hanging up the phone when he interjected.

"Oh, and by the way, Jon, Transcorp has decided that they will cover you in this affair after all and will pay all of the lawyers' fees."

"Sure, now that they know they have nothing to lose." I laughed bitterly.

"Please give them my most insincere thanks, Chaunce." Actually, this was better news than I would admit as the lawyers' fees, though undoubtedly a pittance to a big insurance company like Transcorp were no small matter to me. I then thanked Chauncey for his efforts on my behalf, said my good-byes, hung up the phone and went promptly to bed. I slept well. There were no dreams that night.

THE BEGINNING

"Cry 'Havoc' and let slip the dogs of war."

Shakespeare

The next morning, as if in synchrony with my mood, the sun burst up into an azure sky and the temperature soared into the upper sixties, a gorgeous spring day in northern Vermont. Without conscious thought, I was into my running clothes and out the door to do the daily five miler that had become my habit. These soft spring days along with the days of early to mid fall were engineered for running. The humidity was low, the temperatures mild but not too warm and the sun felt good upon the face as I raced along. Although in my case the word race was probably not that appropriate, it still felt good to be alive and free of lawsuits. As I ran along, I naturally began to think back over the trial and to try to make some sense of what had happened. It dawned on me just then that, in the excitement of having the case against me dismissed, I had completely neglected to ask Chauncey some of the many questions that I had. For example, how exactly had it come about that the lawsuit was dismissed? Was it at the request of Jeff Peterson as per our agreement that he apparently felt that I had broken? Was it as a result of my lawyer making yet another motion for dismissal that the judge had at last granted? Was it by fiat of Judge Prouder because of the collusive activities of Chauncey and Jeff? And why had Kathy Wennar been put up on the stand again as the last witness to accuse a relatively minor witness in the case of lying to keep her job? These were just the most pressing of the questions that I had. I made a mental note to call Chauncey and ask him about all this. Also, I wasn't done trying to find some way to obtain some measure of revenge against Jeff Peterson for bringing this non case against me in the first place. Chauncey had nixed any thoughts I might have had about malicious prosecution but what about incompetence or legal malpractice? Could there be some way that I might make that work for me? I would have to think about it.

Getting back to the house, I ate a quick breakfast of cereal and orange juice, took a shower, and drove off to La Place D'Espere. During the trial, I had not been to see Cassie at all; and even though she had long since stopped communicating with me, I had been assiduous in visiting her almost daily up to that point. I wondered if she had missed me though Gail had told me that the nursing home personnel had noticed no appreciable difference in her behavior when I had stopped showing up. Indeed, when I got there Cassie barely looked up and almost immediately returned her gaze to some far distant place of which only she was cognizant. The only word left in her once formidable vocabulary was "yes," but this morning she said nothing. I had begun to tell her about the trial, more to hear my own voice and to fill the void of silence that separated us when Gail came into the room. She said that she had been trying to finish up some paperwork but had seen me come in and that she wanted to congratulate me on having the case dismissed. I thanked her for that and proceeded to tell her the whole story of the deal that Jeff and Chauncey had made, the mistake that Jeff had made in the questioning, the actions of Dikembe after he apparently had overheard Chauncey and me discussing my further testimony, and the mysterious second appearance on the witness stand of Kathy Wennar. I also added in the warnings that Chauncey had given me concerning the untrustworthiness of Dikembe Nkomo and the contrasting endorsement of Jeff Peterson that he had tendered. What did she make of all this?

At first she should only shake her head in confusion, but after a while she came up with a theory that may have had some merit. She advanced the idea that Chauncey, who was obviously extremely ambitious and was angling for a partnership in his present firm without much success to date, may have been looking for a position in the much bigger and more prestigious firm of Peterson, Falkner and Beiderbeck, perhaps even a partnership if he could manage it. It would make sense that if he could swing a very lucrative case Peterson's way this might go a long way toward achieving those ends. He could easily rationalize the ethical problems by assuring himself that he could do all this and still provide me with the best defense, which, in the final analysis, was his maximum, if not his only, obligation. If Dikembe and the nursing home suffered, well that was of little concern. The nursing home had insurance, and Dikembe was the enemy and a black man on top of that. This sounded quite Machiavellian to me; but I must admit, it did make some kind of sense given the events that had occurred. But what about the strange last minute testimony of Kathy Wennar? What was Gail's take on that one?

Again, she paused for some moments to think about it, but the best idea that she could come up with only mirrored my own. Either Jeff was even more incompetent than we thought, or Judge Prouder had persuaded him that it would be in his interest to sabotage his own case. This sounded even weirder to me than the Chauncey partnership conspiracy theory but we were theorizing the best we could with the facts that we had.

I then asked her how she and Dikembe were feeling about their chances in the upcoming verdict. She said that they both were very optimistic and couldn't imagine the jury returning anything but a "not guilty" verdict but that Dikembe was still concerned that the nursing home was at risk because there was no getting around the fact that Wennar had fallen under their care and that he had a previous and well known history of falls. If the jury bought the idea that the nursing home was negligent despite best efforts, then the theory of proximate cause would mandate that the nursing home was responsible for all of the subsequent bad things that happened. Six million dollars was a lot of risk. Dikembe had told her that, even now, at this late stage of the trial, there was tremendous pressure placed on him by the insurance carrier and even some pressure by the owner of the nursing home to settle the case for a few hundred thousand dollars. This would partially satisfy the plaintiff and her lawyers but would be well within the parameters of settlement that the insurance company could live with. Dikembe felt that this was a rather short sighted position to take as it would open the door for other nursing home suits along similar lines, would encourage the lawyers who, at the worst, would at least make some money for doing a terrible job of litigation, and because of the first two things, would dramatically raise the cost of insurance for all nursing homes and thus the rates that all nursing homes would then have to charge their patients. He was determined to see the case all the way to the verdict if he had his way. I told Gail to give Dikembe my regards and to tell him that I was rooting for both of them. She promised that she would.

Cassie had continued to remain silent through this entire exchange and might just as well have been another piece of furniture for all the reaction that she demonstrated. The saddest thing was that but for the lack of animation in her eyes she still looked the way she always had. On the surface, she was still my Cassie sitting there in that chair. As always, it was very hard for me to admit that she was gone.

Neither Gail nor I even mentioned Cassie's name during that whole interchange, and as we said our goodbyes, neither one of us included Cassie in the leave taking. It was only later that I realized this.

Sunday, as advertised, was a day of rest. I took the time to mow the lawn for the first time that year and to do some of the usual spring chores that come up after a typical Vermont winter. Again, like the day before, the weather was great, and it was good to be outdoors in it. Strangely enough, I didn't think much about the trial that day. Even though the final verdict had not yet been rendered, I found that the trauma of it was just starting to fade from my mind. The rest of the day was running, bagpiping, walking the dog and reading. All the while, as I went through these pleasant activities of leisure, I was considering ways and means of getting my pound of flesh from Jeff Peterson.

When Monday came, I was quickly back into my usual routine, I made rounds at the hospital where I found that two new admissions had come to my service over the weekend. One was a fifty-six year old smoker with a family history of heart disease who had been admitted to the CCU with classical cardiac chest pain. He had been ruled out for a heart attack by serial EKGs and enzymes, but his clinical history and risk factors were so compelling that I felt that a cardiology consult and probably a cardiac catheterization were in order. The other admission was a ninety-two year old woman who came in with a community acquired left lower lobe pneumonia. She was doing well and was already improving on intravenous antibiotics in spite of her age, and I was hoping to transition her to oral antibiotics and to send her home in another day or two. My other in-house patients were also all doing well for a change so rounds were fairly benign, and I got to the clinic early enough to deal with the weekend mail and the paperwork left over from Friday before the first scheduled patient put in an appearance. From there, I didn't have much time to think about anything but the matters at hand. At about eleven forty-five, Rachel informed me that Gail Casperson was on the phone, and I picked up the receiver.

"Jon," she said, "the verdict was not guilty. The jury only deliberated forty-five minutes."

"Fantastic!" I replied. "Were there any surprises?"

"Only on the faces of Kathy Wennar and Jeff Peterson." She answered. "The summations to the jury were pretty cut and dried and a lot shorter than I had anticipated. Jeff didn't even speak about pressure ulcers, nutritional deficiencies, lack of care plans or any of those other things that he had listed in his initial presentation. He restricted himself to the fall and the hip fracture and just harped endlessly on how the nursing home was responsible and negligent because they hadn't prevented the fall. Dikembe then also concentrated mostly on the fall, though he did go through a long list of caretaking measures that the nursing home had implemented as representative of the overall care that the patient received there. He ended up by saying that the only way the fall could realistically have been prevented would have been to have a dedicated person be with the patient at all times, day and night, and that the nursing home just could not reasonably be expected to absorb that cost. He also emphasized that Mrs. Wennar had the means and could easily have hired extra personnel to perform that function but chose not to. I think that made a big impression on the jury."

"It would appear that you are right, my dear." I retorted. "Thanks for telling me. I appreciate it. This makes my day. I only wish that I had been there to see the look on Jeff's face in particular. It does me a world of good to think about the money that they laid out for expert witnesses and other expenses that they are now going to have to eat. It couldn't have happened to a nicer guy. With luck, this will set back the industry of spurious suits a decade or two, at least in this state." With that, we said our goodbyes and I hung up the phone. All's well that ends well.

Still, there were a lot of things about the case that continued to nag at me. I put in calls to Chauncey, Dikembe and Judge Prouder when I got some free time at lunch. Chauncey never did return my call and I never spoke to him again. When Dikembe called back, I congratulated him on the verdict, told him that I thought that he had done a great job and asked him if I could take him, or him and his wife, out to dinner so that we could discuss the case. He thanked me for my congratulations and told me that he would check his schedule and get back to me about the dinner thing. He never did call back, and as of this writing, I have not seen or spoken to him again. Judge Prouder's clerk of courts returned my call in the judge's stead. I told him that I needed to speak to the judge concerning some matters of the recent court case that were deeply disturbing to me and that I needed the judge's advice. He gave me an appointment to see the judge that next Wednesday at ten in the morning.

THE BEGINNING

"Cry 'Havoc' and let slip the dogs of war."

Shakespeare

As I sat across a mammoth desk from Judge Charles Prouder, I couldn't help but think that the inner chambers were something of a let down. There were no magic mirrors, crystal balls or even a phoenix perched over by the door. Chambers was simply a large room with a large desk, walls lined with book shelves which in turn were filled with what appeared to be legal tomes and a few plush chairs facing the aforementioned desk. There was what appeared to be a bathroom off the east side of the room. I say "appeared" because I never got to go in there and so am only guessing. Whether there was also a shower or a Jacuzzi is also open to conjecture.

I started the conversation by joking with the judge that the real reason that I wanted this appointment to talk to him was so that I could finally see for myself the mysterious insides of "chambers" where all the lawyers and judges went for intimate discussions during those courtroom breaks. This did get a laugh from him so I knew that we were off to a good start. I forged ahead.

I began by recounting to the judge the entire story of the deal that Chauncey had originally suggested to me and to which Jeff had agreed. No part of which I was aware was left out, and I was careful to include the way in which I had agreed to shade my own testimony to comply with the wishes of the plaintiff's attorney so that the judge wouldn't think that I was trying to put the best face on my part in the conspiracy. Basically, I laid the facts as I understood them out before the judge and asked that he comment upon them. I told him that, not being a lawyer myself, I had relied on the advice of my lawyer who had assured me that these deals are made all the time and that there was nothing illegal or unethical about them.

When I had concluded my tale, the judge leaned back in his seat, looked me in the eye and said, "Look, Doctor, you may have noticed that there are three tables in that courtroom. Not two tables. Three tables. This is for a reason. The litigants sitting at those three tables are three separate parties. Even though two of them may be named as defendants in a lawsuit, this doesn't mean that they are in it together or that they are buddies. As your lawyer told you, his job is to defend your interests in any way that he can short of breaking the law himself. This means that he is allowed to talk to any of the other litigants and to make any deal with them that he so desires, provided, of course, that he doesn't subvert the truth or do anything that is outside the law. As long as you are not required to give false testimony, you may shade your statements in any way that you find compatible with your conscience. That is the legal truth of it. You see all of these books on the shelves around you? They are filled with the letter of the law. Everything about the law, however, is not in these books, many though they may be. There remains room for gamesmanship in the courtroom. There always has been, and I suspect that there always will be. Jeff Peterson certainly understands this as he alluded to the concept of gamesmanship several times when we were discussing certain rulings that I was making in here. So, to directly answer your question, yes, what you lawyer did was perfectly legal and what Jeff Peterson did was also. You may not have liked it, and it may have made you uncomfortable, but it wasn't something that would get you in trouble with the legal system. If a third party, in this case the lawyer for the nursing home, gets cut out and is victimized by the deal, that is just another example of gamesmanship. He is also allowed to make his own deals within the system you see."

I thanked the judge for his information and told him that it made me feel a lot better to know that I hadn't been led astray by my legal counsel since I was beginning to think that I couldn't trust my own lawyer at that point, and he acknowledged my thanks with a nod of his head. He then looked at me expectantly as if encouraging me to go on.

"Also, Judge Prouder, I am just wondering how it is that the plaintiff's lawyer can keep me in court for an entire week without even really bringing a reasonable case against me. First of all, Peterson never deposed me so he didn't bother to get my side of the story before the trial that I had done nothing wrong in his opinion. Thirdly, except for some vague allegations that were made by Dr. Howard Friedman on that videotape, I was never accused of anything by anyone in that courtroom. Still, I was required to give up a week of my life when I could have been productively seeing patients, doing some good and making some money. Instead, I am forced to waste my time for no good reason. If it was the case that Peterson needed me as a witness against the nursing home and intended to pit me against them, then he should have simply called me as an expert witness. I could have testified for the hour or two that would have taken and been done with it."

The judge paused briefly and again brought his gaze to bear on me directly.

"I absolutely agree with you here, Doctor Ziebaska. Unfortunately, our legal system is such that these plaintiff's lawyers can just about do anything they want with impunity. There is no incentive for them to do otherwise. What we need is tort reform, something along the order of what they have in Great Britain where, if a lawsuit is judged ultimately to be without merit, the lawyer that brings that suit must at least pay the court costs of anyone involved. This would provide something of a brake on the power of these lawyers who at the moment can run roughshod over the citizenry just as what happened to you here. Too bad that the trial lawyers have such a strong lobby in Congress and that such tort reform is not likely to occur in our lifetimes. Honestly though, I believe that that is the only way that the system will change and that is the only way that a problem such as yours might be addressed. Again, it's too bad, but that's the way it is."

It was nice to know that the judge was on my side, but since there was nothing that he could practically do about it, this was small consolation. Again, I thanked him for taking the time to talk to me. He had addressed the major issues of my concern, and though I hadn't exactly gotten complete satisfaction, at least I knew then that Jeff and Chauncey hadn't made a chump out of me. That was somewhat helpful. The judge and I shook hands and parted on mutually respectful and friendly terms.

As I walked down to my car, I continued to fume inside about the way Jeff Peterson had tried to manipulate me during the trial and, most especially, about the way he had wasted my time and caused me no considerable anguish and anxiety by involving me in a trial in which I never should have been involved. If he hadn't been so incompetent or so lazy as to have not taken my deposition, he might have realized the error of his ways before he did that. There had to be some way that I could make things difficult for him but I had yet to see my way clear to such a solution.

THE BEGINNING

"Cry 'Havoc' and let slip the dogs of war."

Shakespeare

Sitting across the table from the "most beautiful girl in the whole wide world" in the Lavender Moon, a fine restaurant in the town of Swanton, Vermont, my ego couldn't help but feel a bit inflated in spite of the fact that I was only all too well aware of the grasping and malevolent intelligence that lay not so deeply below the beautiful façade. I had reserved the table and had come early to set the stage and to lay the groundwork for my campaign, and so was witness to Kathy Wennar's entrance, which was something of a minor production for at least 50% of the restaurant's patrons. Since it was only two weeks or so from the end of the trial, she again wore black but only by a long stretch of the imagination could her present attire be seen as mourning garb. This dress was soft and clingy, with a deep U neckline that exposed considerably more than the tops of her magnificent breasts and gave a visual promise of more to come. It was cut to mid-thigh length and showed to great advantage a pair of long and moderately muscled legs that seemed to stretch out into the infinity of every man's desire. As she moved across the room to join me at our table, the fabric moved deliciously and tantalizingly around those milky thighs as if to say, "Lift me up, lift me up." And you can just bet that every man that room was thinking just that. The thoughts of the women are more opaque to me, but I have a good imagination.

When she sat to join me and bestowed upon me that "Have a small piece of my glorious incandescence." Smile, it was all I could do not to preen with male pride. I knew that all eyes were upon us and that most were envious of my position, but I had gotten to know the person that Kathy was, and that knowledge was some protection from her physical persona. The male mantis is besotted with his mate, but when he quite literally loses his head over his infatuation he probably has second thoughts.

We greeted one another and ordered drinks, a glass of an imported rose for her, a 7+7 for me. We made some small talk about the fine spring weather that had arrived at last, hopefully to stay for some time, and then I revealed my idea. I began by telling Kathy that, in spite of the fact that she had lost the case, I thought that she had done a good thing in general by bringing the suit against the nursing home. I myself had seen many instances where elderly people who were frequent fallers had been moved into a nursing home to protect them, but because of over interpretation of the "no restraint" policy and lack of staffing to allow constant one-on-one supervision in certain instances, these people had continued to fall in the nursing homes and, in fact, some of them had gone on to break hips or other bones and had then had all of the attendant complications leading in some instances to an earlier death, not unlike the case of her late husband. I told her that I knew that the money wasn't all that important to her, but that I thought she had gotten a raw deal, and that I had a way that she might finally be able to make some money out of the situation.

Up to this point in the conversation, Kathy had remained politely attentive, but I could see those lovely cerulean blue eyes begin to glaze over as I went on about how her suit could actually bring some future improvement to the lot of elderly nursing home patients. At this first mention of cold hard cash, however, there was an instant and profound change in her demeanor. I could see the pupils of her eyes dilate suddenly as if some infinitely older and more grasping intelligence had manifested itself and was eagerly waiting its chance to pounce. Her breathing actually stopped for a few moments as I continued.

"I'm quite sure that your lawyers committed legal malpractice in this case, and I think that you have a good case if you sue them," I said. I then went on to tell her that her lawyers hadn't even bothered to depose me although I was named a co-defendant in the suit and was probably the major witness in the case. Because of their failure to depose me, they had many misconceptions about the medical facts of the case and so were vulnerable in their position. Not only that but since they had not questioned me in advance they had no idea what I was going to say on the stand and so were not able to prepare a decent cross examination or rebut anything that I did say. This hurt her case tremendously and, in fact, was probably the deciding factor in the jury's decision to acquit (Naturally, I did not mention the fact that the jury also probably saw right through her own testimony and by the end of the trial was quite convinced that she was a lying low-life who was only out to collect some money for her husband's death.). On top of all that, her lawyers had not bothered to depose any of the nursing home employees involved in the case, from the nurses to the physical therapists to the dietary and other ancillary personnel so, consequently, they were not able to deal with the testimony which any of those folks gave either!

I ended my argument by reminding her that she had asked for 6 million dollars and had ended up with nothing, a considerable difference in amounts, and I told her that I had run the basics of the case by several lawyers in town all of whom had opined that she would have a very good case of legal malpractice against the lawyers whom she had used. Of course, none of these lawyers were too interested in taking the case themselves as they did business with the firm in question on an almost monthly basis and lived in the same legal community. This was not a barrier to a contemplated suit, however. At this point, I pulled a business envelope out of my jacket.

"In this envelope," I said, "is a list of lawyers who specialize in suing other lawyers for malpractice. I got it from the Internet last night." For, indeed, it was true. Just as there is an entire legal industry that now specializes in suing nursing homes, another that specializes in medical malpractice cases, another that specializes in accident victims, another that specializes in work related injuries, there is also an entire legal industry that has devoted itself to legal malpractice cases. "Have you been injured by the failure of your lawyer to perform in an acceptable manner? Call us now at this number. We can get you the money that you deserve!" This to me was poetic justice and true earthly retribution. I would get my personal satisfaction by having Kathy Wennar sue Jeff Peterson and his firm for legal malpractice just as she had sued me for medical malpractice.

At this point, the waitress came by to take our orders. Since she was not a male, Kathy's physical aura was wasted on her and she actually tended to ignore Kathy and concentrate on me, the male member of the party, as many waitresses tend to do when waiting on a couple. Needles to say, this did not suit La Dame Wennar very well, but there was absolutely nothing that she could do about it. In any event, the suggestions that I had planted in her little head probably blunted the effects of this minor rejection, and she appeared not to take it too badly. She was able to order her tossed salad and other glass of wine without biting off anyone's head, and I after I ordered a tuna fish sandwich on rye and a coke, the waitress departed with a smile directed at me and with all of her appendages intact.

From this point, we said very little as we both mulled over our future actions. Kathy asked a few questions about the nitty-gritty of contacting the law firms that were advertising on the Internet and about the general activities of lawyers in regard to suits in which they might be involved. I did my best to answer her questions but was not really much interested. I had said my piece, shot my bolt, planted my seed, and was eager to move on. Not that I wasn't interested at some level on prolonging my lunch with the "most beautiful woman in the whole wide world," but the fact was that I just wasn't terribly impressed with her basic personality and moral foundation.

When our food came, I bolted mine quickly, almost to the point of rudeness. I added up the bill in my head, noted the cost of the most expensive dessert on the menu and added that amount, added a 20% tip and removed that total of money from my wallet.

"Kathy," I said, "this lunch has been a real pleasure, and it was really nice talking to you, but I'm afraid that I have to leave early as I have a prior engagement and my time is a little short. Feel free to stay and have a nice dessert on me. And have a good rest of the day." With that, I placed the cash on the table and stood to leave.

She feigned disappointment though I could see that at this point she would rather be alone to contemplate her own future legal course, and offered me her exquisite hand to shake. She then thanked me for my help, and as I turned to leave, she winked broadly in my direction and again produced that million watt smile that caught me like a breaking wave and surfed me out of the restaurant into the street. I climbed into the little yellow Volkswagon and drove off.

There was one more thing that I had to do before going home, and that led me once again to La Place D'Espere, the nursing home which had lately been playing such a large role in my life. This had become the place where my beloved Cassandra would probably be spending her final days and was also the place where the woman who had become my new companion and confidant spent most of her working day. This was also the institution that had shared with me the risk and the ignominy of the recent lawsuit. I had pressing business there.

I parked the bug in the lot, walked briskly to the front door and entered decisively through the automatic doors. I had made some decisions. Without further ado, I strode across the lobby and knocked on Gail Casperson's door. Luckily, she was at her desk as I don't think I could have held my words in any longer, and, in any event, they came tumbling out in a torrent before I could take any of them back.

"Gail," I blurted, "I've decided that you were right all along and that I need to change Cassie's resuscitation status to Do Not Resuscitate. I agree that it would not be reasonable or appropriate to use extraordinary measures of any kind to prolong her life now just because of a promise that I made to her in another time when she was in her right mind and we were much younger, in a different world. Things have changed, and it's up to me to address those changes and to do what's right."

Gail looked up at me with some concern rather than triumph in her eyes.

"I think you're doing the right thing, Jon, of course, but are you sure in your own mind that this is what you want?"

"Yes, I've given it a lot of thought. In fact, I've been thinking of almost nothing else lately. This has been weighing on my mind for some time, and I'm sure that it's the right decision." In fact, know that I had actually said the words and the thought had become a reality, I felt as though the proverbial great weight had been lifted from my shoulders. The decision was a good one, the best one, the correct one.

"Also, Gail, I've given some other things a lot of thought as well." Gail's eyebrows arched up a bit at this, and she replied, "Oh?"

"Yes." I responded. "I think that you and I have some unfinished business and that I need to take you out to dinner tonight so that we can start taking care of it."

"Hummmm. A bit presumptuous of you, isn't it? You know I lead an incredibly busy life and that my evenings are rarely free. However, it just so happens that this particular evening I am free and would love to take you up on your invitation."

"Fine." I replied. "I'll pick you up at 7 sharp." "It's a deal." she said.

With that, I took my leave and walked down the hall to room 207 where my ruined wife now spent the eternity of her days. I found her sitting in her rocker, slowly bobbing and staring out the window with her eyes unfocussed. I crossed the room and took her soft hand gently on my own. She looked up at me with no sign of recognition in those familiar brown eyes, but at least there was no fear there and I was thankful for that. I asked her how she was doing, and she said, "Yes." I asked her how her day had gone, and she responded, "Yes." I asked if she was feeling well, and she said, "Yes." I asked if I could do anything for her, and she again answered, "Yes." There was nothing else. If this had been new to me, I might have broken down, cried or given voice to my despair, but it was all too familiar now, all too much a part of her, all too much a part of both of us. I had thought about this a lot also. Could I have a life with Gail now? Could I divorce my Cassie and marry another woman even with the situation as it was? I still didn't think that I could do this, to abandon my wife in that way, even though she wasn't the wife that I once knew. "'Til death do us part." still echoed in my head. Even so, I needed some life of my own outside of this horror, and it had become my hope that Gail would still have me under these circumstances. She was a good woman, and I strongly suspected that she would. I knew that we had a strong connection and that it had even been made stronger with the recent stresses and strains that we had undergone together. We both had our independent lives and did not require a formal marriage for financial security or other more sectarian reasons so this would not be an impediment. And, after all, this was "The Place of Hope."

I left my wife's room. She took no notice of my departure. I walked down the hallway, out into the lobby and out the automatic doors. I stepped out into the softness of that bright spring day. The sun fell down brilliantly on my upturned face. Hope rose like an expanding bubble in the center of my chest.

WEDDING BELLS

"One's tootings at the wedding of the soul. Occur as they occur."

Wallace Stevens

Tate in October of the year 2004, Jeffrey Edward Peterson, a partner in the law firm of "Peterson, Faulkner and Beiderbeck. Attorneys at Law, Specialists in Medical Malpractice" was diligently if grudgingly reviewing the long winded and somewhat arcane deposition of a consultant neurosurgeon when his secretary, Holly Everybody, entered his office with a thick business envelope in her hand. The return address on the outside of the envelope said, "Therrien, Johnson, Crestman and Pelkey, Attorneys at Law, Specialists in Legal Malpractice." Mr. Peterson, without bothering to reach over and grab his gold plated letter opener in the shape of a labrador retriever, ripped open the envelope with his meaty and rather sweaty hands as he gave vent to the utterance of a few choice four letter words. Inside was a thin sheet of paper which said, "Please make available to the above mentioned attorneys any and all records pursuant to the matter of Martin Wennar and Katherine Wennar vs. Place D'Espere Nursing Home and Jon Zabieska, M.D." Peterson's eyes widened and his mouth gaped open like that of a fish on dry land. The next four years would be a nightmare...

THE BEGINNING

"Cry 'Havoc' and let slip the dogs of war."

Shakespeare

Texandra, my elder daughter and aviculturist, called me the other day to relate the latest in the saga of Little Joe. Since his second escape attempt, he had been relegated to quarters of his own outside the main gorilla exhibit. This consisted basically of a solitary, though large, two room cell with an outer section with a barred front wall and an inner section which contained a sleeping area where Joe could get a little privacy if he so desired. The sleeping area backed onto a corridor on three sides where the zoo-keepers could move around freely and do their work, store supplies and access the sleeping area through a large metal door on one of the sides of the enclosure. One day while one of Alexandra's fellow keepers was moving around some equipment in the back corridor, she caught out of the corner of her eye what she initially thought was a large black snake curling up the back wall of Little Joe's cage. When she turned to face that wall, however, it became obvious that this was the right arm of Joe himself. He had painstakingly by hand removed one of the cinder blocks from the back wall of his cell and was sticking his arm out to investigate the situation before, presumably, enlarging the opening and making his third attempt at freedom. After recovering from her initial shock and surprise, the keeper got on her two-way radio and reported the problem. A large number of keepers responded to the alarm, and poor Joe was quickly sedated once again and moved to a more secure location. Some keepers claimed that there was a poster of Marilyn Monroe in Joe's cage that he kept there to hide the results of his labors from the eyes of his captors, but this was judged by most to be an apocryphal exaggeration of his gorilla intelligence. The fact remains, though, that he hasn't given up, and that the thought of freedom continues to burn brightly down deep somewhere in that simian brain.

www.ingramcontent.com/pod-product-compliance
Lightning Source LLC
Chambersburg PA
CBHW021616120626
46545CB00001B/258